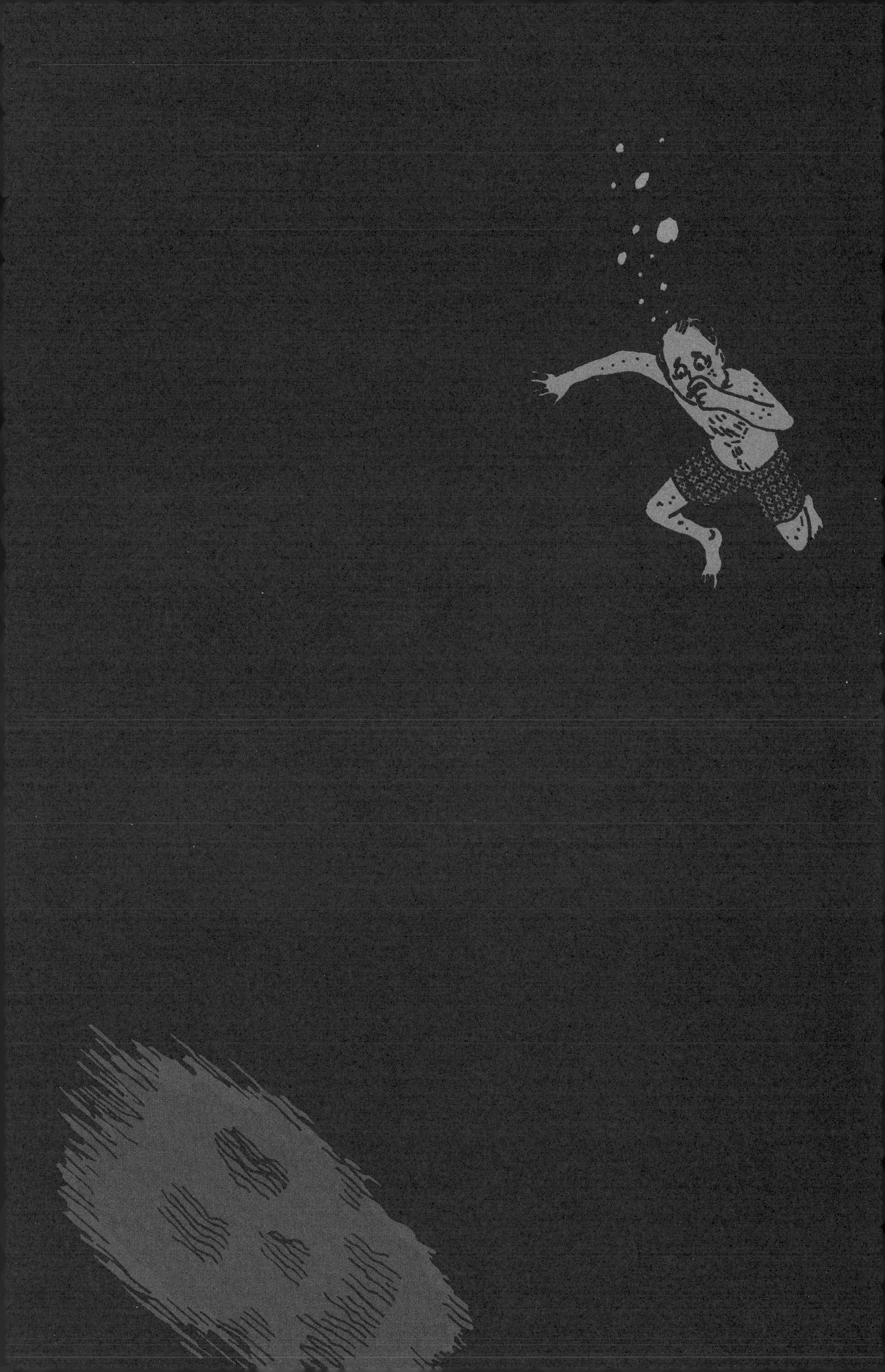

AS A CARTOONIST

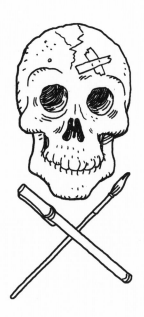

☑ COMICS SAVED
MY LIFE

☑ COMICS WILL
KILL ME

NOAH VAN SCIVER

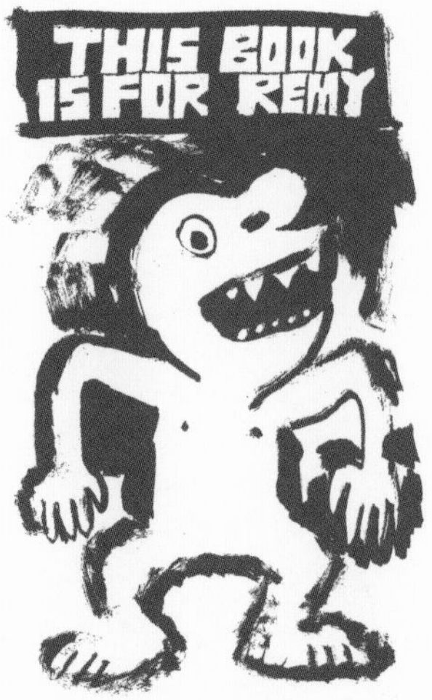
THIS BOOK IS FOR REMY

FANTAGRAPHICS BOOKS INC.
7563 Lake City Way NE
Seattle, Washington, 98115
www.fantagraphics.com

DESIGN: Kayla E. & Noah Van Sciver
PRODUCTION: Paul Baresh
PROMOTION: Jacquelene Cohen
VP / ASSOCIATE PUBLISHER / EDITOR: Eric Reynolds
PRESIDENT / PUBLISHER: Gary Groth

ISBN: 978-1-68396-561-9
LIBRARY OF CONGRESS CONTROL NUMBER: 2021951587
FIRST PRINTING: June 2022
PRINTED IN CHINA

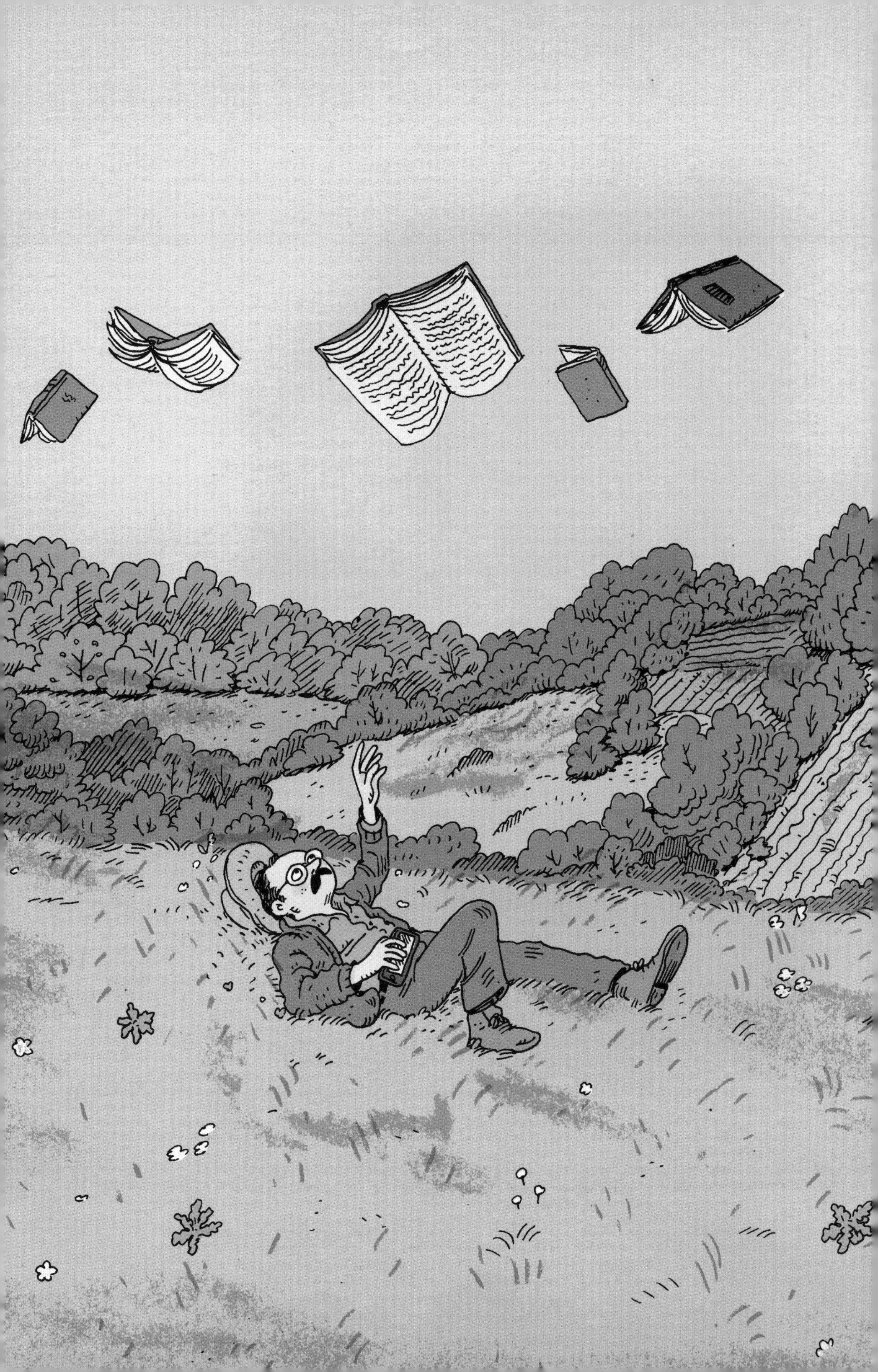

AS A
CARTOONIST

NOAH VAN SCIVER

Jackie Ormes

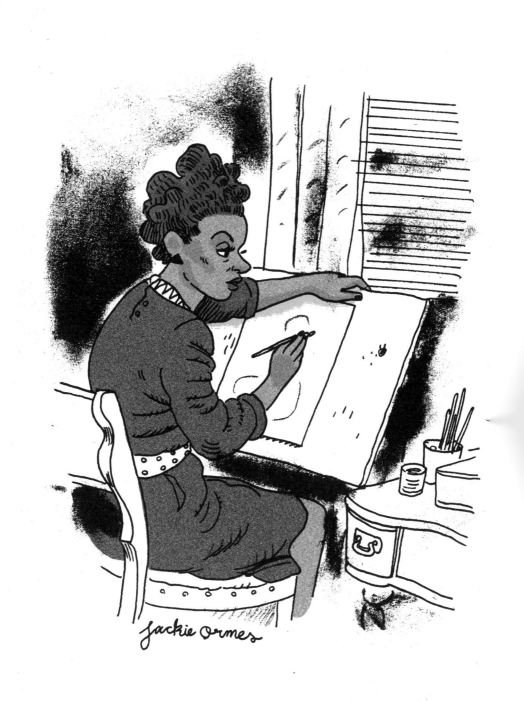

H. T. Webster

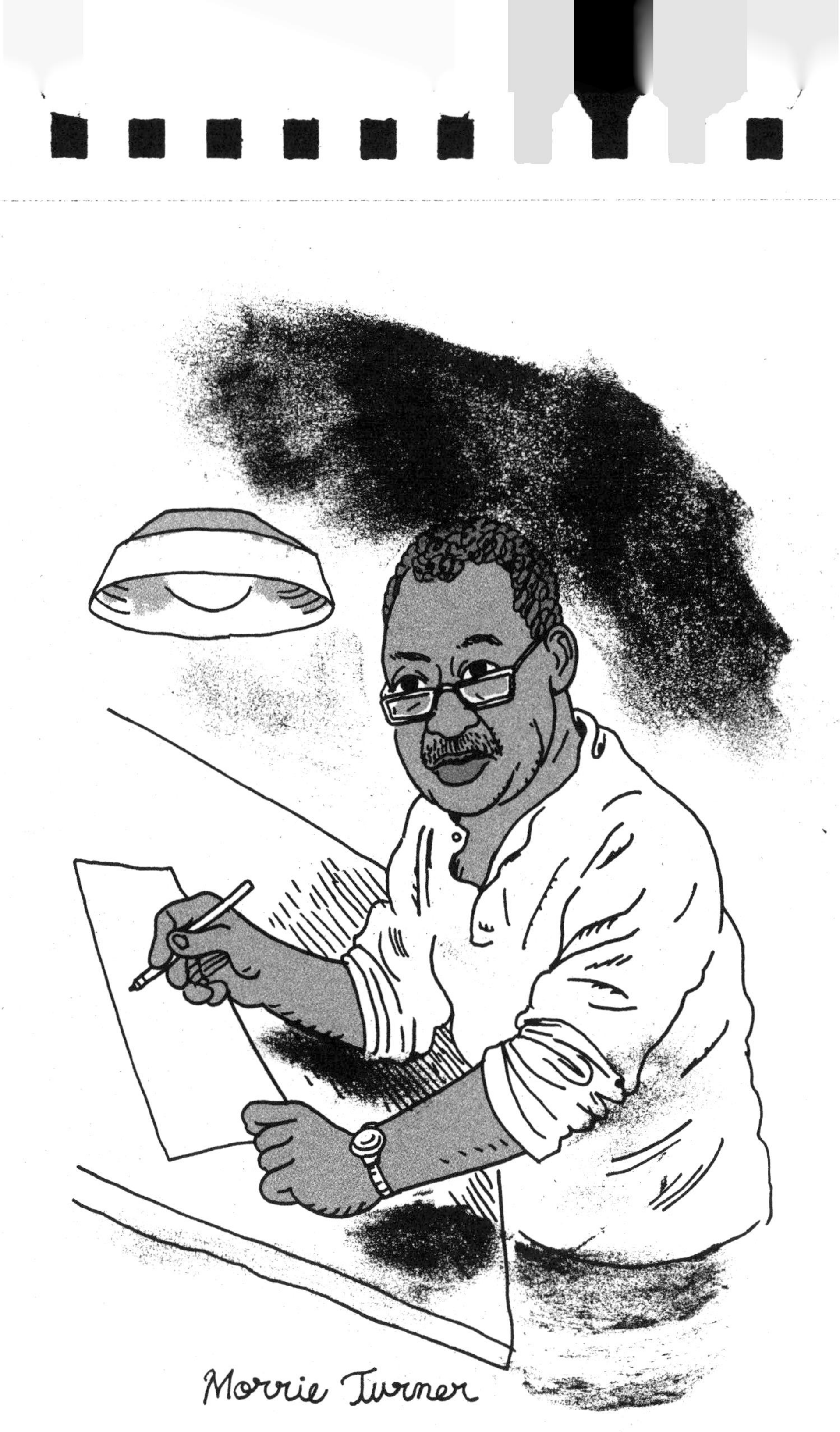
Morrie Turner

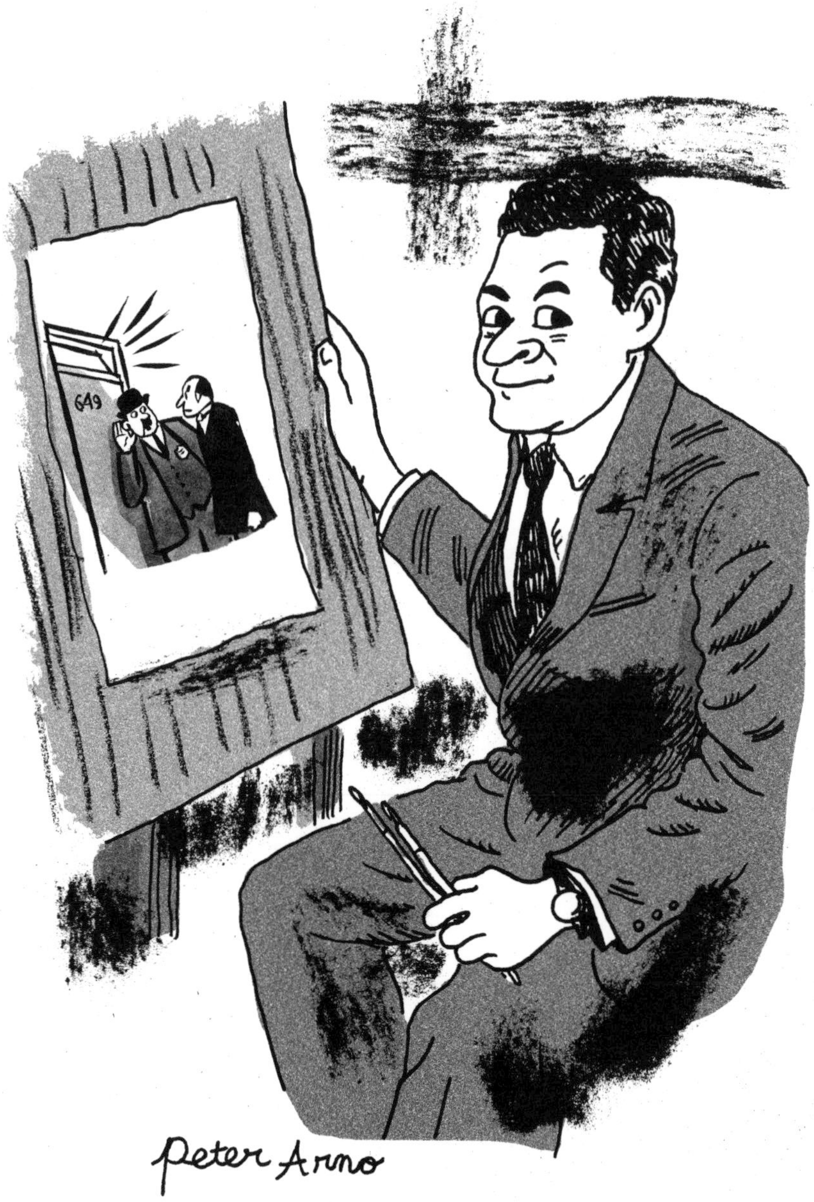
649
Peter Arno

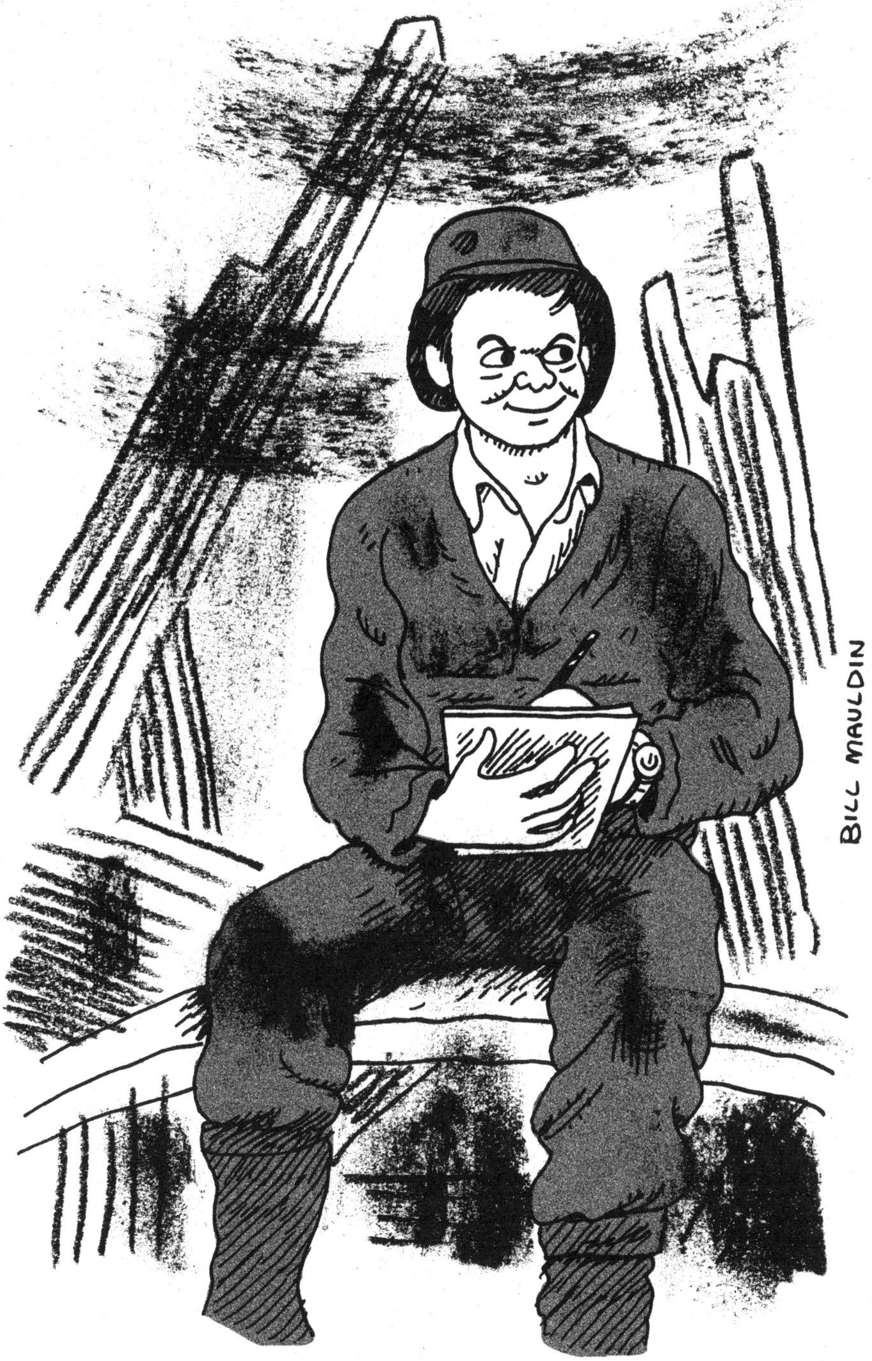
BILL MAULDIN

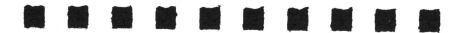

MASTER CARTOONIST
(actual name lost)

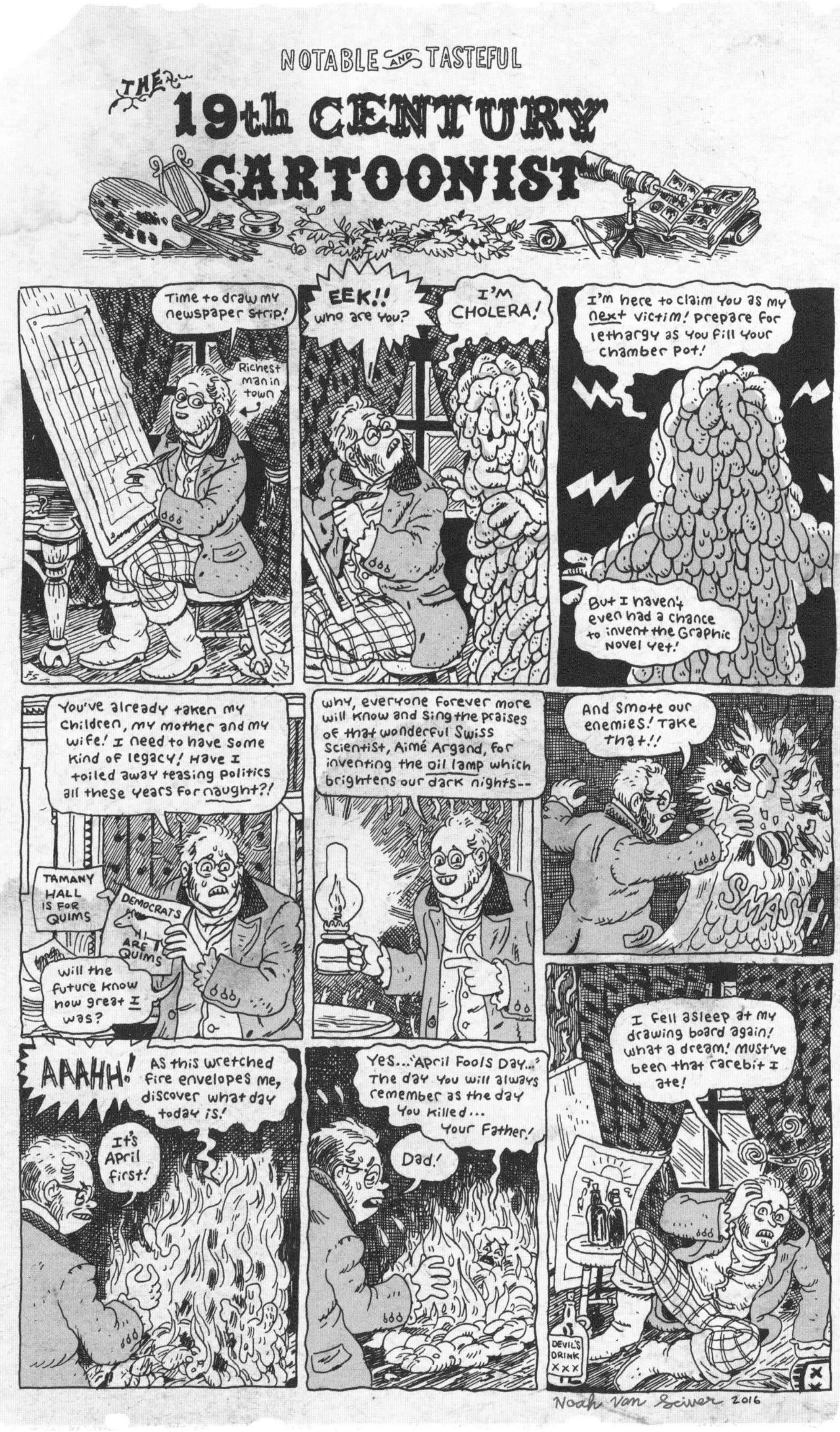
NOTABLE AND TASTEFUL
THE 19th CENTURY CARTOONIST
Time to draw my newspaper strip!
Richest man in town
EEK!! who are you?
I'M CHOLERA!
I'm here to claim you as my next victim! prepare for lethargy as you fill your chamber pot!
But I haven't even had a chance to invent the Graphic Novel yet!
You've already taken my children, my mother and my wife! I need to have some kind of legacy! Have I toiled away teasing politics all these years for naught?!
TAMANY HALL IS FOR QUIMS
DEMOCRATS ARE QUIMS
will the future know how great I was?
why, everyone forever more will know and sing the praises of that wonderful Swiss Scientist, Aimé Argand, for inventing the oil lamp which brightens our dark nights--
And smote our enemies! Take that!!
SMASH!
AAAHH!
As this wretched fire envelopes me, discover what day today is!
It's April first!
Yes... 'April Fools Day...' The day you will always remember as the day you killed... Your Father!
Dad!
I fell asleep at my drawing board again! what a dream! Must've been that rarebit I ate!
DEVIL'S DRINK XXX
Noah Van Sciver 2016

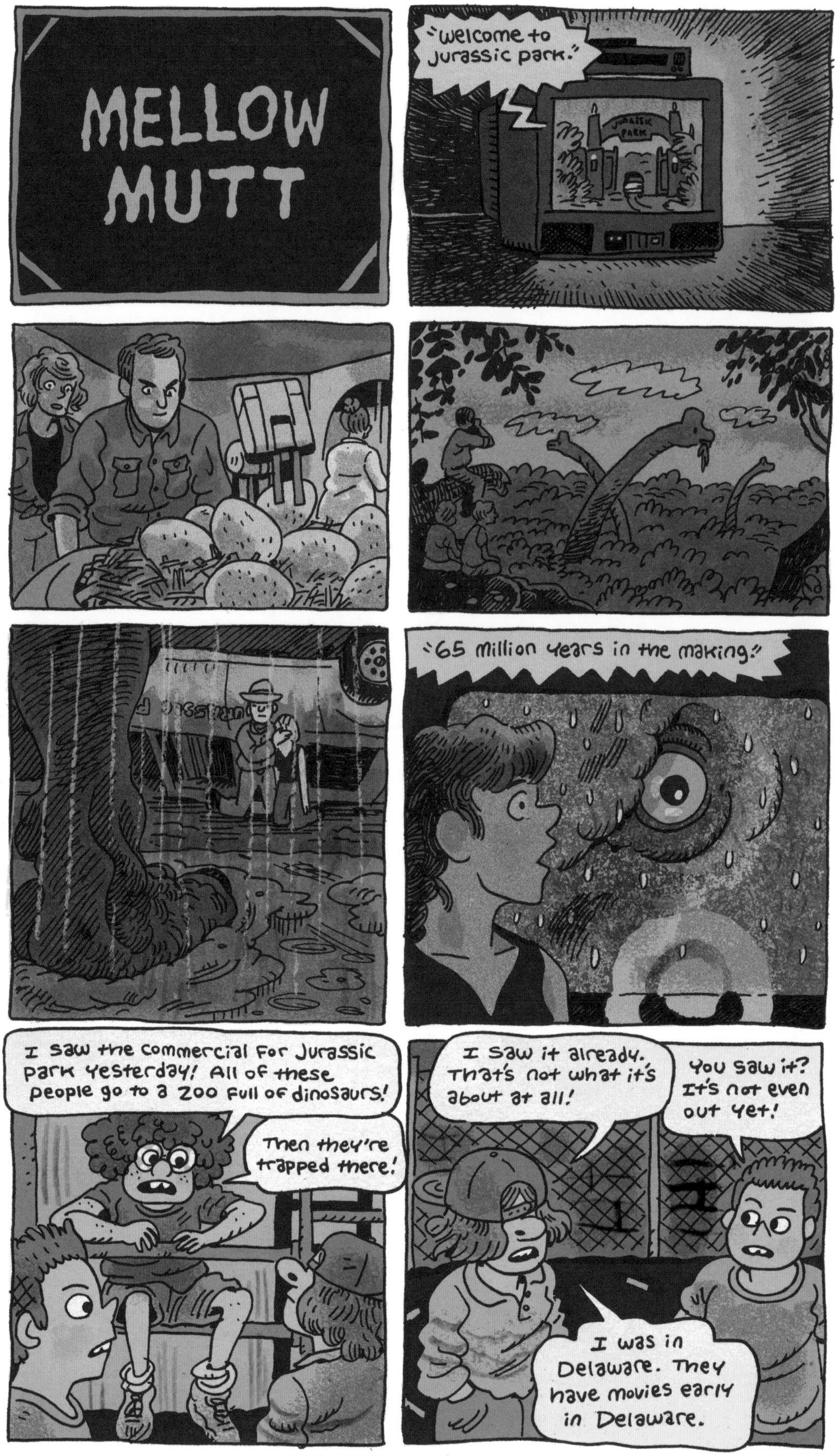
MELLOW MUTT
"Welcome to Jurassic park."
"65 million years in the making."
I saw the commercial for Jurassic park yesterday! All of these people go to a zoo full of dinosaurs!
Then they're trapped there!
I saw it already. That's not what it's about at all!
You saw it? It's not even out yet!
I was in Delaware. They have movies early in Delaware.

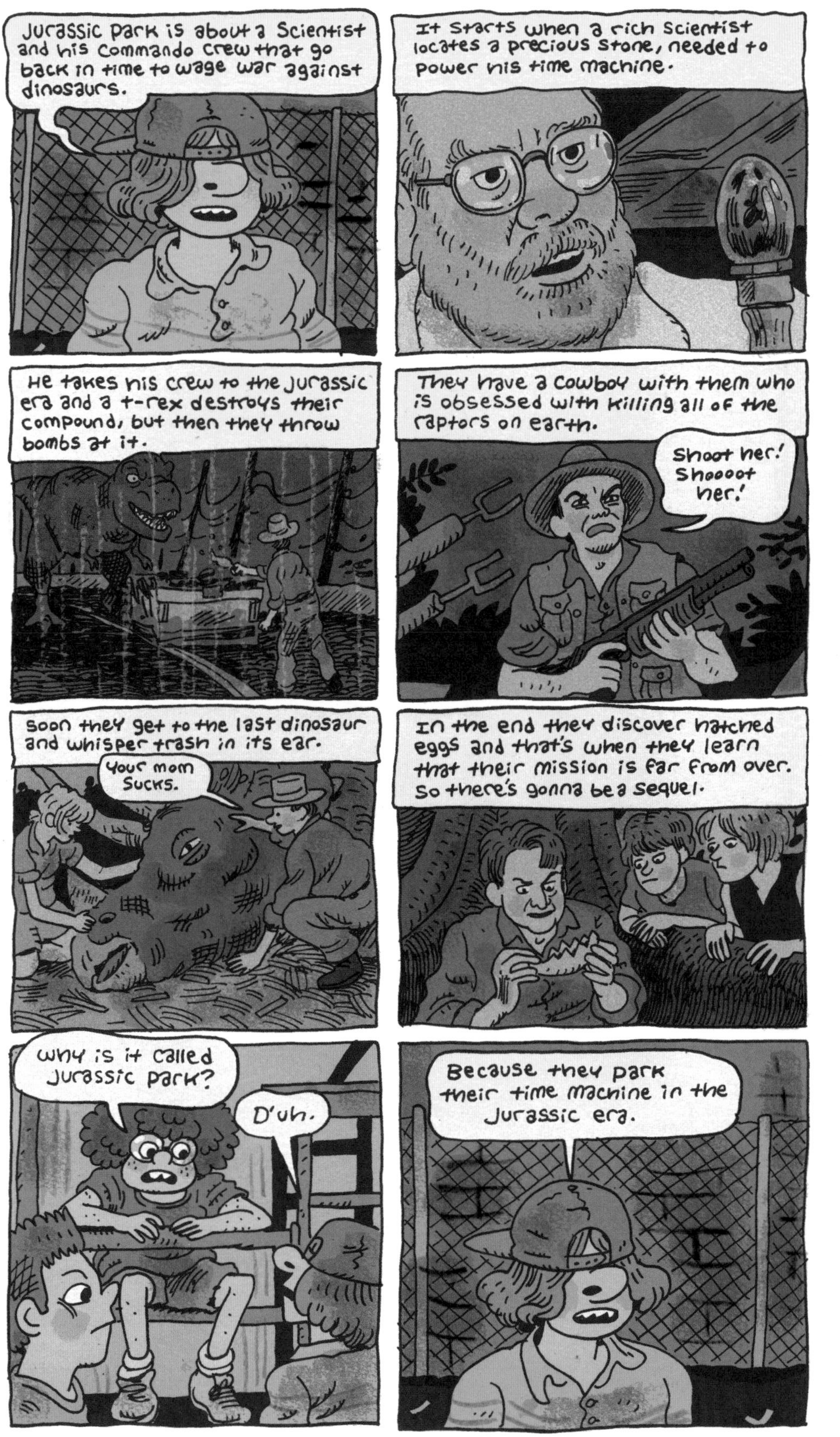
Jurassic Park is about a Scientist and his Commando crew that go back in time to wage war against dinosaurs.
It Starts when a rich Scientist locates a precious Stone, needed to power his time machine.
He takes his crew to the Jurassic era and a t-rex destroys their compound, but then they throw bombs at it.
They have a cowboy with them who is obsessed with killing all of the raptors on earth.
Shoot her! Shoooot her!
Soon they get to the last dinosaur and whisper trash in its ear.
Your mom Sucks.
In the end they discover hatched eggs and that's when they learn that their mission is far from over. So there's gonna be a sequel.
Why is it called Jurassic park?
D'uh.
Because they park their time machine in the Jurassic era.

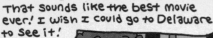

That sounds like the best movie ever! I wish I could go to Delaware to see it!

me too!

Yeah well...

Not everybody's parents divorce so you can have two homes.

weeks later...

Gimmie!

Happy birthday!

Gimmie!

RIP

SHRED

ELLIE

JURASSIC PARK

Ellie Sattler with firing grappling hook and limited edition movie collector card!

plus a triceratops hatchling!

Thanks, mom!

"we've come all this way and we aren't leaving until every single one of those dinos begs for a comet to end their suffering!"

BANG BANG!

Now it's your turn, hatchling! prepare to meet God in the celestial kingdom!

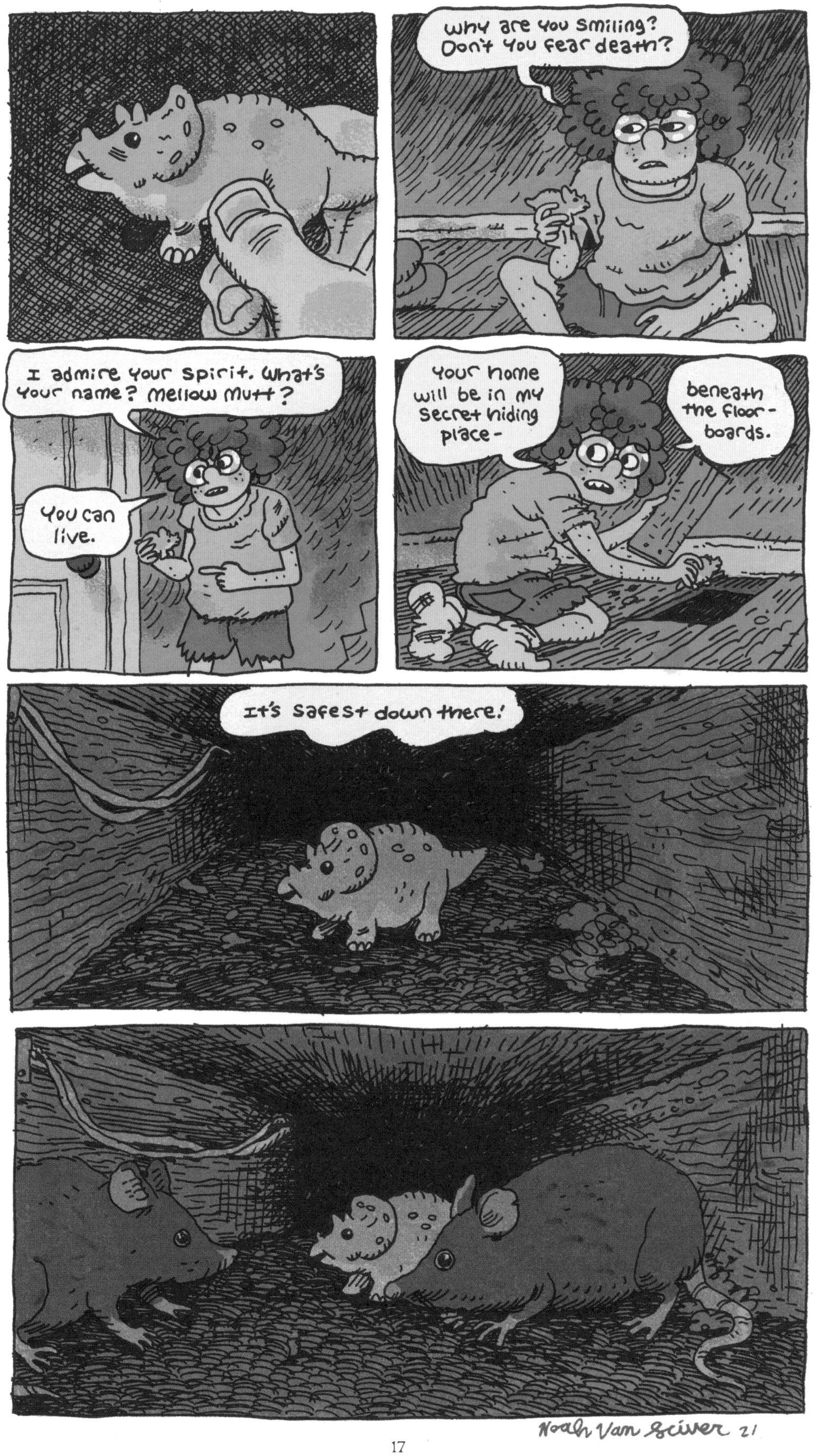
Why are you smiling? Don't you fear death?
I admire your spirit. What's your name? Mellow Mutt?
You can live.
Your home will be in my secret hiding place-
beneath the floor-boards.
It's safest down there!
Noah Van Sciver 21

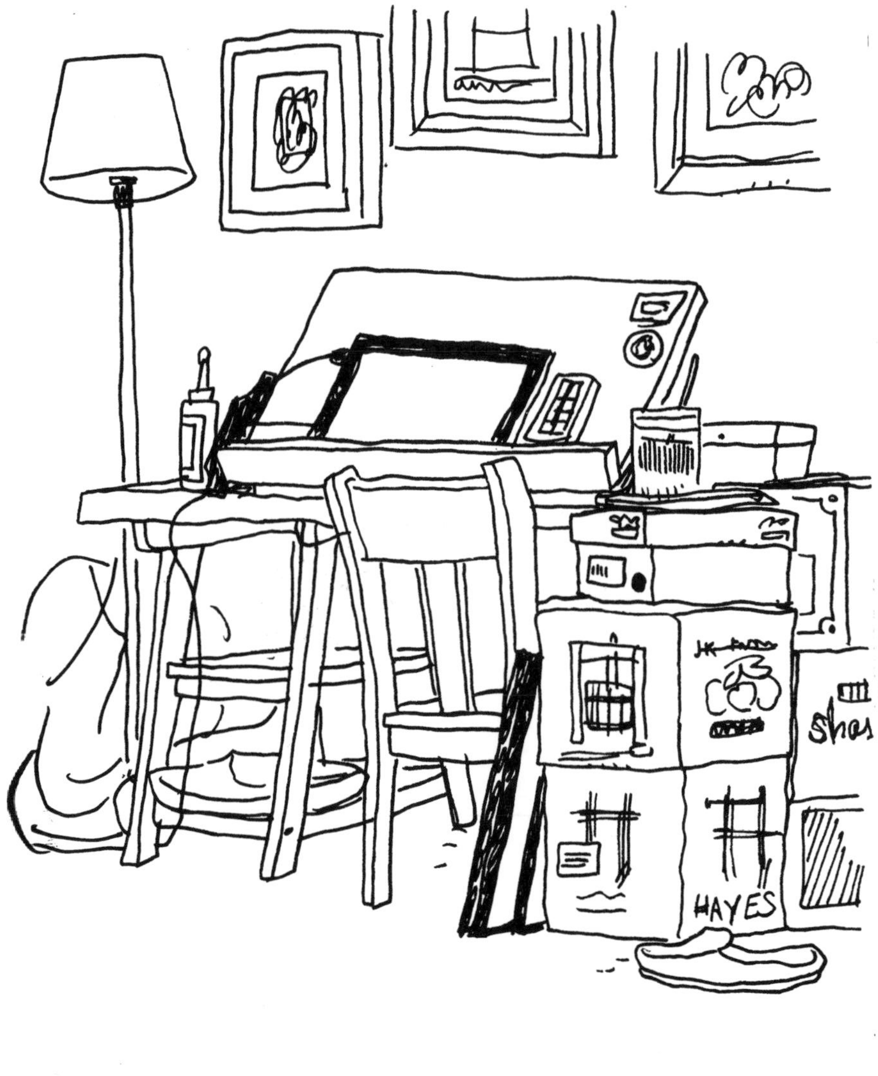
HAYES

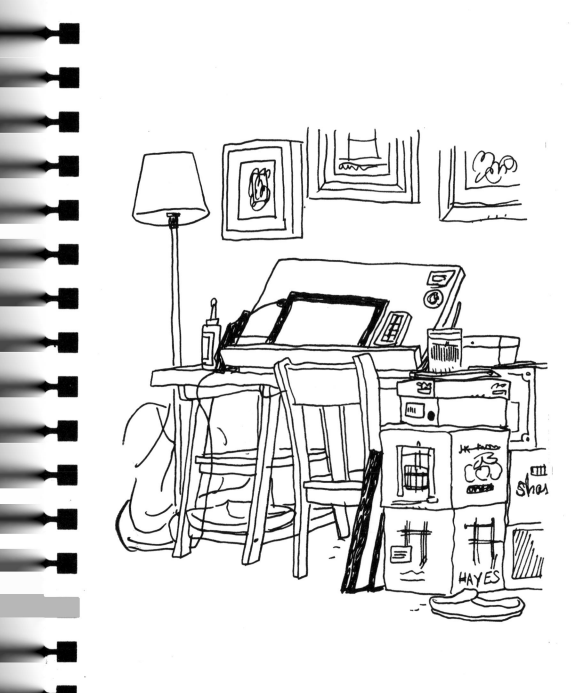

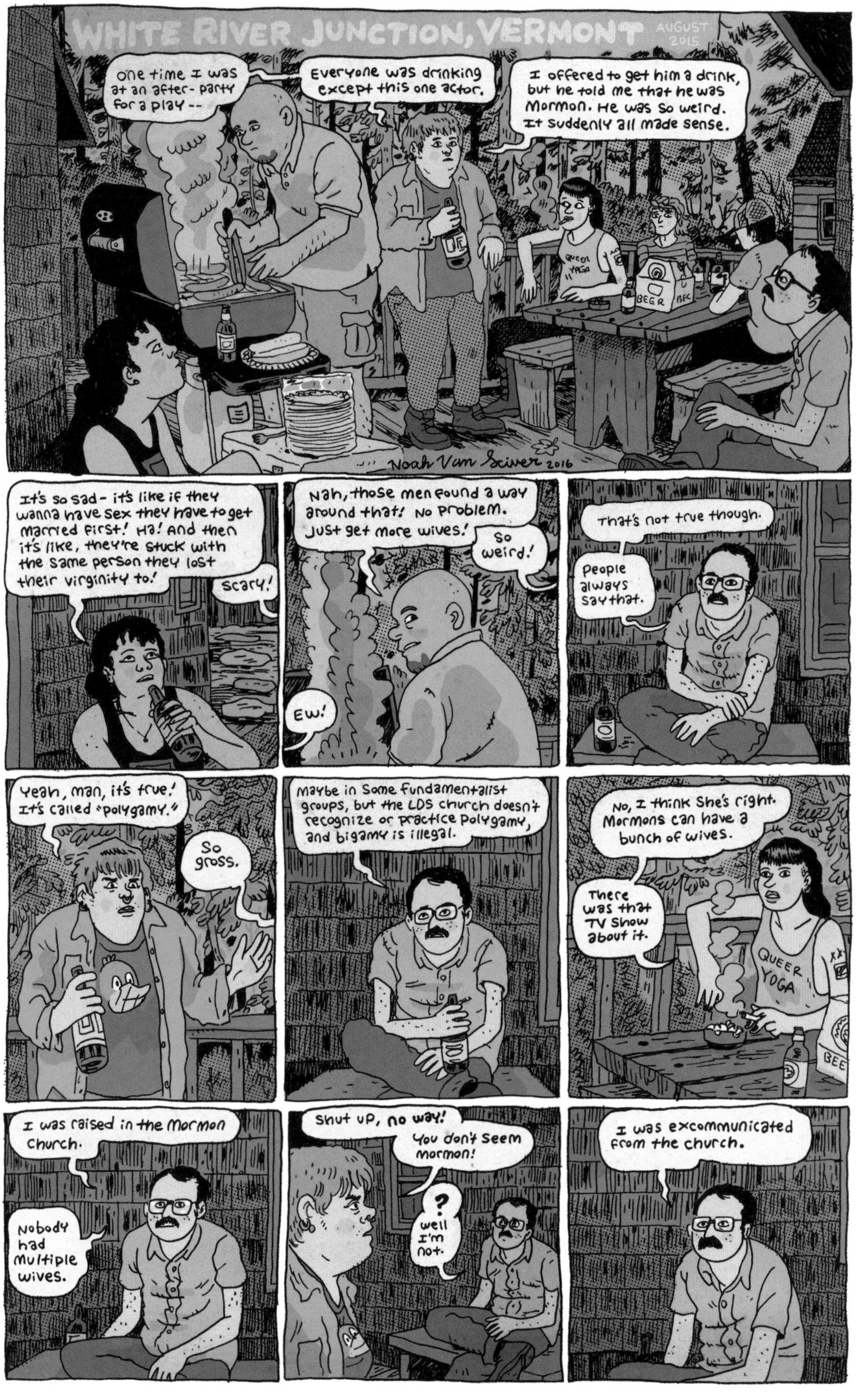
WHITE RIVER JUNCTION, VERMONT
AUGUST 2015
One time I was at an after-party for a play --
Everyone was drinking except this one actor.
I offered to get him a drink, but he told me that he was Mormon. He was so weird. It suddenly all made sense.
QUEER YOGA
BEER
Noah Van Sciver 2016
It's so sad - it's like if they wanna have sex they have to get married first! Ha! And then it's like, they're stuck with the same person they lost their virginity to!
Scary!
Nah, those men found a way around that! No problem. Just get more wives!
So weird!
Ew!
That's not true though.
People always say that.
Yeah, man, it's true! It's called "polygamy."
So gross.
Maybe in some fundamentalist groups, but the LDS church doesn't recognize or practice polygamy, and bigamy is illegal.
No, I think she's right. Mormons can have a bunch of wives.
There was that TV show about it.
QUEER YOGA
I was raised in the Mormon church.
Nobody had multiple wives.
Shut up, no way!
You don't seem mormon!
?
Well I'm not.
I was excommunicated from the church.

Whoa, how'd you pull that off?

I didn't do anything. My parents got divorced.

After the split my mother left the church and had any of her children still living with her taken out as well.

That included me.

What? You're Mormon? Did you believe in Joseph Smith and the "Golden plates" and all that stuff?

BEER

BEER

Well yeah, I mean as a kid I had no reason not to. It's what I was taught.

Yuck, man. Mormons are like Scientologists!

OK! Come get your franks!

How many are vegan friendly?

These people are weird. I miss Denver. I feel like it was a mistake moving here.

1993: I'm in my childhood home in Merchantville, New Jersey. It's Sunday and I'm watching all of the kids in my neighborhood play from the bathroom window.

In our household it was forbidden to go outside on a Sunday. My father insisted that we stay in and "keep the Sabbath day holy."

I was expected to read the scriptures and study them. But as a kid I couldn't understand them and I thought they were boring. Instead I would watch others play from the window.

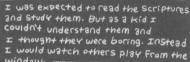

So there I am watching, when something metallic and disc-shaped flies by the window! Right past my face!

I swear it looked just like a U.F.O. from a 1950's movie. Nobody in the street noticed a thing.

It was just something strange that only I saw. Just for me. But what the heck was it?

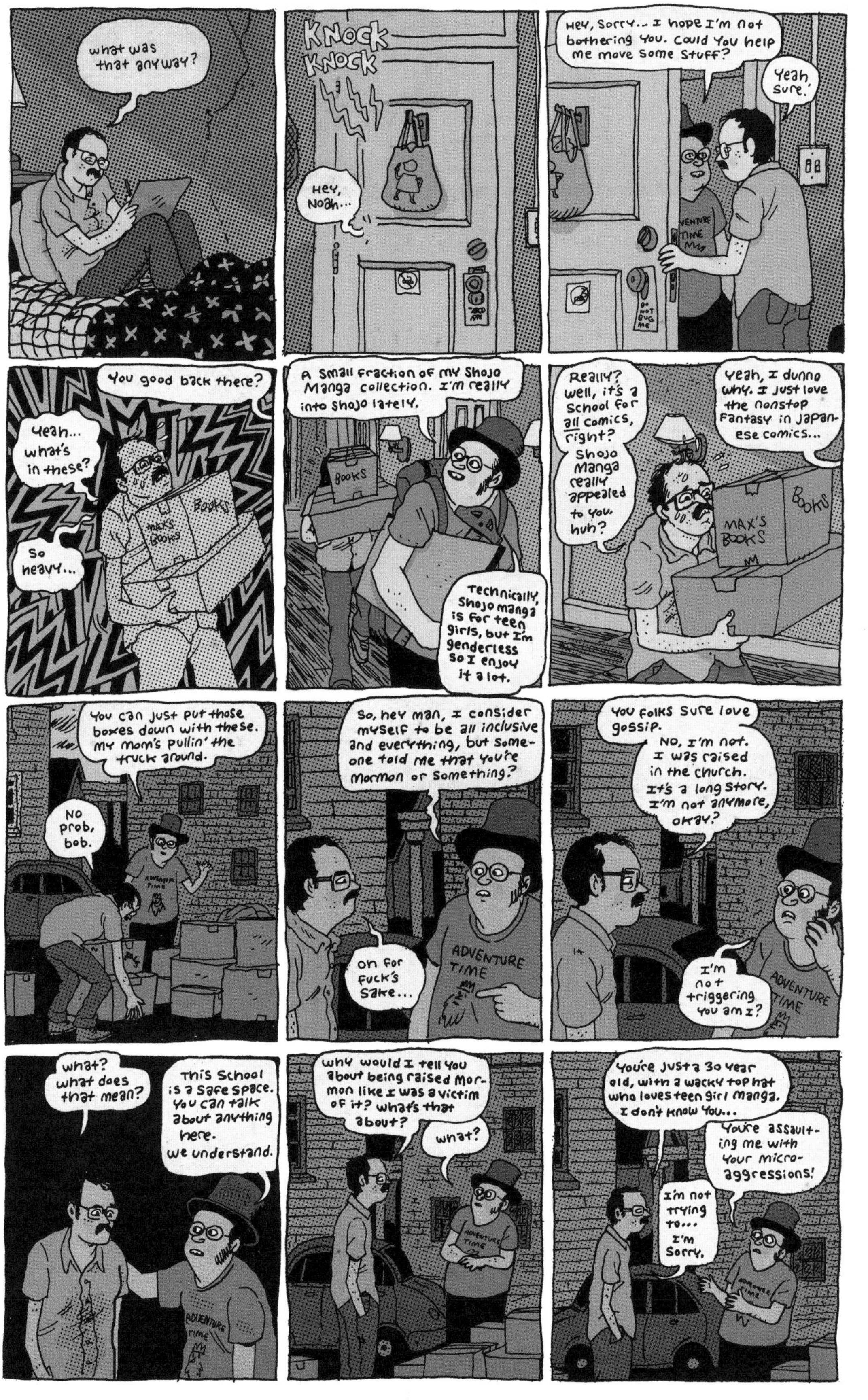
what was that anyway?
KNOCK KNOCK
Hey, Noah...
Hey, Sorry... I hope I'm not bothering you. Could you help me move some stuff?
Yeah, sure.
You good back there?
Yeah... what's in these?
So heavy...
MAX'S BOOKS
BOOKS
A small fraction of my Shojo Manga collection. I'm really into Shojo lately.
Technically, Shojo manga is for teen girls, but I'm genderless so I enjoy it a lot.
Really? Well, it's a school for all comics, right?
Shojo Manga really appealed to you, huh?
Yeah, I dunno why. I just love the nonstop fantasy in Japanese comics...
You can just put those boxes down with these. My mom's pullin' the truck around.
No prob, bob.
So, hey man, I consider myself to be all inclusive and everything, but someone told me that you're Mormon or something?
Oh for fuck's sake...
ADVENTURE TIME
You folks sure love gossip.
No, I'm not. I was raised in the church. It's a long story. I'm not anymore, okay?
I'm not triggering you am I?
what? what does that mean?
This school is a safe space. You can talk about anything here. We understand.
Why would I tell you about being raised Mormon like I was a victim of it? What's that about?
what?
You're just a 30 year old, with a wacky top hat who loves teen girl manga. I don't know you...
You're assaulting me with your micro-aggressions!
I'm not trying to... I'm sorry.

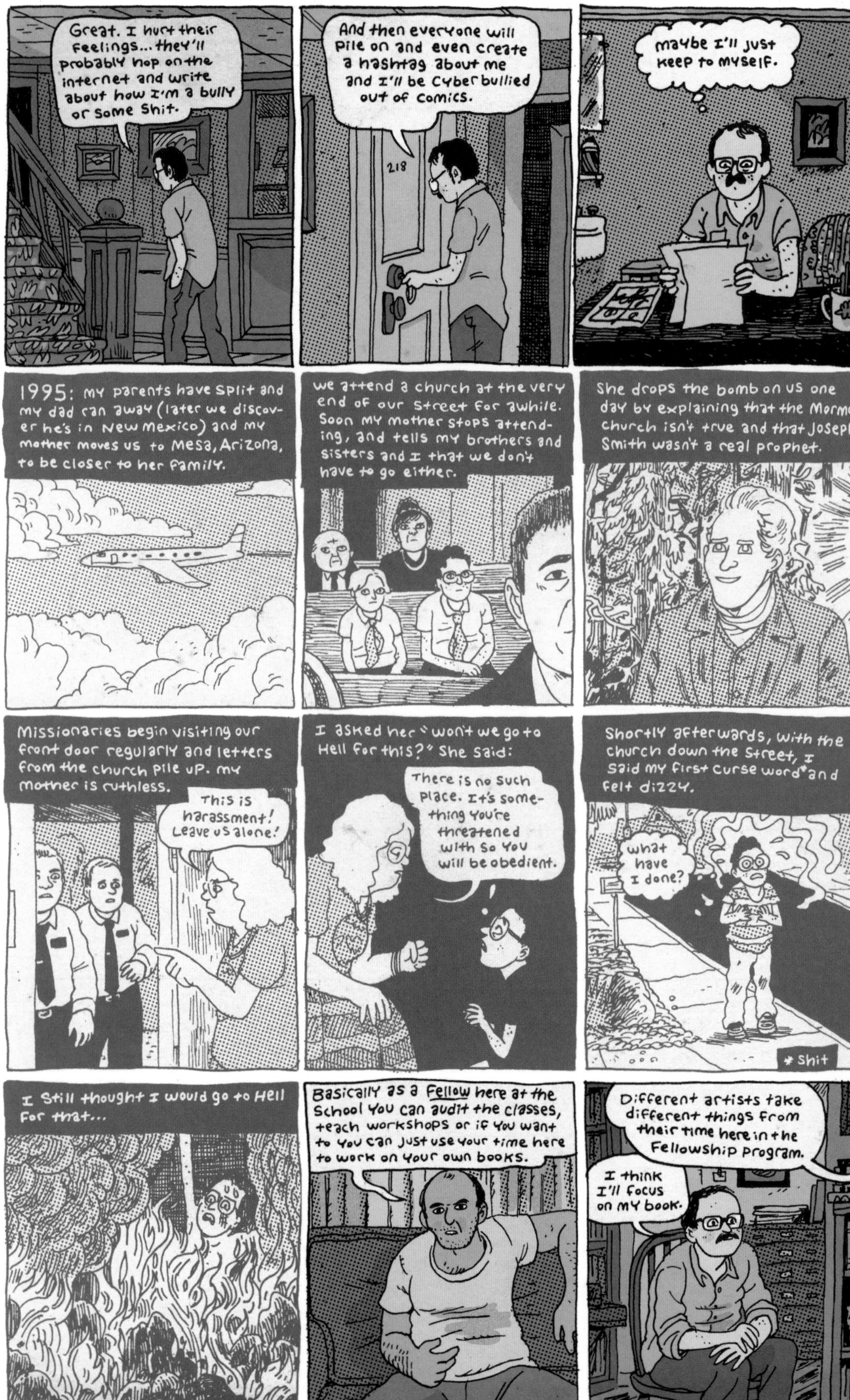
Great. I hurt their feelings... they'll probably hop on the internet and write about how I'm a bully or some shit.
And then everyone will pile on and even create a hashtag about me and I'll be cyberbullied out of comics.
218
maybe I'll just keep to myself.
1995: my parents have split and my dad ran away (later we discover he's in New Mexico) and my mother moves us to Mesa, Arizona, to be closer to her family.
we attend a church at the very end of our street for awhile. Soon my mother stops attending, and tells my brothers and sisters and I that we don't have to go either.
She drops the bomb on us one day by explaining that the Mormon church isn't true and that Joseph Smith wasn't a real prophet.
Missionaries begin visiting our front door regularly and letters from the church pile up. my mother is ruthless.
This is harassment! Leave us alone!
I asked her "won't we go to Hell for this?" She said:
There is no such place. It's something you're threatened with so you will be obedient.
Shortly afterwards, with the church down the street, I said my first curse word* and felt dizzy.
what have I done?
*Shit
I still thought I would go to Hell for that...
Basically as a Fellow here at the School you can audit the classes, teach workshops or if you want to you can just use your time here to work on your own books.
Different artists take different things from their time here in the Fellowship program.
I think I'll focus on my book.

That's totally cool. Okay, so, the key to living here in this town is to get out as much as possible.

Fortunately New York City is only 5 hours away...

I think he's right about that. There's nothing to do around here. I guess that's why the school is here...

There's no chance of being distracted.

I act like such an asshole sometimes. I snapped at that Top hat person.

Let's see what's up this hill...

I get so sick of comics that are obviously just cartoon Network pitches. Like having a show is the endgame of comics...

SILLY FARTING ROBOT & PALS!

But on the other hand I've done a mountain of comics that are goofy... and I think people should do whatever makes them happy.

It's just when I'm feeling anxiety, I focus in on something and pick it apart and get riled up over nothing.

An old graveyard!

2004: my first roommate, Pat, and I decide to go to the sunday service of the local LDS church as a goof.

That'd be funny. Let's go.'

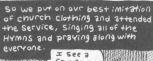

So we put on our best imitation of church clothing and attended the service, singing all of the hymns and praying along with everyone.

I see a few new faces here today.

Though I acted like it was all a joke, actually I was searching for a feeling there. I wanted to know if it felt right. I didn't feel anything and that was the last time I went to church.

"In Memory of Deacon Eben Dewey Died October 19 1794 82 Years"

Wow!

I can't read the name on this one...
" loving Son Died 1811"

This place has been inhabited for a long time!

That's really cool.

How have you been enjoying White River Junction?

So far so good I think. I've begun working on a new book so mostly I've been locking myself away in the old studio...

Listen, I asked you to meet with me because some of the students are concerned you may be intolerant.

"Intolerant?" What are you talking about? I've barely spoken to any of the students! Intolerant in what way?

Okay— There's no reason to raise your voice. The students issued a complaint about your negativity towards manga readers and expressive clothing!

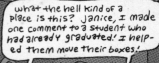

What the hell kind of a place is this? Janice, I made one comment to a student who had already graduated! I helped them move their boxes!

They were wearing a top hat!

Your comments about their hat and their books made them feel very unsafe, and apparently many of the current students are now concerned.

It's my job to let you know.

That does it! I don't want anything to do with these people! This is ridiculous!

I can't believe this.

"Unsafe!" That's so silly.

Fuck! I told myself I would avoid all drama while I was here!

24

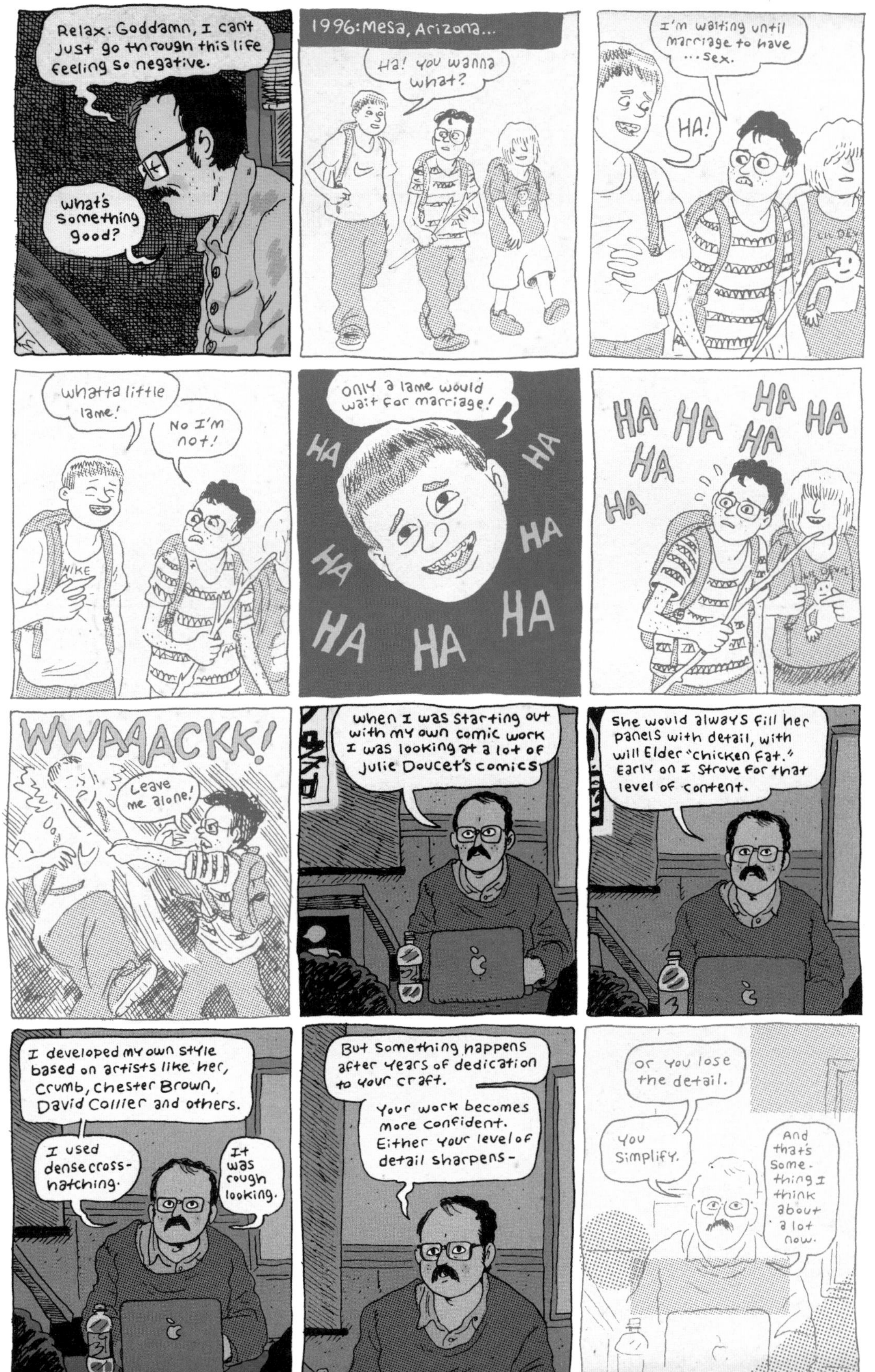
Relax. Goddamn, I can't just go through this life feeling so negative.
What's something good?
1996: Mesa, Arizona...
Ha! You wanna what?
I'm waiting until marriage to have ...sex.
HA!
Whatta little lame!
No I'm not!
Only a lame would wait for marriage!
HA HA HA HA HA HA HA
HA HA HA HA HA HA HA HA
WWAAACKK!
Leave me alone!
When I was starting out with my own comic work I was looking at a lot of Julie Doucet's comics
She would always fill her panels with detail, with Will Elder "chicken fat." Early on I strove for that level of content.
I developed my own style based on artists like her, Crumb, Chester Brown, David Collier and others.
I used dense cross-hatching.
It was rough looking.
But something happens after years of dedication to your craft.
Your work becomes more confident. Either your level of detail sharpens-
Or you lose the detail.
You simplify.
And that's some-thing I think about a lot now.

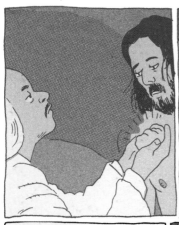

You are excrement. But you can turn yourself into gold.

The fish thinks about his hunger. Not about the fisherman.

This movie is incredible. *

* The Holy Mountain

I still haven't figured out how to draw nature well...

maybe I've spent too much time in a city...

They're like sticks in the ground...

Why don't I go out and make some sketches? I imagined myself doing things like that before I came here.

Okay, yeah, a little nature would be good for my rotten soul.

maybe I can do a lot of nature sketches and print a little mini comic of them.

I should check my social medias real quick.

Then I'll head out.

2 HOURS LATER...

"The Holy Mountain is based on 'Ascent of Mount Carmel' by John of the Cross..."

maybe I have no peace of mind because I have no religion.

maybe God will appear to me in the woods and then I'll be a new American prophet.

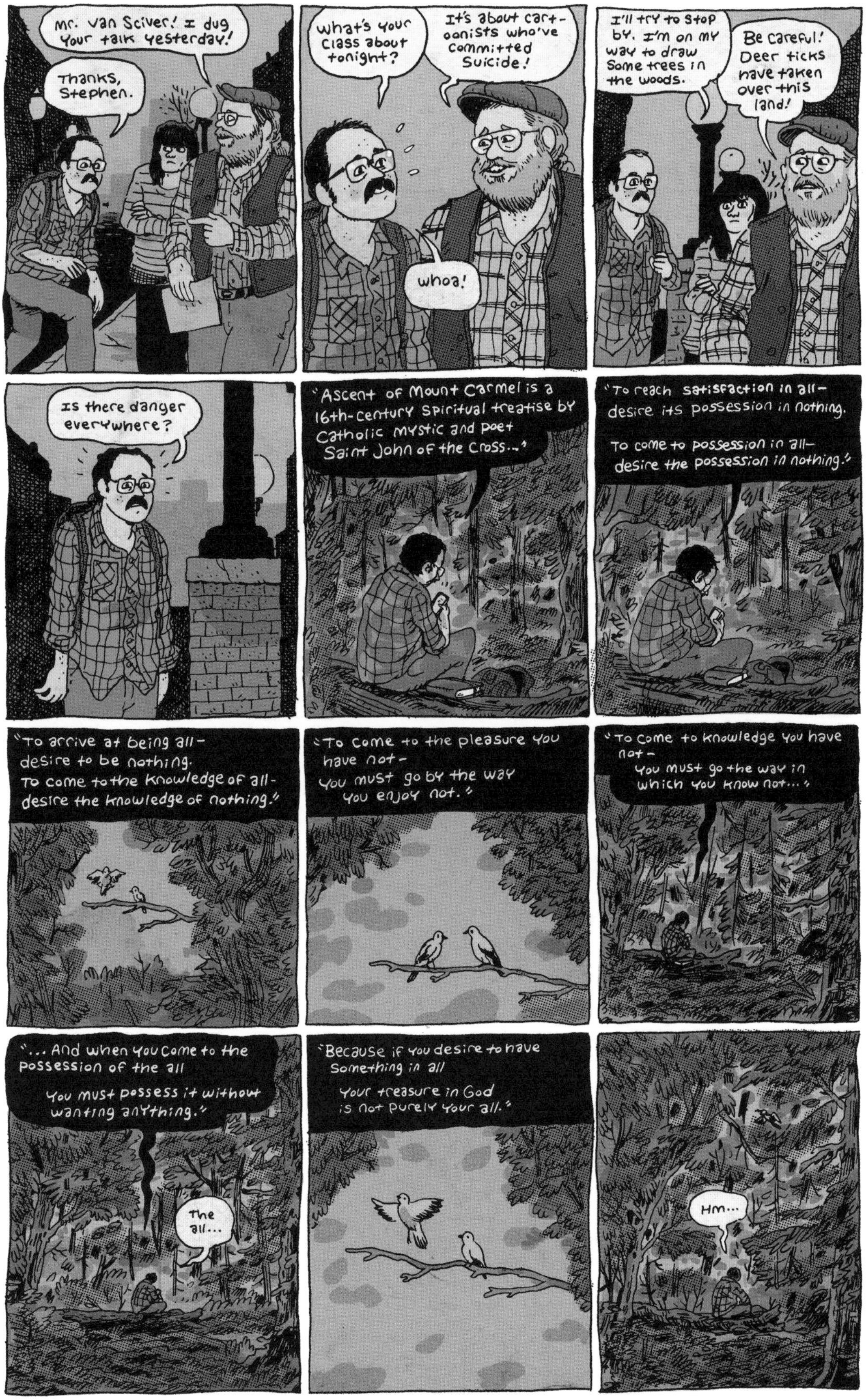
Mr. van Sciver! I dug your talk yesterday!
Thanks, Stephen.
What's your class about tonight?
It's about cartoonists who've committed suicide!
Whoa!
I'll try to stop by. I'm on my way to draw some trees in the woods.
Be careful! Deer ticks have taken over this land!
Is there danger everywhere?
"Ascent of Mount Carmel is a 16th-century spiritual treatise by Catholic mystic and poet Saint John of the Cross..."
"To reach satisfaction in all- desire its possession in nothing.
To come to possession in all- desire the possession in nothing."
"To arrive at being all- desire to be nothing.
To come to the knowledge of all- desire the knowledge of nothing."
"To come to the pleasure you have not- you must go by the way you enjoy not."
"To come to knowledge you have not- you must go the way in which you know not..."
"... And when you come to the possession of the all you must possess it without wanting anything."
The all...
"Because if you desire to have something in all your treasure in God is not purely your all."
Hm...

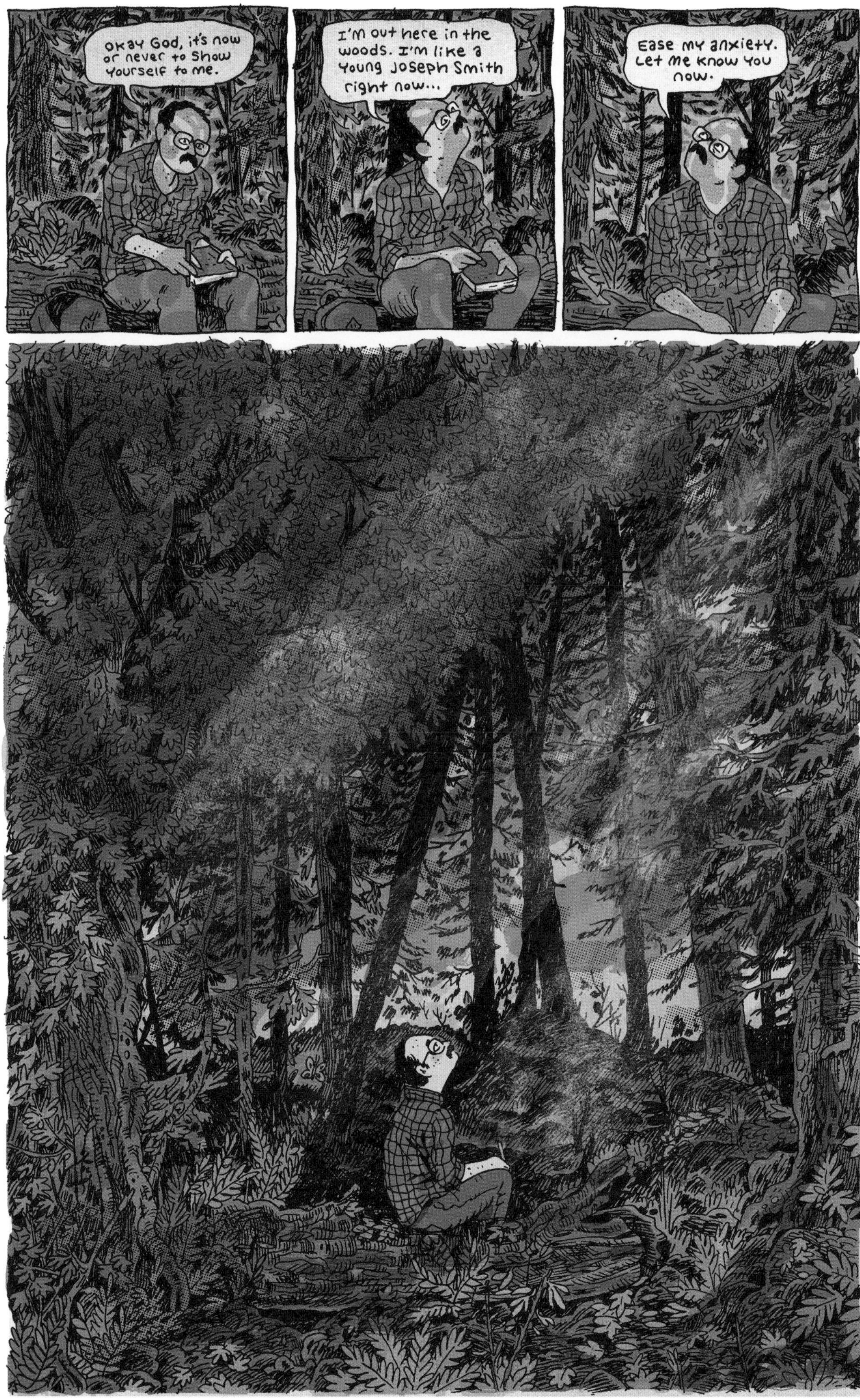
Okay God, it's now or never to show yourself to me.
I'm out here in the woods. I'm like a young Joseph Smith right now...
Ease my anxiety. Let me know you now.

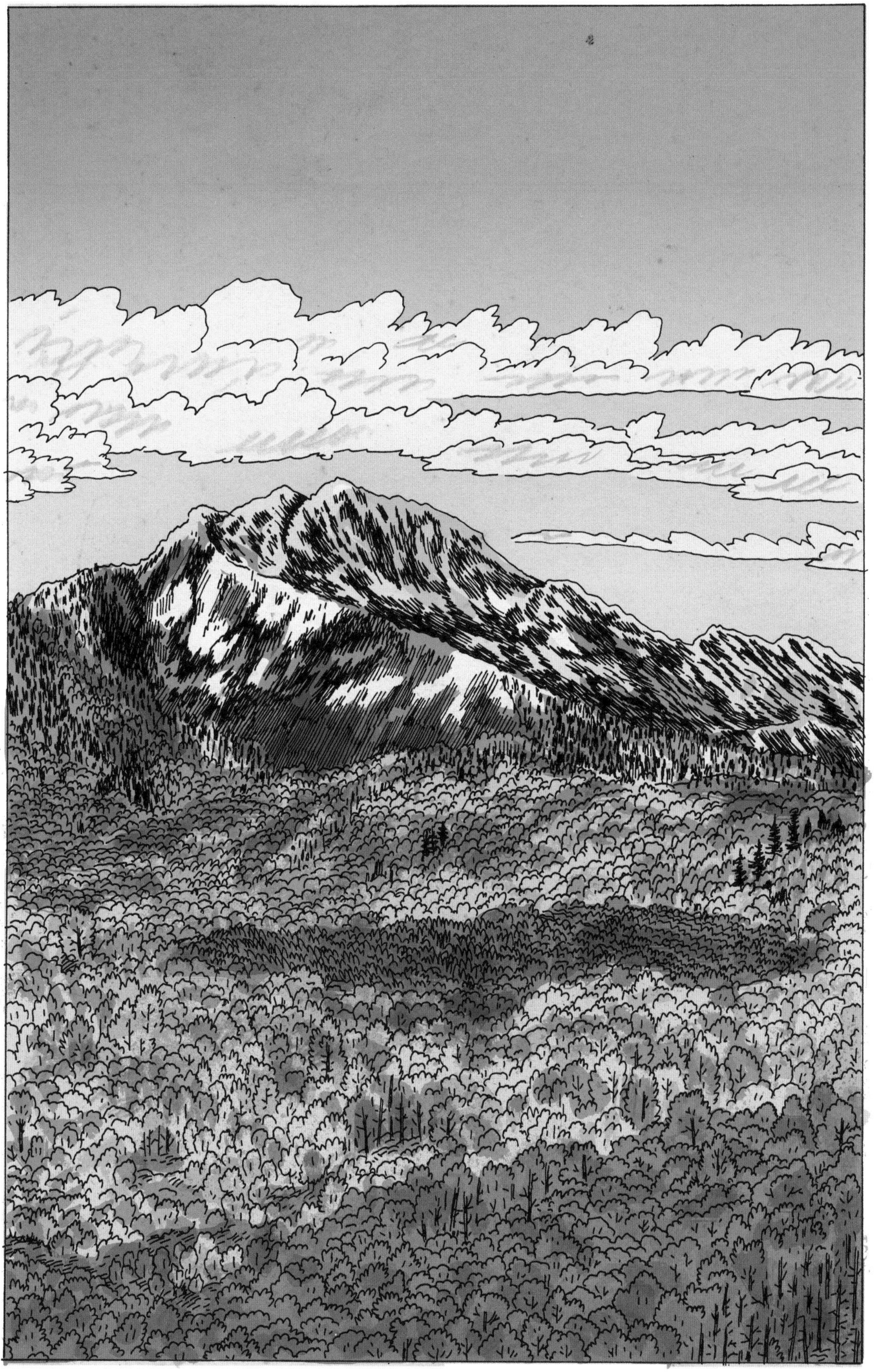

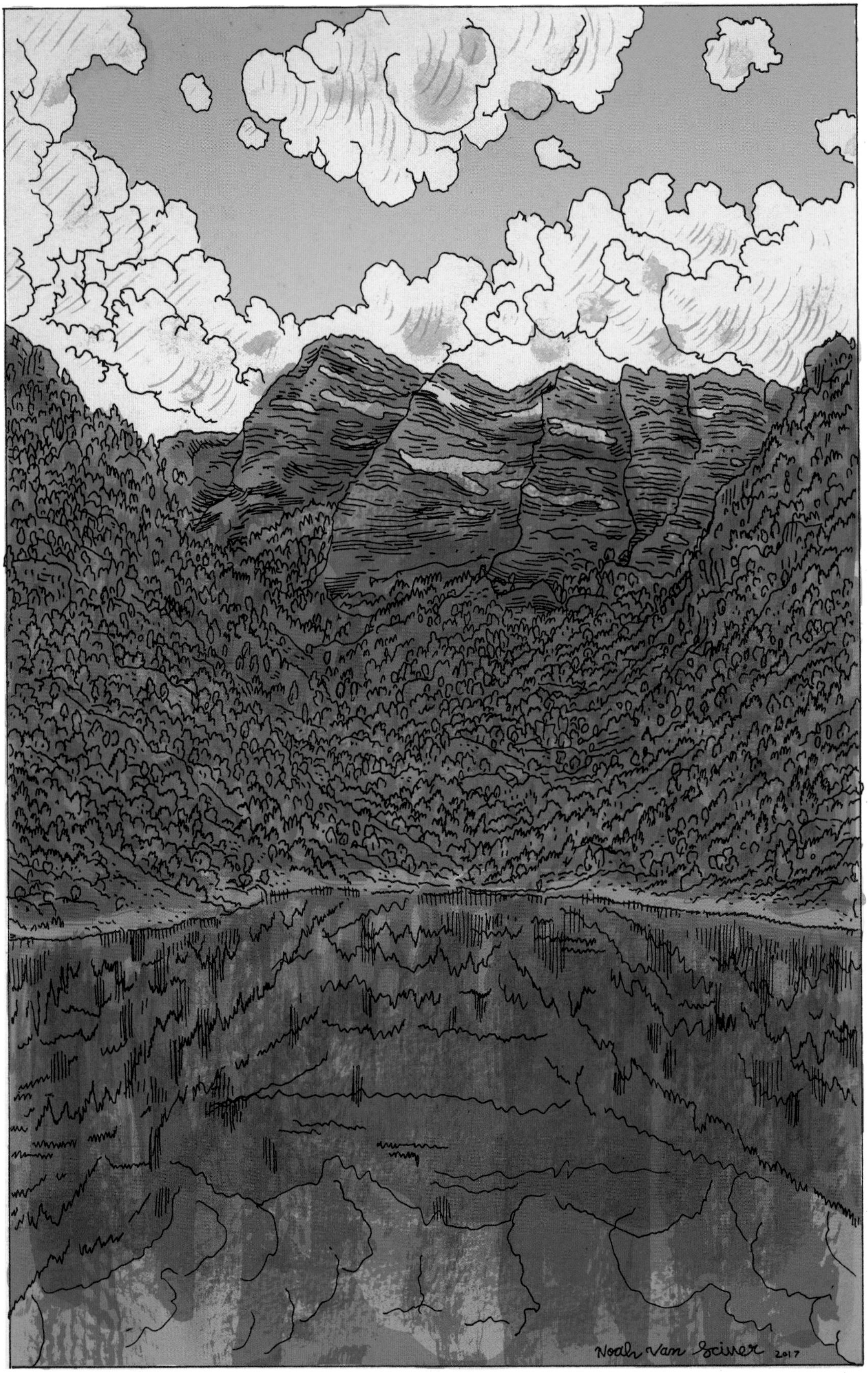
Noah Van Sciver 2017

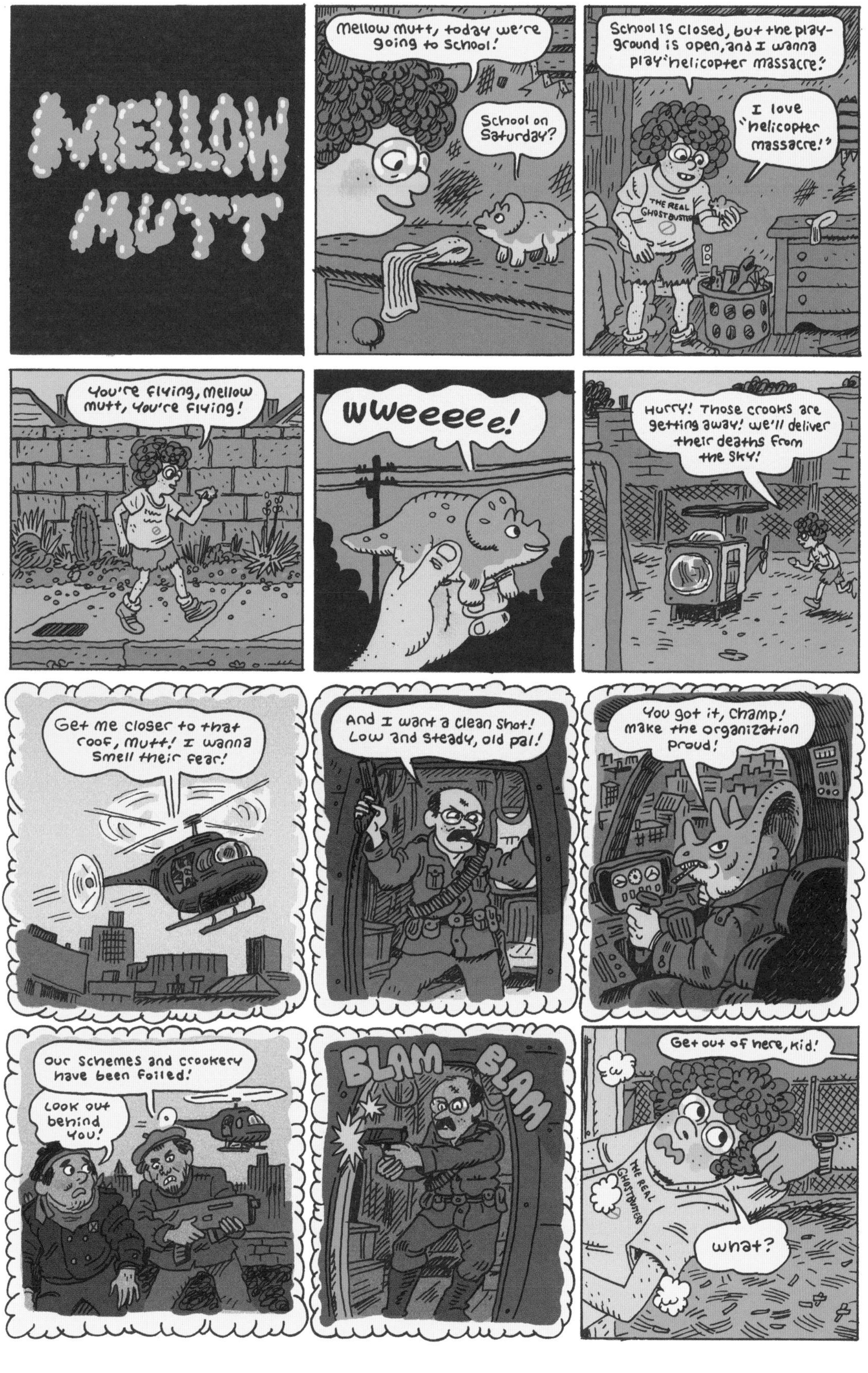
MELLOW MUTT
Mellow mutt, today we're going to school!
School on Saturday?
School is closed, but the playground is open, and I wanna play "helicopter massacre."
I love "helicopter massacre!"
THE REAL GHOSTBUSTERS
You're flying, mellow mutt, you're flying!
WWeeeee!
Hurry! Those crooks are getting away! We'll deliver their deaths from the sky!
Get me closer to that roof, Mutt! I wanna smell their fear!
And I want a clean shot! Low and steady, old pal!
You got it, champ! Make the organization proud!
Our schemes and crookery have been foiled!
Look out behind you!
BLAM BLAM
Get out of here, kid!
THE REAL GHOSTBUSTERS
What?

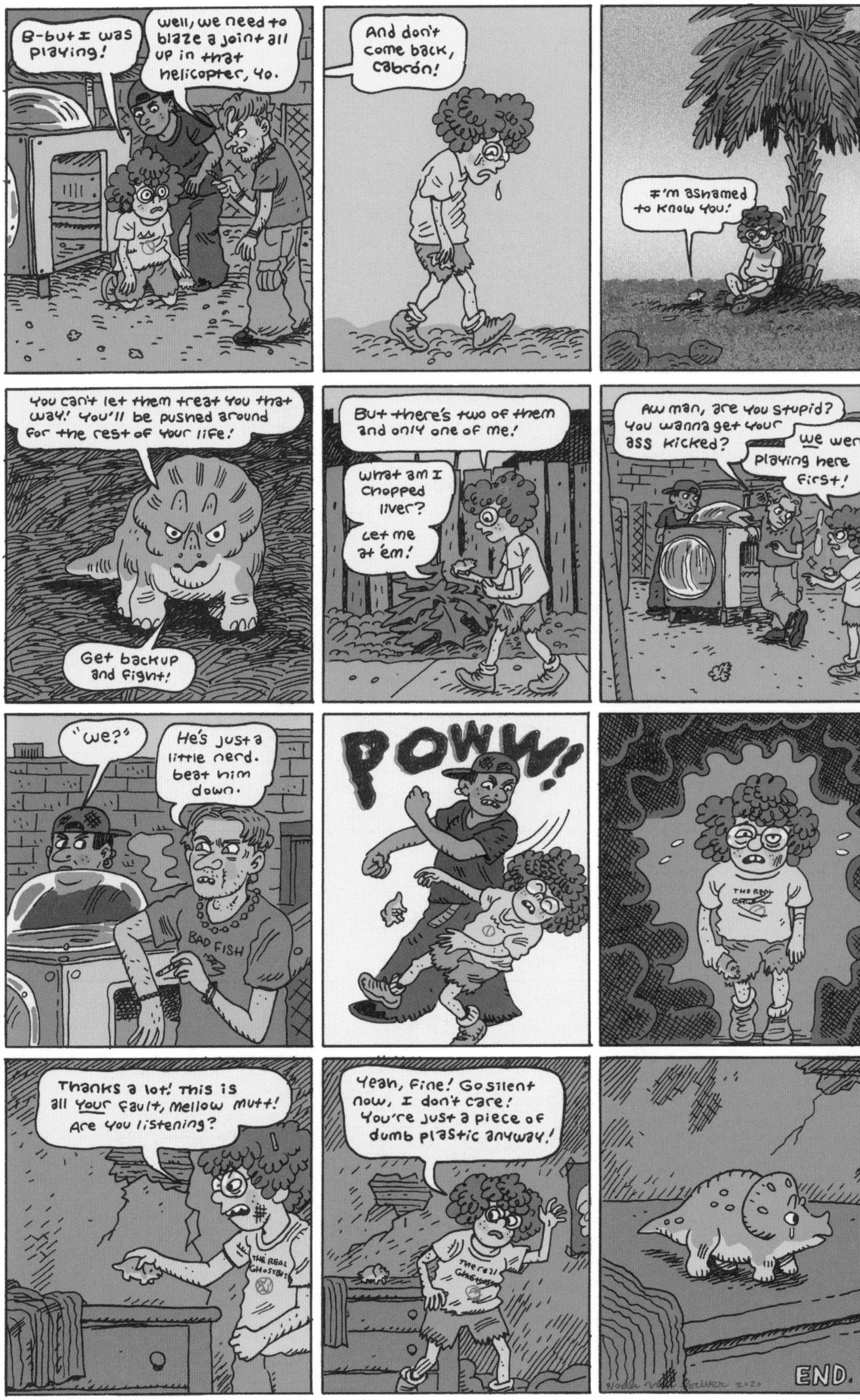

B-but I was playing!
Well, we need to blaze a joint all up in that helicopter, yo.
And don't come back, cabrón!
I'm ashamed to know you!
You can't let them treat you that way! You'll be pushed around for the rest of your life!
Get backup and fight!
But there's two of them and only one of me!
What am I chopped liver?
Let me at 'em!
Aw man, are you stupid? You wanna get your ass kicked?
We were playing here first!
"We?"
He's just a little nerd. Beat him down.
BAD FISH
POWW!
Thanks a lot! This is all YOUR fault, Mellow Mutt! Are you listening?
Yeah, fine! Go silent now, I don't care! You're just a piece of dumb plastic anyway!
END.

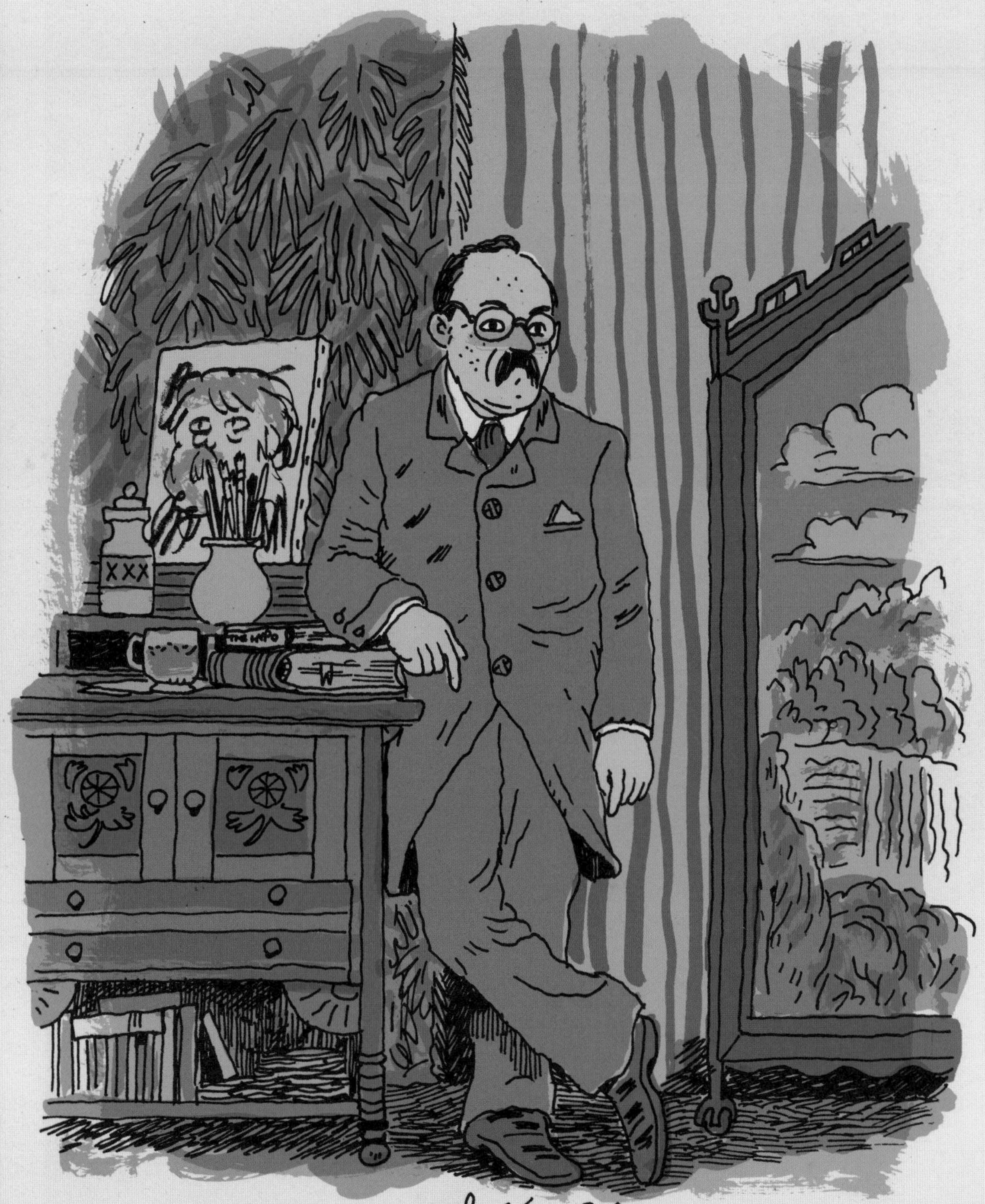
XXX
THE HYPO
Noah Van Sciver 2017

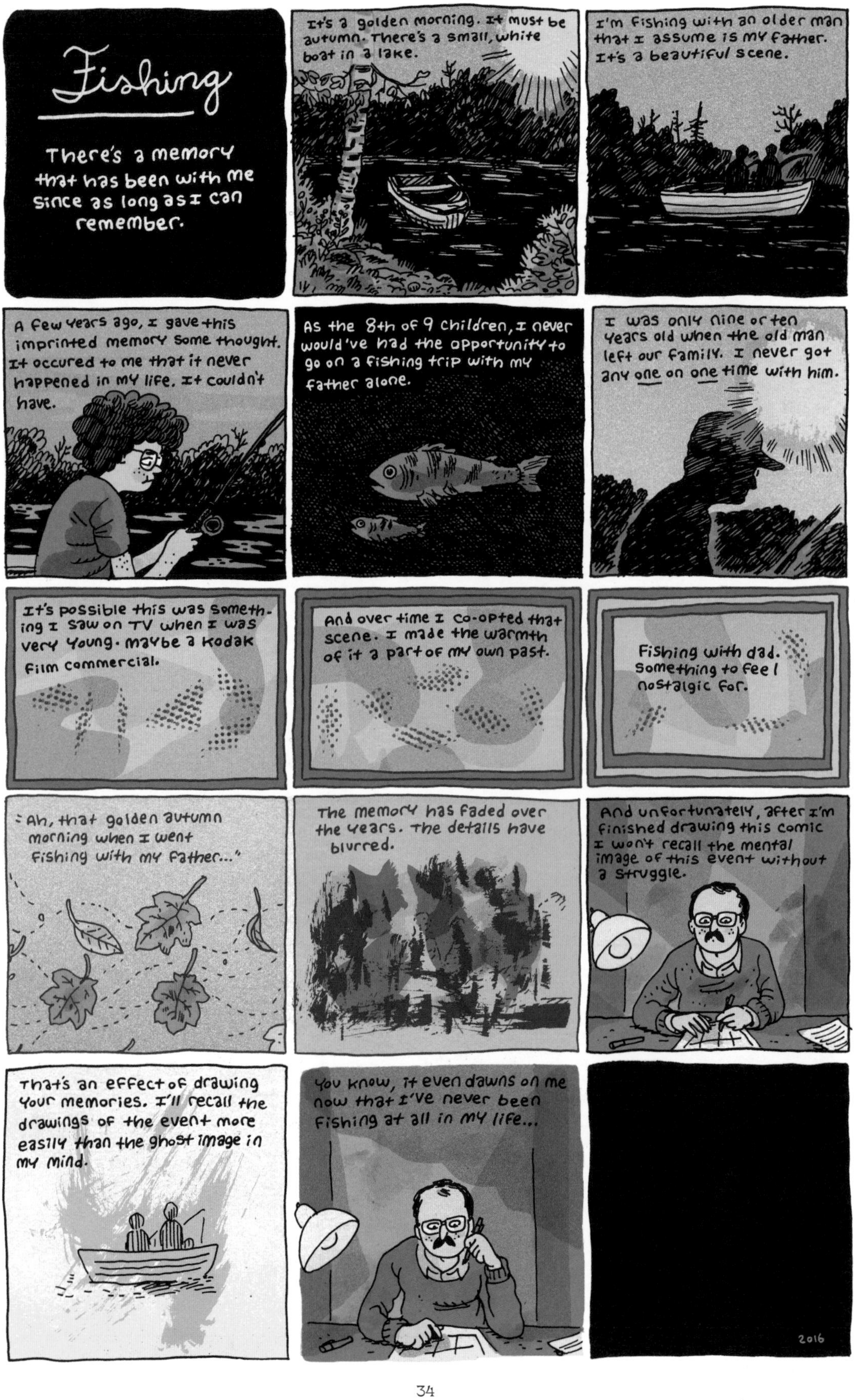
Fishing
There's a memory that has been with me since as long as I can remember.
It's a golden morning. It must be autumn. There's a small, white boat in a lake.
I'm fishing with an older man that I assume is my father. It's a beautiful scene.
A few years ago, I gave this imprinted memory some thought. It occured to me that it never happened in my life. It couldn't have.
As the 8th of 9 children, I never would've had the opportunity to go on a fishing trip with my father alone.
I was only nine or ten years old when the old man left our family. I never got any one on one time with him.
It's possible this was something I saw on TV when I was very young. Maybe a Kodak film commercial.
And over time I co-opted that scene. I made the warmth of it a part of my own past.
Fishing with dad. Something to feel nostalgic for.
"Ah, that golden autumn morning when I went fishing with my father..."
The memory has faded over the years. The details have blurred.
And unfortunately, after I'm finished drawing this comic I won't recall the mental image of this event without a struggle.
That's an effect of drawing your memories. I'll recall the drawings of the event more easily than the ghost image in my mind.
You know, it even dawns on me now that I've never been fishing at all in my life...
2016

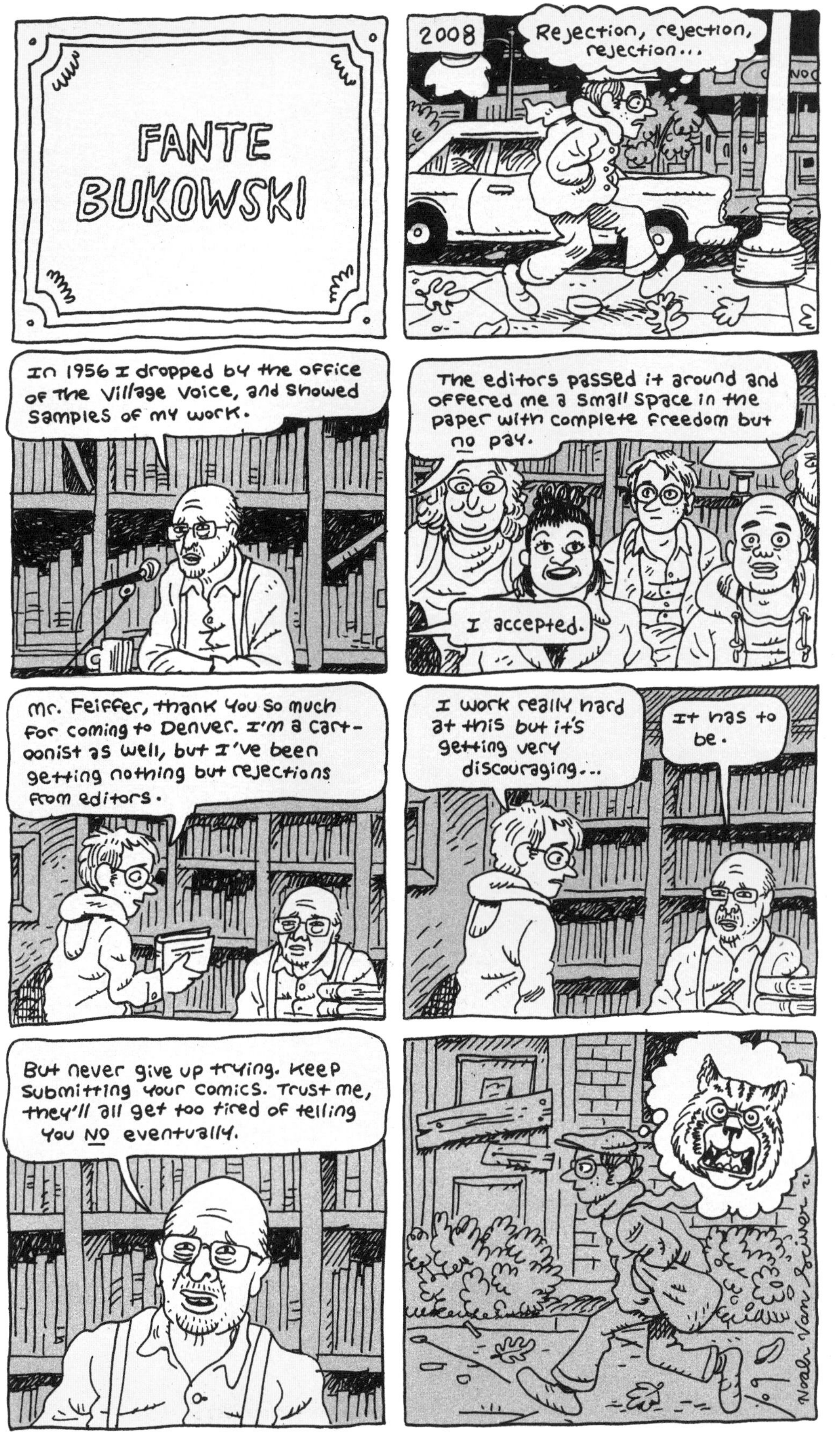
FANTE BUKOWSKI
2008
Rejection, rejection, rejection...
In 1956 I dropped by the office of The Village Voice, and showed samples of my work.
The editors passed it around and offered me a small space in the paper with complete freedom but no pay.
I accepted.
Mr. Feiffer, thank you so much for coming to Denver. I'm a cartoonist as well, but I've been getting nothing but rejections from editors.
I work really hard at this but it's getting very discouraging...
It has to be.
But never give up trying. Keep submitting your comics. Trust me, they'll all get too tired of telling you NO eventually.
Noah Van Sciver

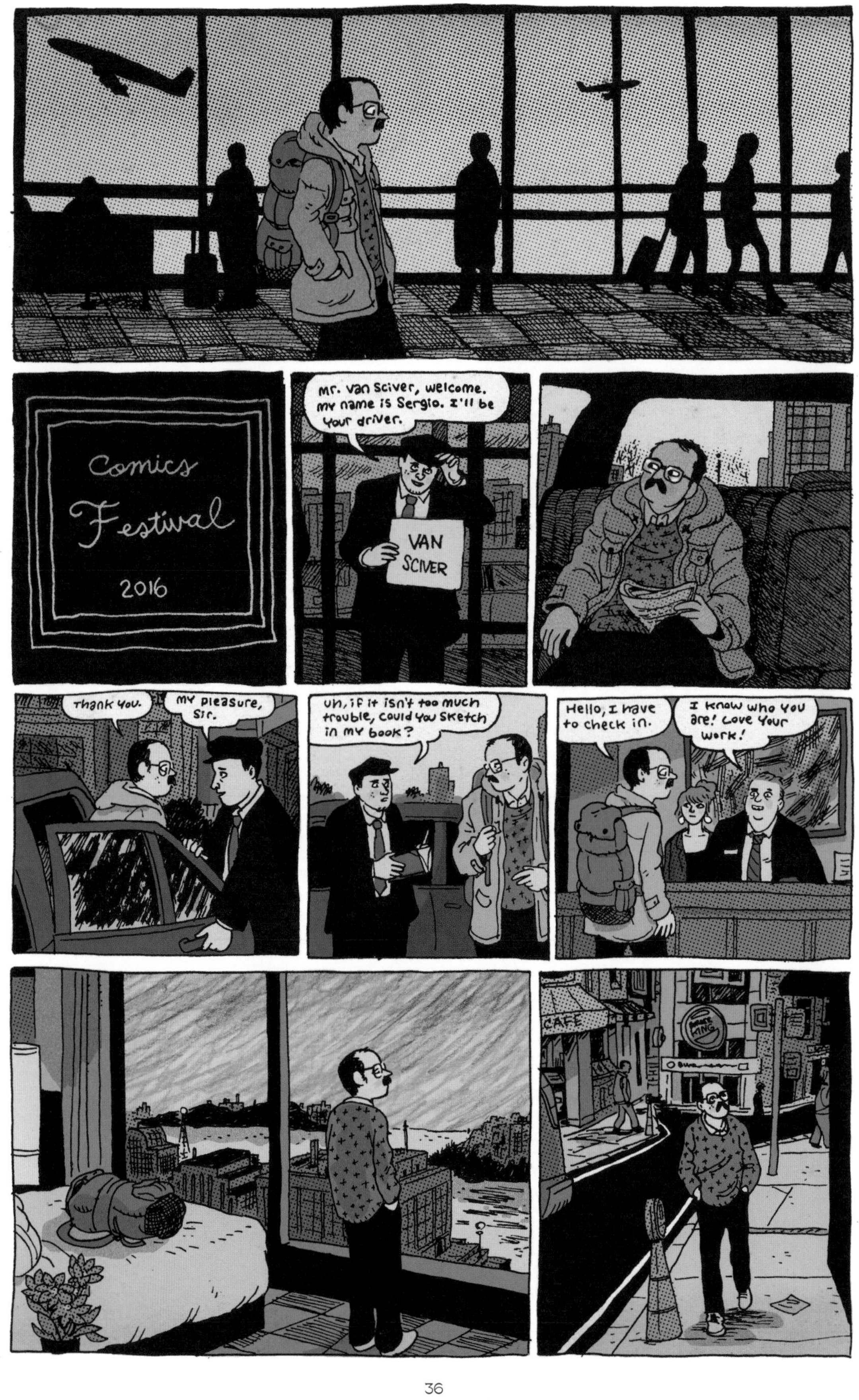
Comics Festival 2016
Mr. Van Sciver, welcome. My name is Sergio. I'll be your driver.
VAN SCIVER
Thank you.
My pleasure, sir.
Uh, if it isn't too much trouble, could you sketch in my book?
Hello, I have to check in.
I know who you are! Love your work!
CAFE

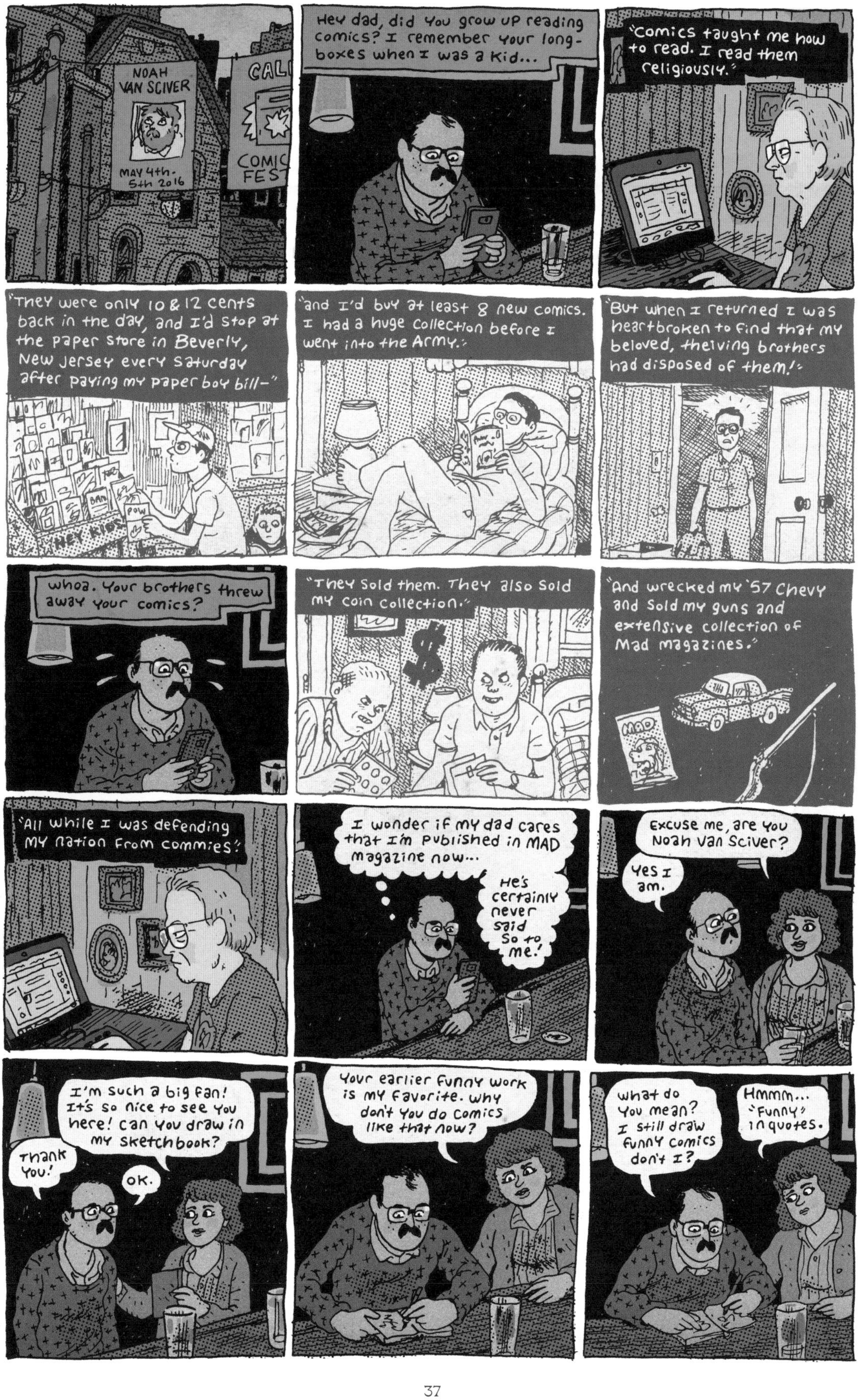
NOAH VAN SCIVER
MAY 4th. 5th 2016
COMIC FEST
Hey dad, did you grow up reading comics? I remember your long-boxes when I was a kid...
"Comics taught me how to read. I read them religiously."
"They were only 10 & 12 cents back in the day, and I'd stop at the paper store in Beverly, New Jersey every Saturday after paying my paper boy bill–"
POW
HEY KIDS
"and I'd buy at least 8 new comics. I had a huge collection before I went into the Army."
"But when I returned I was heartbroken to find that my beloved, thelving brothers had disposed of them!"
whoa. Your brothers threw away your comics?
"They sold them. They also sold my coin collection."
"And wrecked my '57 Chevy and sold my guns and extensive collection of Mad magazines."
MAD
"All while I was defending my nation from commies!"
I wonder if my dad cares that I'm published in MAD magazine now...
He's certainly never said so to me!
Excuse me, are you Noah Van Sciver?
Yes I am.
I'm such a big fan! It's so nice to see you here! Can you draw in my sketchbook?
Thank you!
OK.
Your earlier funny work is my favorite. Why don't you do comics like that now?
What do you mean? I still draw funny comics don't I?
Hmmm... "Funny" in quotes.

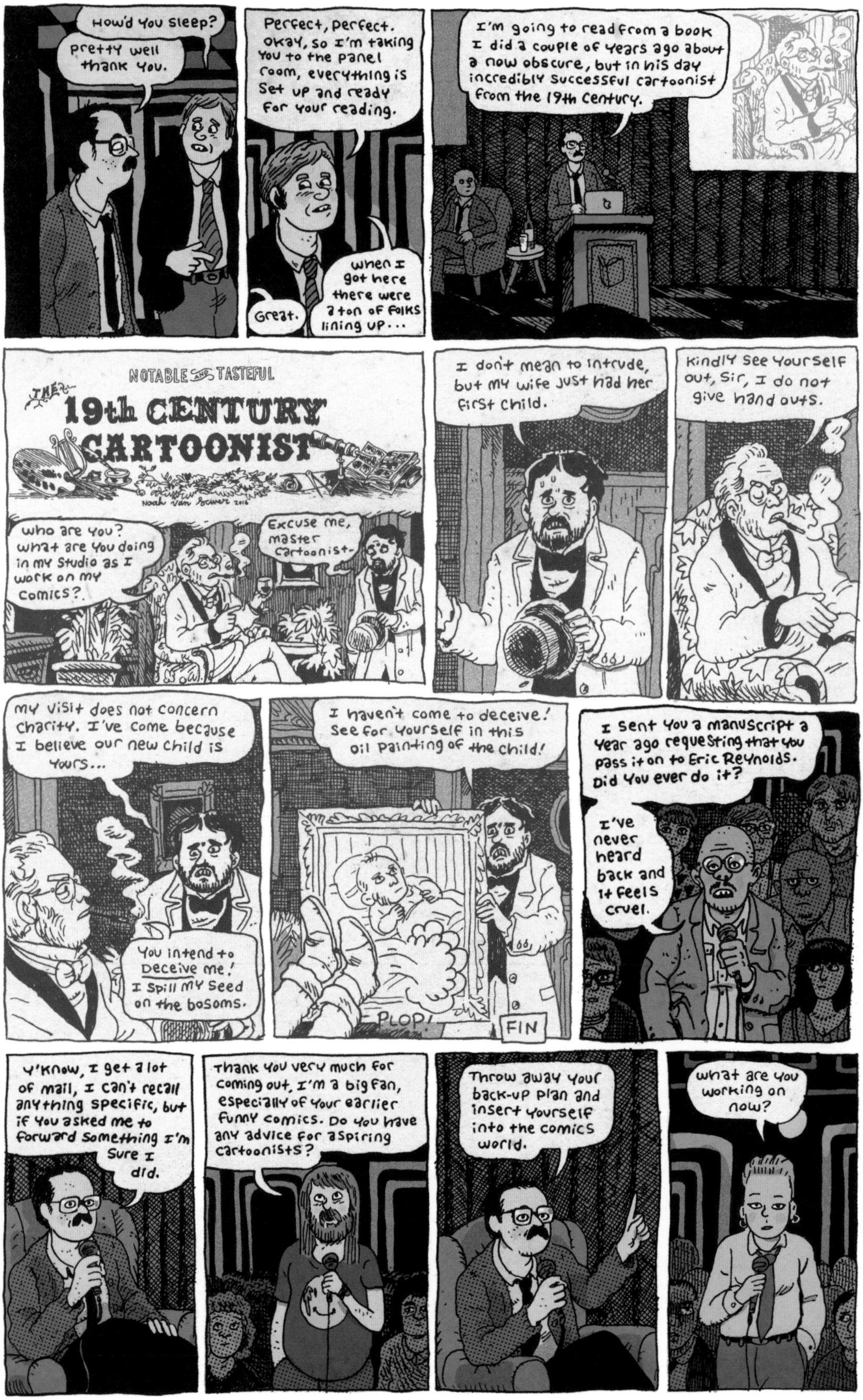
How'd you sleep?
Pretty well thank you.
Perfect, perfect. Okay, so I'm taking you to the panel room, everything is set up and ready for your reading.
When I got here there were a ton of folks lining up...
Great.
I'm going to read from a book I did a couple of years ago about a now obscure, but in his day incredibly successful cartoonist from the 19th century.
NOTABLE AND TASTEFUL
THE 19th CENTURY CARTOONIST
Noah Van Sciver 2016
Who are you? What are you doing in my studio as I work on my comics?
Excuse me, master cartoonist-
I don't mean to intrude, but my wife just had her first child.
Kindly see yourself out, sir, I do not give hand outs.
My visit does not concern charity. I've come because I believe our new child is yours...
You intend to deceive me! I spill my seed on the bosoms.
I haven't come to deceive! See for yourself in this oil painting of the child!
PLOP!
FIN
I sent you a manuscript a year ago requesting that you pass it on to Eric Reynolds. Did you ever do it?
I've never heard back and it feels cruel.
Y'know, I get a lot of mail, I can't recall anything specific, but if you asked me to forward something I'm sure I did.
Thank you very much for coming out, I'm a big fan, especially of your earlier funny comics. Do you have any advice for aspiring cartoonists?
Throw away your back-up plan and insert yourself into the comics world.
What are you working on now?

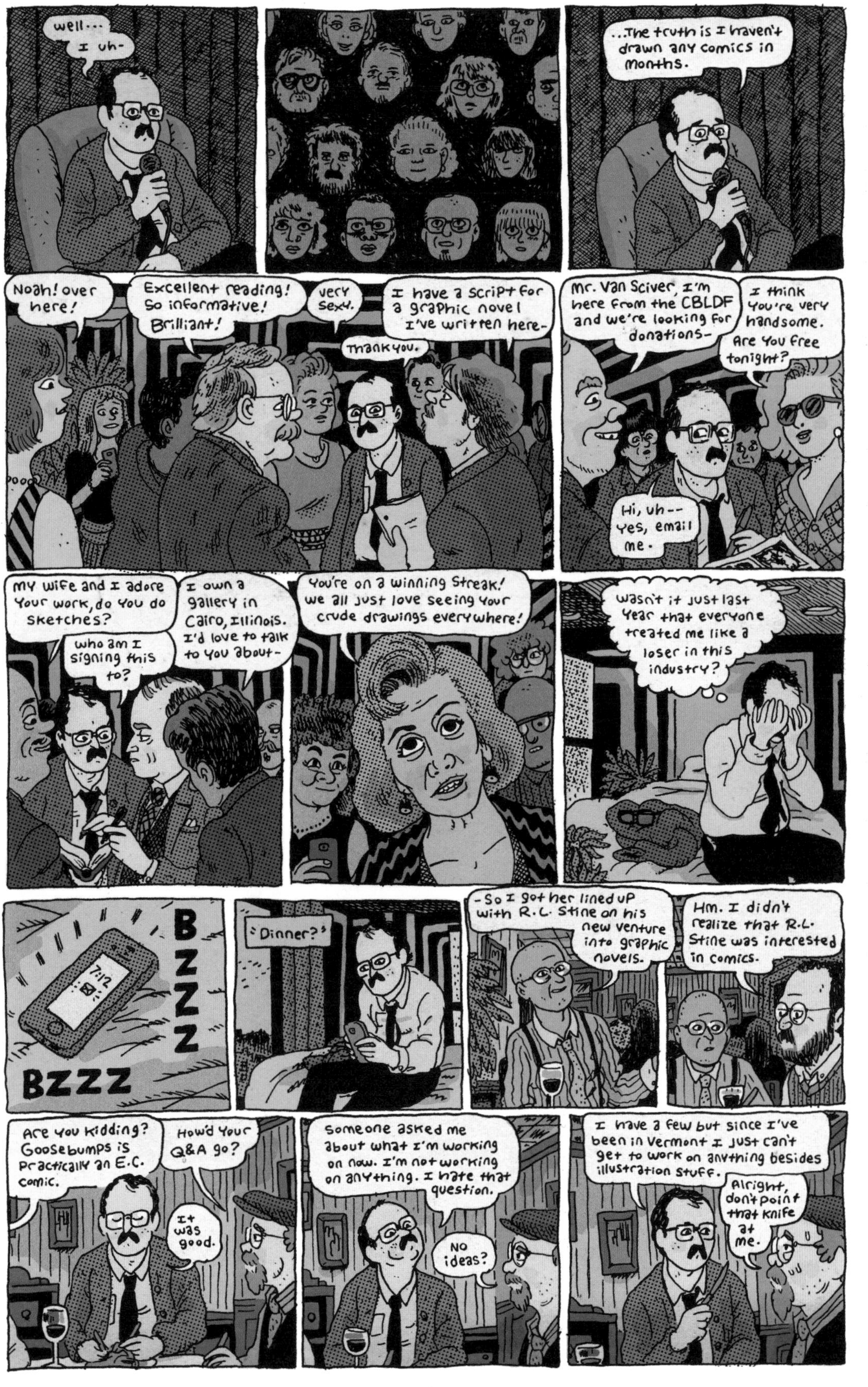
well...
I uh-
...The truth is I haven't drawn any comics in months.
Noah! over here!
Excellent reading! So informative! Brilliant!
very sexy.
I have a script for a graphic novel I've written here-
Thank you.
Mr. Van Sciver, I'm here from the CBLDF and we're looking for donations-
I think you're very handsome. Are you free tonight?
Hi, uh-- yes, email me.
My wife and I adore your work, do you do sketches?
who am I signing this to?
I own a gallery in Cairo, Illinois. I'd love to talk to you about-
You're on a winning streak! We all just love seeing your crude drawings everywhere!
Wasn't it just last year that everyone treated me like a loser in this industry?
7:12
BZZZ
BZZZ
Dinner?
-So I got her lined up with R.L. Stine on his new venture into graphic novels.
Hm. I didn't realize that R.L. Stine was interested in comics.
Are you kidding? Goosebumps is practically an E.C. comic.
How'd your Q&A go?
It was good.
Someone asked me about what I'm working on now. I'm not working on anything. I hate that question.
No ideas?
I have a few but since I've been in Vermont I just can't get to work on anything besides illustration stuff.
Alright, don't point that knife at me.

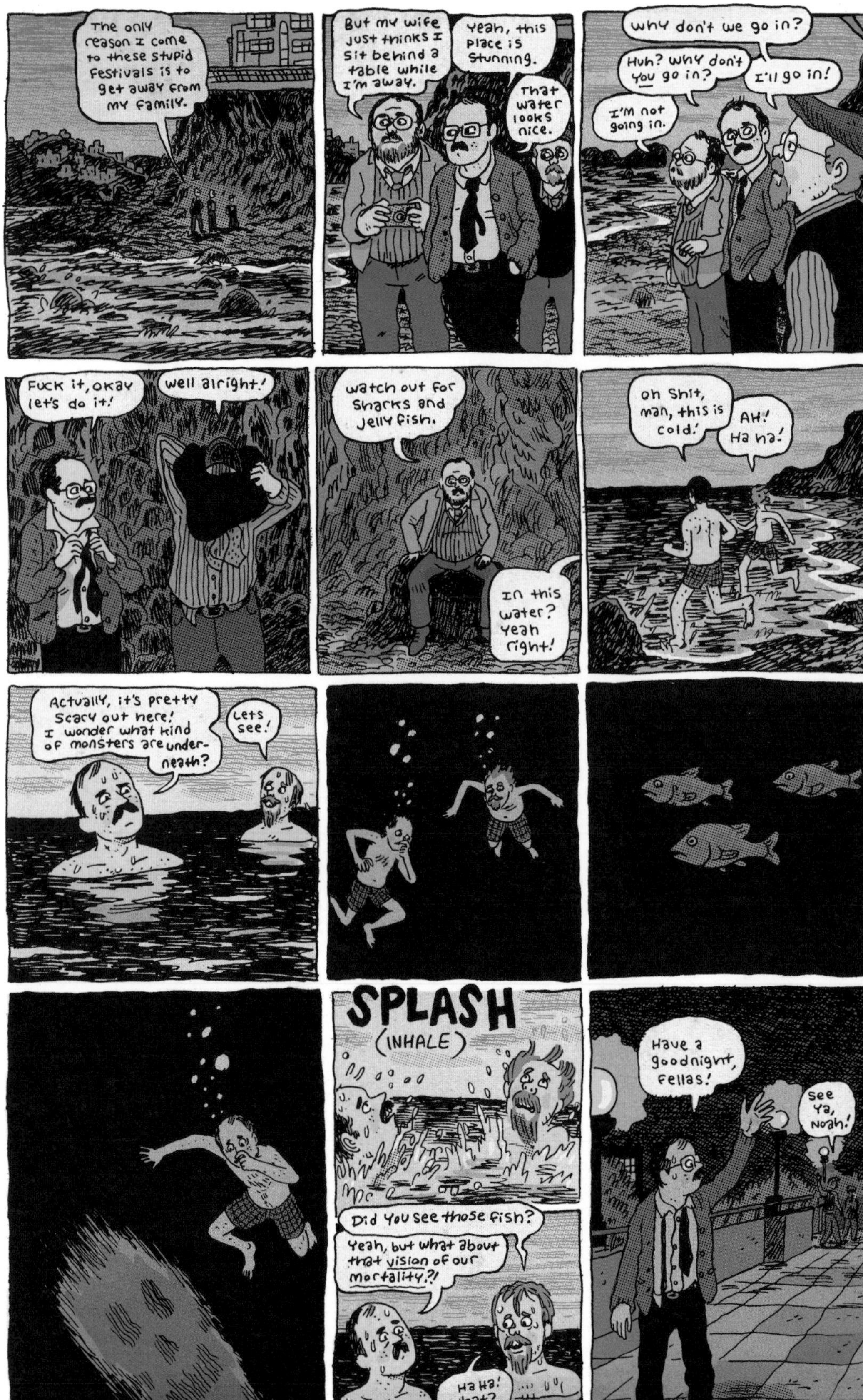
The only reason I come to these stupid festivals is to get away from my family.
But my wife just thinks I sit behind a table while I'm away.
Yeah, this place is stunning.
That water looks nice.
Why don't we go in?
Huh? Why don't you go in?
I'll go in!
I'm not going in.
Fuck it, okay let's do it!
Well alright!
Watch out for sharks and jelly fish.
In this water? Yeah right!
Oh shit, man, this is cold!
AH! Ha ha!
Actually, it's pretty scary out here! I wonder what kind of monsters are underneath?
Lets see!
SPLASH
(INHALE)
Did you see those fish?
Yeah, but what about that vision of our mortality?!
Ha ha! What?
Have a goodnight, fellas!
See ya, Noah!

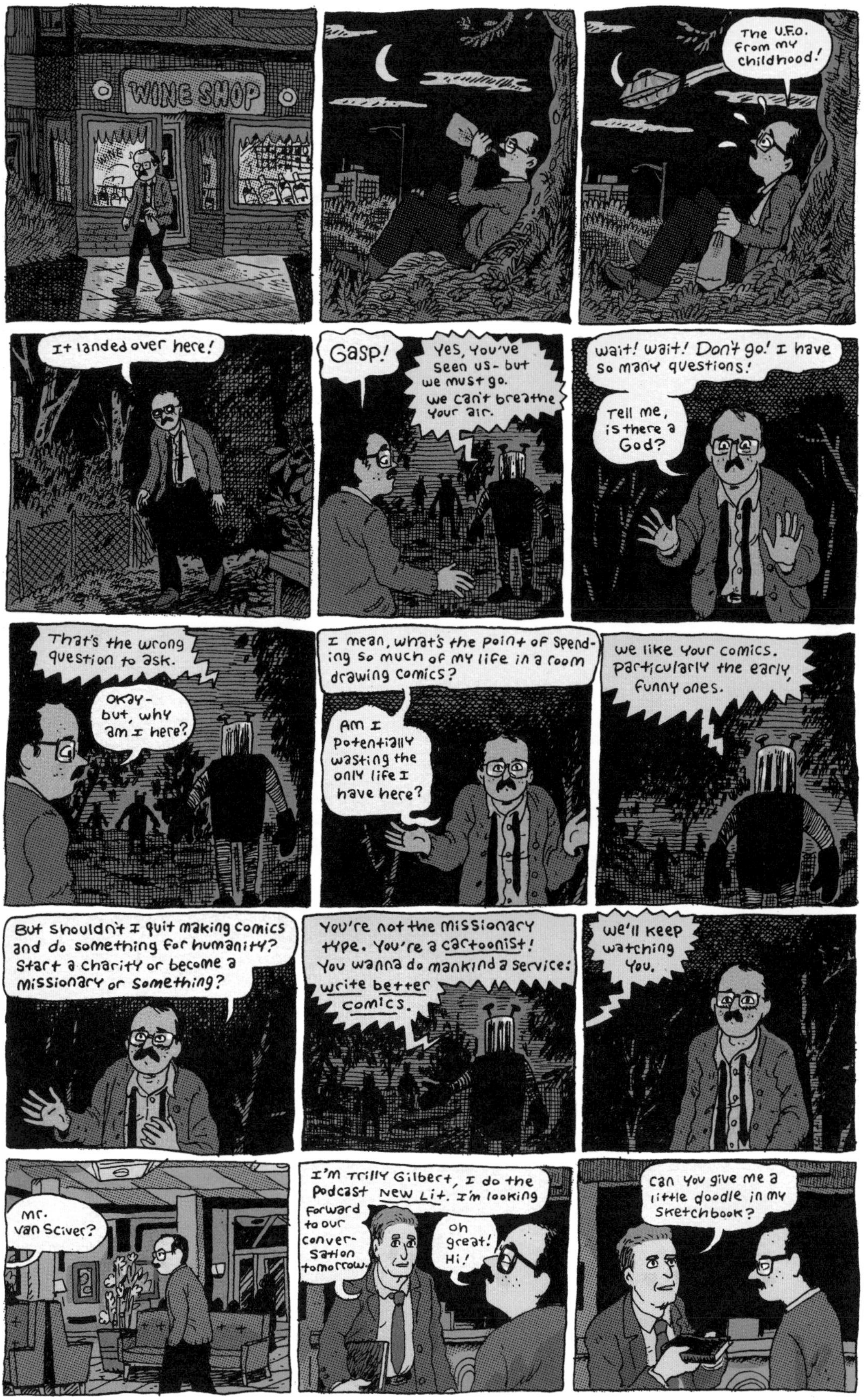
WINE SHOP
The U.F.O. from my childhood!
It landed over here!
Gasp!
Yes, you've seen us- but we must go. We can't breathe your air.
Wait! Wait! Don't go! I have so many questions!
Tell me, is there a God?
That's the wrong question to ask.
Okay- but, why am I here?
I mean, what's the point of spending so much of my life in a room drawing comics?
Am I potentially wasting the only life I have here?
We like your comics. Particularly the early, funny ones.
But shouldn't I quit making comics and do something for humanity? Start a charity or become a missionary or something?
You're not the missionary type. You're a cartoonist! You wanna do mankind a service: write better comics.
We'll keep watching you.
Mr. van Sciver?
I'm Trilly Gilbert, I do the podcast New Lit. I'm looking forward to our conversation tomorrow.
Oh great! Hi!
Can you give me a little doodle in my sketchbook?

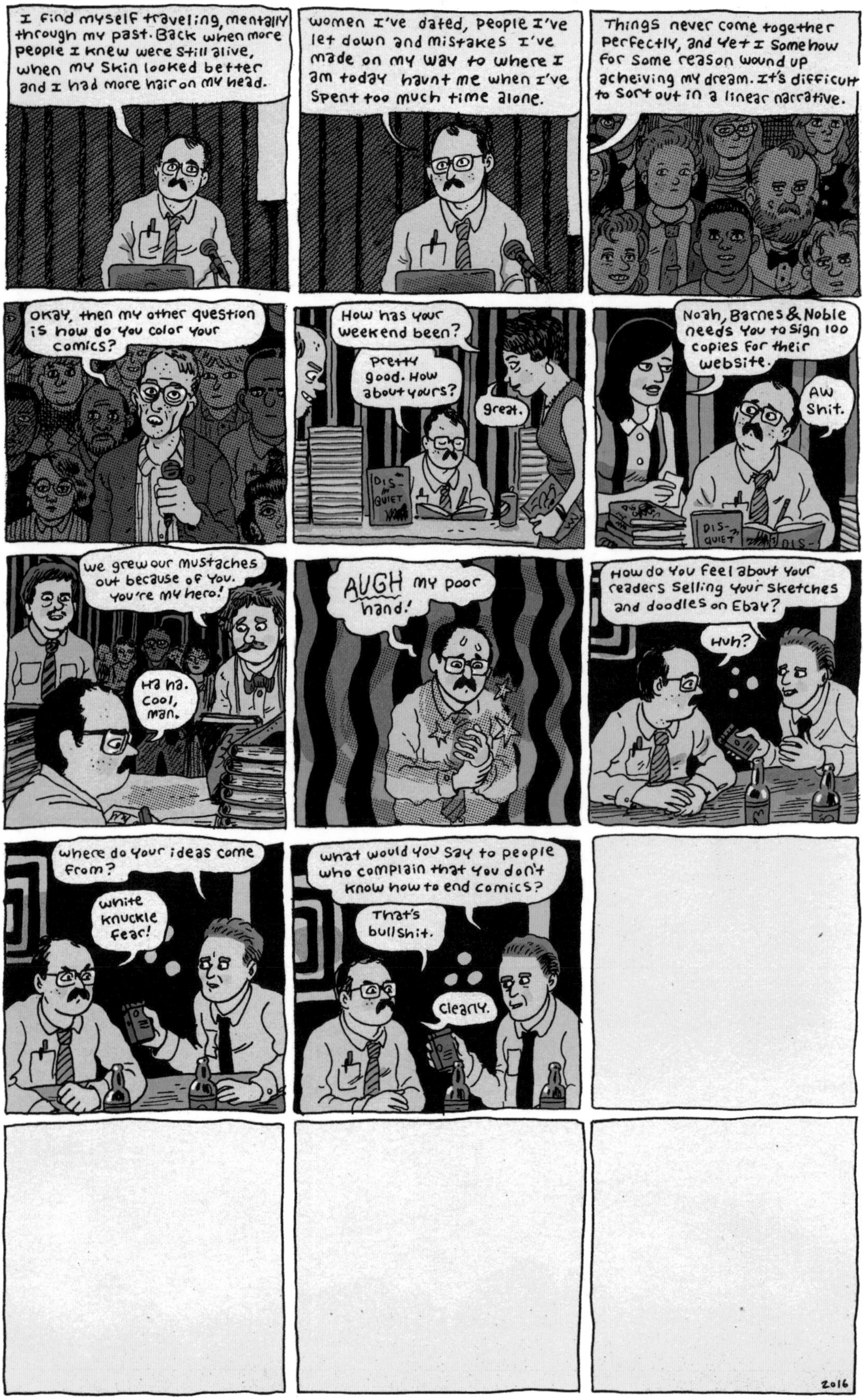
I find myself traveling, mentally through my past. Back when more people I knew were still alive, when my skin looked better and I had more hair on my head.
women I've dated, people I've let down and mistakes I've made on my way to where I am today haunt me when I've spent too much time alone.
Things never come together perfectly, and yet I somehow for some reason wound up acheiving my dream. It's difficult to sort out in a linear narrative.
Okay, then my other question is how do you color your comics?
How has your weekend been?
Pretty good. How about yours?
Great.
DIS-QUIET
Noah, Barnes & Noble needs you to sign 100 copies for their website.
Aw shit.
DIS-QUIET
we grew our mustaches out because of you. You're my hero!
Ha ha. cool, man.
AUGH my poor hand!
How do you feel about your readers selling your sketches and doodles on Ebay?
Huh?
where do your ideas come from?
white knuckle fear!
what would you say to people who complain that you don't know how to end comics?
That's bullshit.
Clearly.
2016

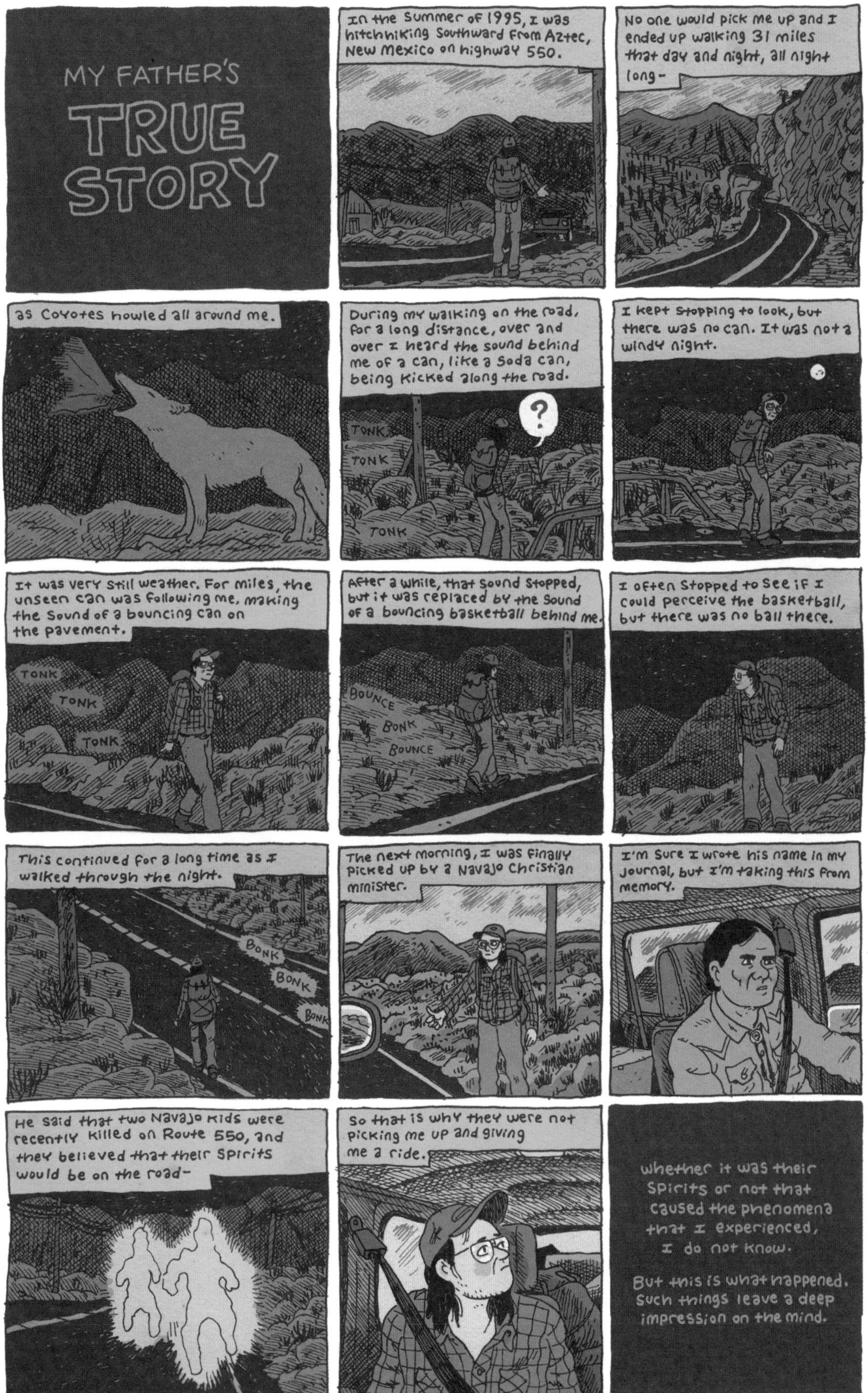
MY FATHER'S
TRUE STORY
In the summer of 1995, I was hitchhiking southward from Aztec, New Mexico on highway 550.
No one would pick me up and I ended up walking 31 miles that day and night, all night long-
as Coyotes howled all around me.
During my walking on the road, for a long distance, over and over I heard the sound behind me of a can, like a soda can, being kicked along the road.
TONK
TONK
TONK
?
I kept stopping to look, but there was no can. It was not a windy night.
It was very still weather. For miles, the unseen can was following me, making the sound of a bouncing can on the pavement.
TONK
TONK
TONK
After a while, that sound stopped, but it was replaced by the sound of a bouncing basketball behind me.
BOUNCE
BONK
BOUNCE
I often stopped to see if I could perceive the basketball, but there was no ball there.
This continued for a long time as I walked through the night.
BONK
BONK
BONK
The next morning, I was finally picked up by a Navajo Christian minister.
I'm sure I wrote his name in my journal, but I'm taking this from memory.
He said that two Navajo kids were recently killed on Route 550, and they believed that their spirits would be on the road-
So that is why they were not picking me up and giving me a ride.
whether it was their spirits or not that caused the phenomena that I experienced, I do not know.
But this is what happened. Such things leave a deep impression on the mind.
Noah Van Sciver 2016

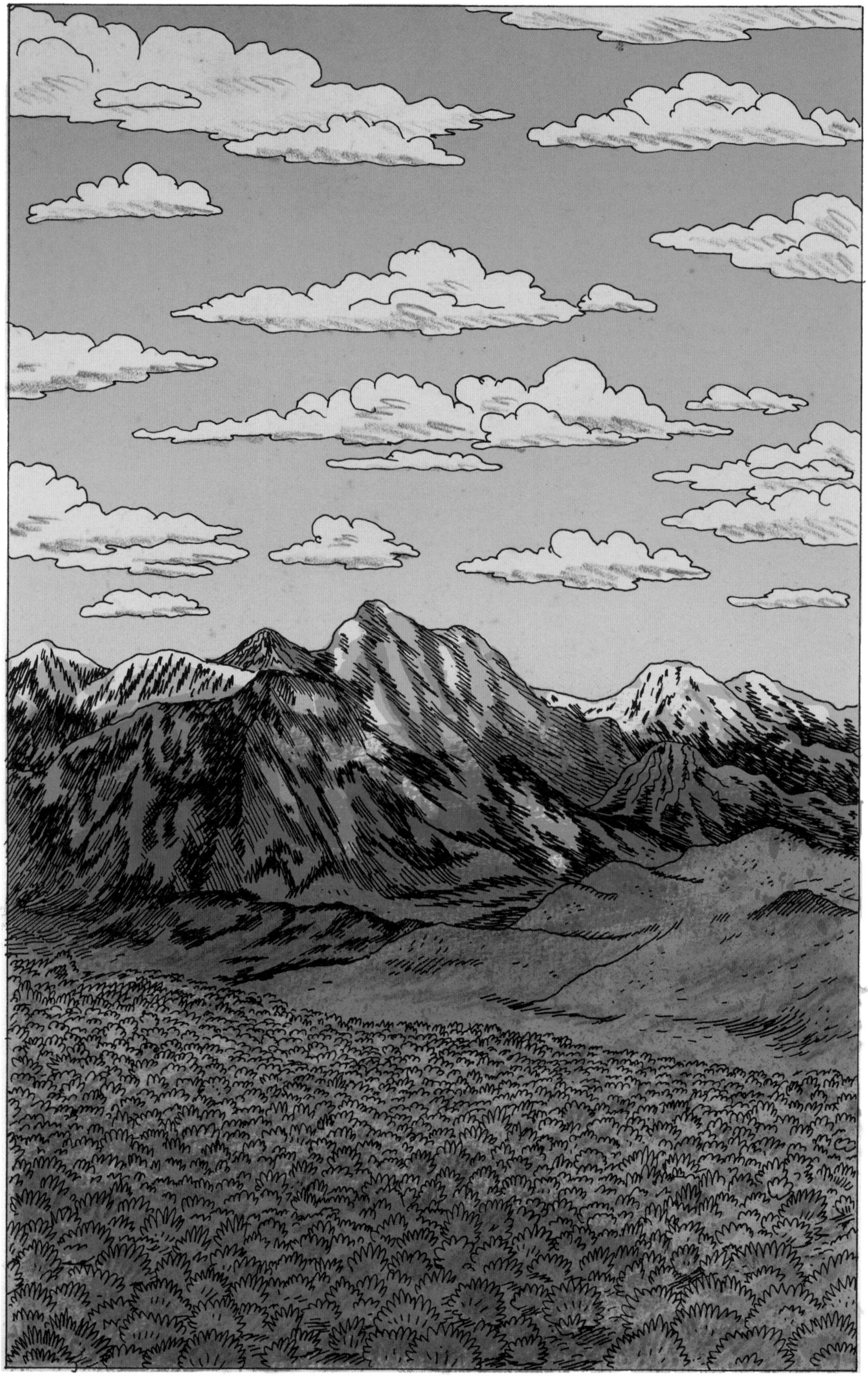

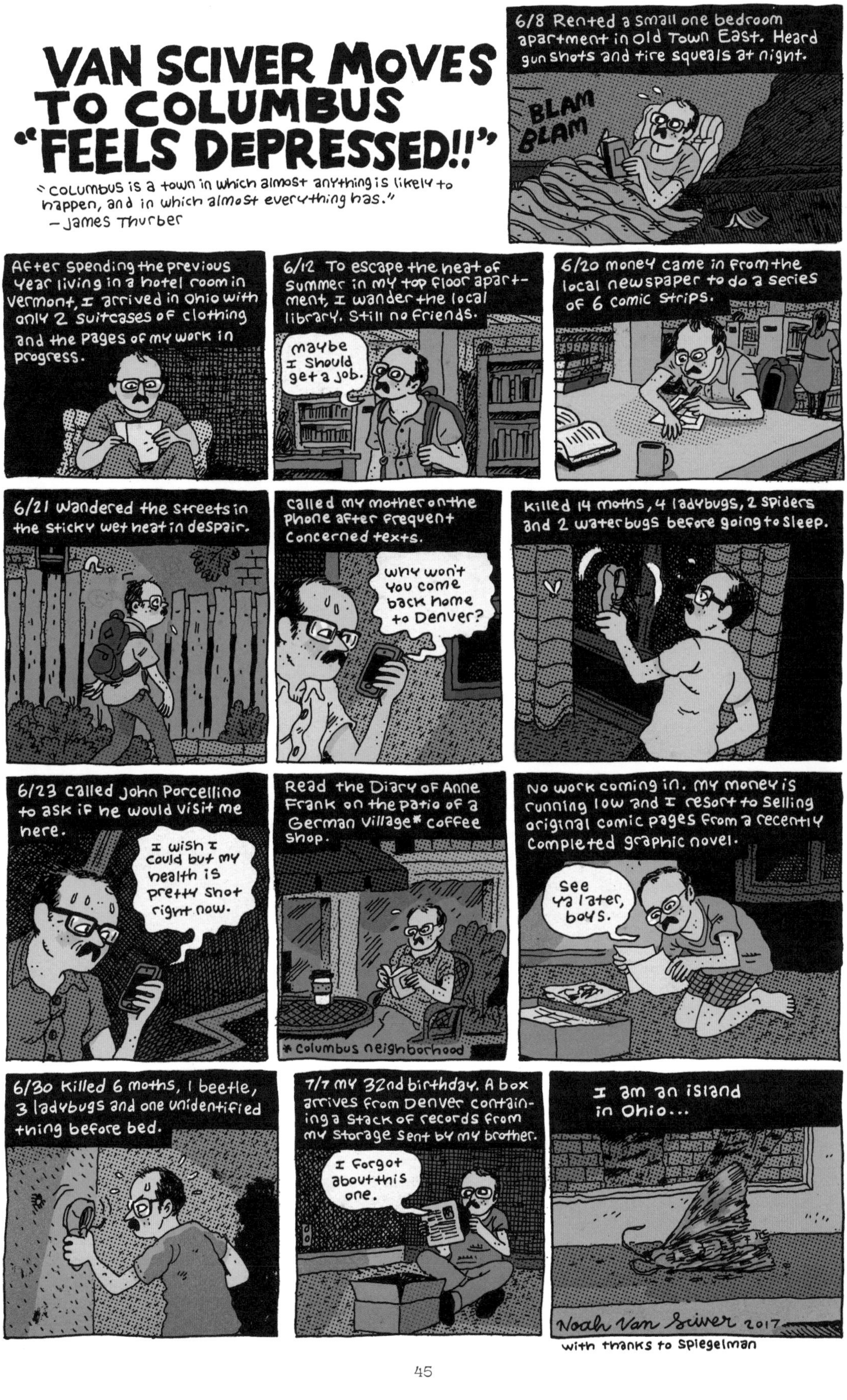
VAN SCIVER MOVES TO COLUMBUS "FEELS DEPRESSED!!"
"Columbus is a town in which almost anything is likely to happen, and in which almost everything has." —James Thurber
6/8 Rented a small one bedroom apartment in Old Town East. Heard gun shots and tire squeals at night.
BLAM BLAM
After spending the previous year living in a hotel room in Vermont, I arrived in Ohio with only 2 suitcases of clothing and the pages of my work in progress.
6/12 To escape the heat of summer in my top floor apartment, I wander the local library. Still no friends.
maybe I should get a job.
6/20 money came in from the local newspaper to do a series of 6 comic strips.
6/21 Wandered the streets in the sticky wet heat in despair.
Called my mother on the phone after frequent concerned texts.
why won't you come back home to Denver?
Killed 14 moths, 4 ladybugs, 2 spiders and 2 waterbugs before going to sleep.
6/23 Called John Porcellino to ask if he would visit me here.
I wish I could but my health is pretty shot right now.
Read the Diary of Anne Frank on the patio of a German Village* coffee shop.
*Columbus neighborhood
No work coming in. My money is running low and I resort to selling original comic pages from a recently completed graphic novel.
See ya later, boys.
6/30 Killed 6 moths, 1 beetle, 3 ladybugs and one unidentified thing before bed.
7/7 My 32nd birthday. A box arrives from Denver containing a stack of records from my storage sent by my brother.
I forgot about this one.
I am an island in Ohio...
Noah Van Sciver 2017
with thanks to Spiegelman

Sep 12 2016

Tom Spurgeon took me to lunch with
Evan Dorkin (who is visiting Columbus).

Slave Labor Graphics was a great
publisher back in the day. My royalty
deal was 60/40! Can you believe
that? Imagine...

Evan talked about the discrepancy between
a cartoonist's social media follower numbers
and their actual book sales. He told me:

Everyone wants to come to your
party but they don't wanna pitch
in for the alcohol!

I thought
that was
great.

I still only have $46 to my name.
This is getting tough and maybe living here
is making it tougher. If things don't improve
in the next few days I'll go find a job at
a coffee shop.

Back at my apartment I took a nap, checked
my email, then made some noodles and
listened to "Another Side of Bob Dylan."

I hadn't listened to this record in so long,
and hearing it again took me back to a time
when I didn't feel like I was fighting
through the wilderness...

what the hell am I doing?

Noah Van Sciver

THE HYPO

Hm. Look at that. This is my very first graphic novel on the bargain cart.

HEY KIDS!

I never look at this book... Actually, I don't even have a copy, do I? HHMm...

Five dollars? That's depressing.

what the hell, I may as well pick it up. At the very least to rescue it from that cart!

BOOK FAIR

Later

...So that's Klaus Janson inking Miller. And that's the only issue I was missing.

You found this today?

PABST

Yeah for 2 dollars at Half-Price Books. You were there too?

Earlier. But I just got some boring stuff...

NYPD

I dunno.

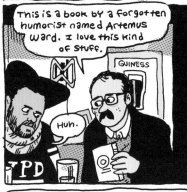

This is a book by a forgotten humorist named Artemus Ward. I love this kind of stuff.

GUINESS

Huh.

PD

-and then a copy of my first book. I found a copy there for five bucks.

what?

Bruh. You bought your own book?

un huh. what? It's not against the law!

PABST

THE HYPO

Can't you get one from the publisher? what if somebody had bought that copy at the store and connected with it? You probably lost a fan!

PABST

Y- you really think so?

Facts. You made a bad move taking that from the store.

Damn. You're right...

PA

49

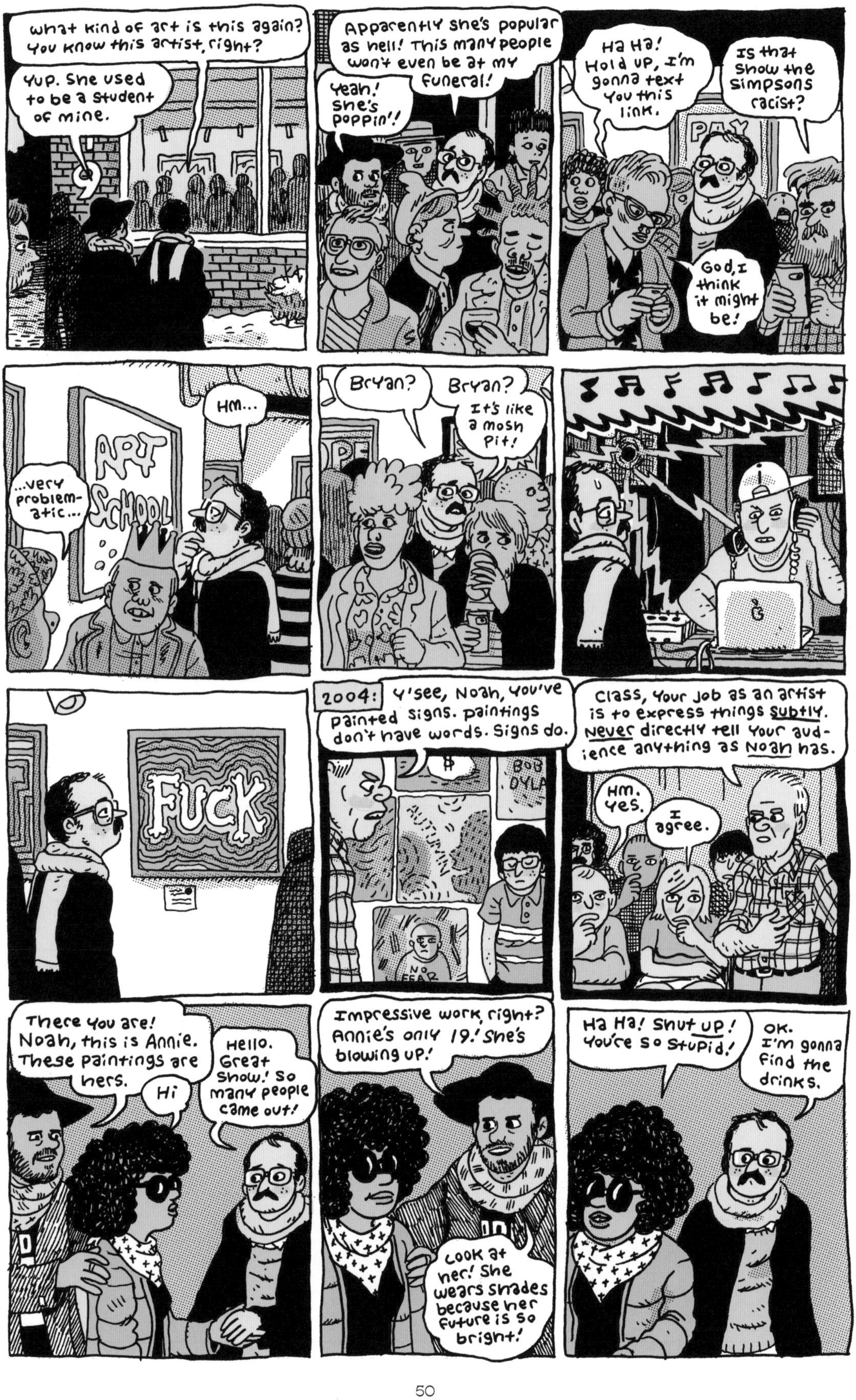

What kind of art is this again? You know this artist, right?
Yup. She used to be a student of mine.
9
Apparently she's popular as hell! This many people won't even be at my funeral!
Yeah! She's poppin'!
Ha Ha! Hold up, I'm gonna text you this link.
Is that show the Simpsons racist?
PAY
God, I think it might be!
...very problem-atic...
HM...
ART SCHOOL
Bryan?
Bryan?
It's like a mosh pit!
FUCK
2004:
Y'see, Noah, you've painted signs. Paintings don't have words. Signs do.
BOB DYLA
NO FEAR
Class, your job as an artist is to express things subtly. Never directly tell your audience anything as Noah has.
HM. Yes.
I agree.
There you are! Noah, this is Annie. These paintings are hers.
Hi
Hello. Great show! So many people came out!
Impressive work, right? Annie's only 19! She's blowing up!
Look at her! She wears shades because her future is so bright!
Ha Ha! Shut up! You're so stupid!
OK. I'm gonna find the drinks.

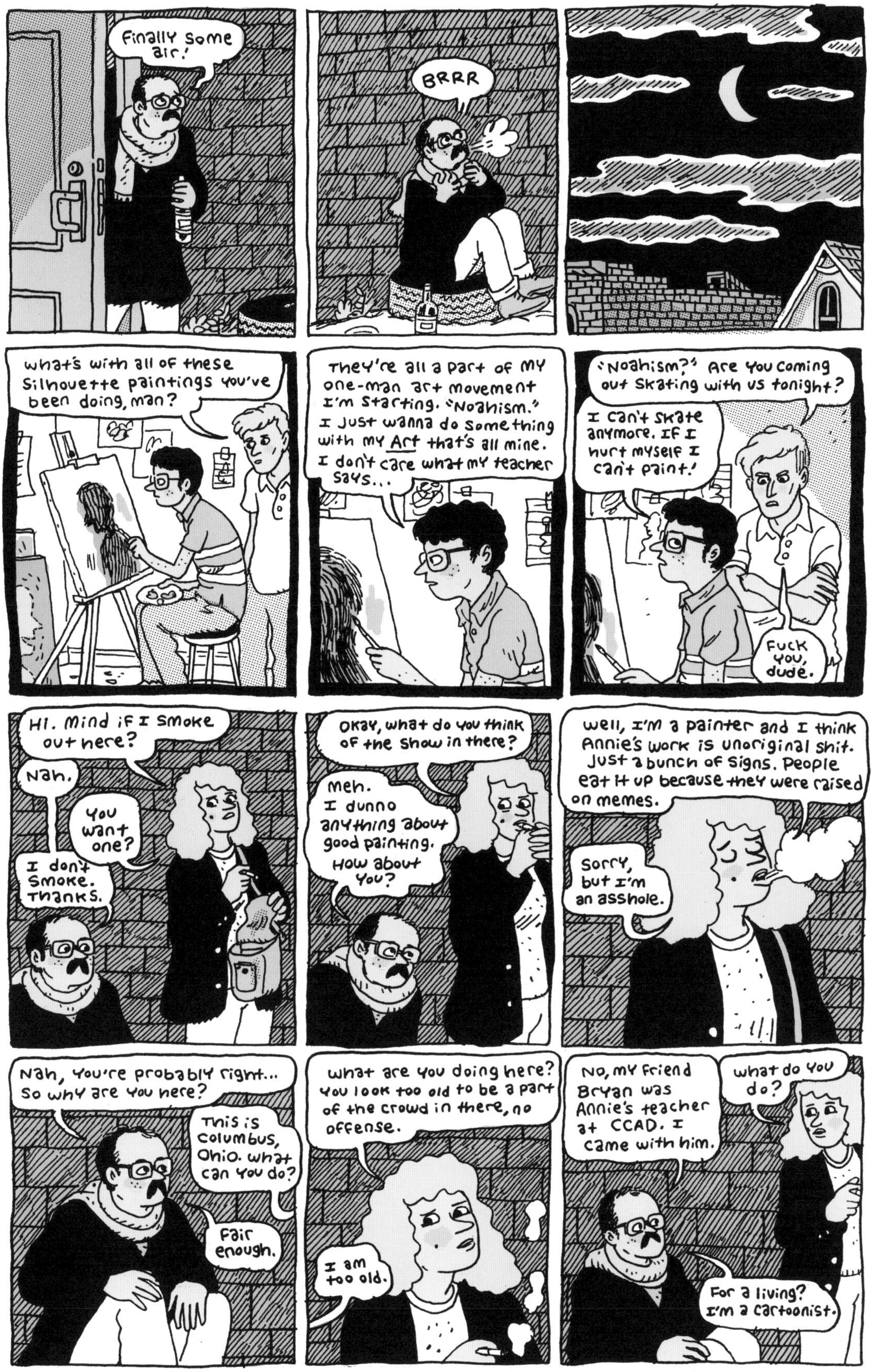

Finally some air!
BRRR
What's with all of these Silhouette paintings you've been doing, man?
They're all a part of my one-man art movement I'm starting. "Noahism." I just wanna do something with my Art that's all mine. I don't care what my teacher says...
"Noahism?" Are you coming out skating with us tonight?
I can't skate anymore. If I hurt myself I can't paint!
Fuck you, dude.
Hi. Mind if I smoke out here?
Nah.
You want one?
I don't smoke. Thanks.
Okay, what do you think of the show in there?
Meh. I dunno anything about good painting. How about you?
Well, I'm a painter and I think Annie's work is unoriginal shit. Just a bunch of signs. People eat it up because they were raised on memes.
Sorry, but I'm an asshole.
Nah, you're probably right... So why are you here?
This is Columbus, Ohio. What can you do?
Fair enough.
What are you doing here? You look too old to be a part of the crowd in there, no offense.
I am too old.
No, my friend Bryan was Annie's teacher at CCAD. I came with him.
What do you do?
For a living? I'm a cartoonist.

A cartoonist, huh? What's your name? I like comics.

Noah Van Sciver.

I know you! You do the comic in the Columbus ALIVE right?

That's me.

I love that.

Don't sit out here too long! It's freezing!

I'm just getting my beer cold!

Ha. Alright, have a good night!

Bye.

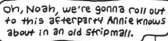

Oh, Noah, we're gonna roll out to this afterparty Annie knows about in an old stripmall.

I think I'm gonna take off, I wanna try to draw a little tonight.

Alright, good hanging out.

Noah?

Yes sir. How's your night?

Good, my friend, good. How are you?

I'm good. I was just at an art show back there.

Ah, art is good.

RING RING

I used to put words in my paintings and boy did I get shamed for that!

Excuse me, it's my wife.

I have to answer.

OK.

RING RING

Ha ha it can be. That stuff wasn't so great. It reminded me of my days taking art classes when I was a teenager.

RING RING

Haa aniga iyo xaaskeyga?

Joojiyaan wadidda nin caddaan ku wareegsan iyo guriga ku soo noqon!

waxaan doono!

52

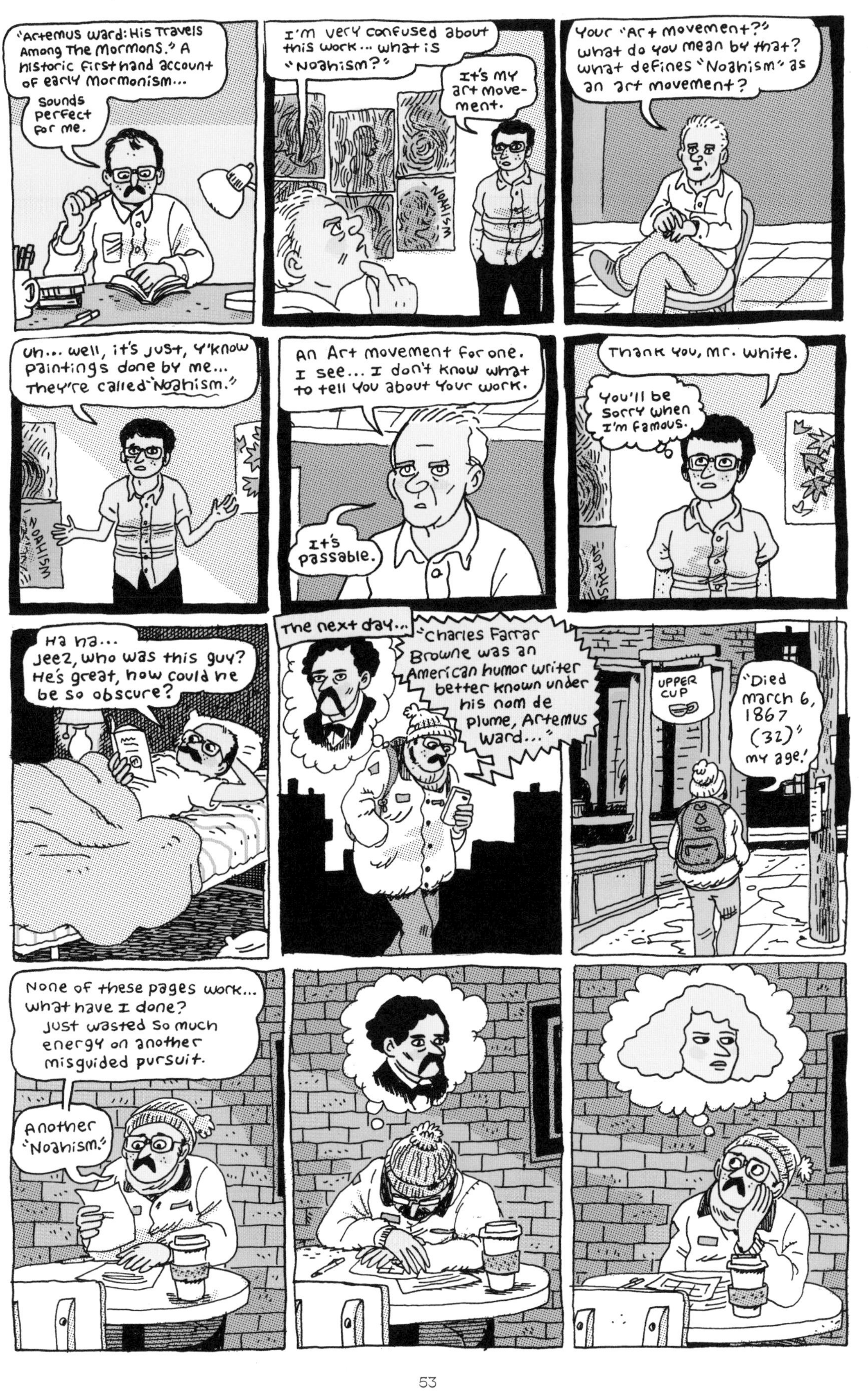
"Artemus Ward: His Travels Among the Mormons." A historic first hand account of early Mormonism...
Sounds perfect for me.
I'm very confused about this work... what is "Noahism?"
It's my art movement.
NOAHISM
Your "Art movement?" what do you mean by that? what defines "Noahism" as an art movement?
Uh... well, it's just, y'know paintings done by me... they're called "Noahism."
NOAHISM
An Art movement for one. I see... I don't know what to tell you about your work.
It's passable.
Thank you, Mr. White.
You'll be sorry when I'm famous.
Ha ha... Jeez, who was this guy? He's great, how could he be so obscure?
The next day...
"Charles Farrar Browne was an American humor writer better known under his nom de plume, Artemus Ward..."
UPPER CUP
"Died March 6, 1867 (32)" my age!
None of these pages work... what have I done? Just wasted so much energy on another misguided pursuit.
Another "Noahism."

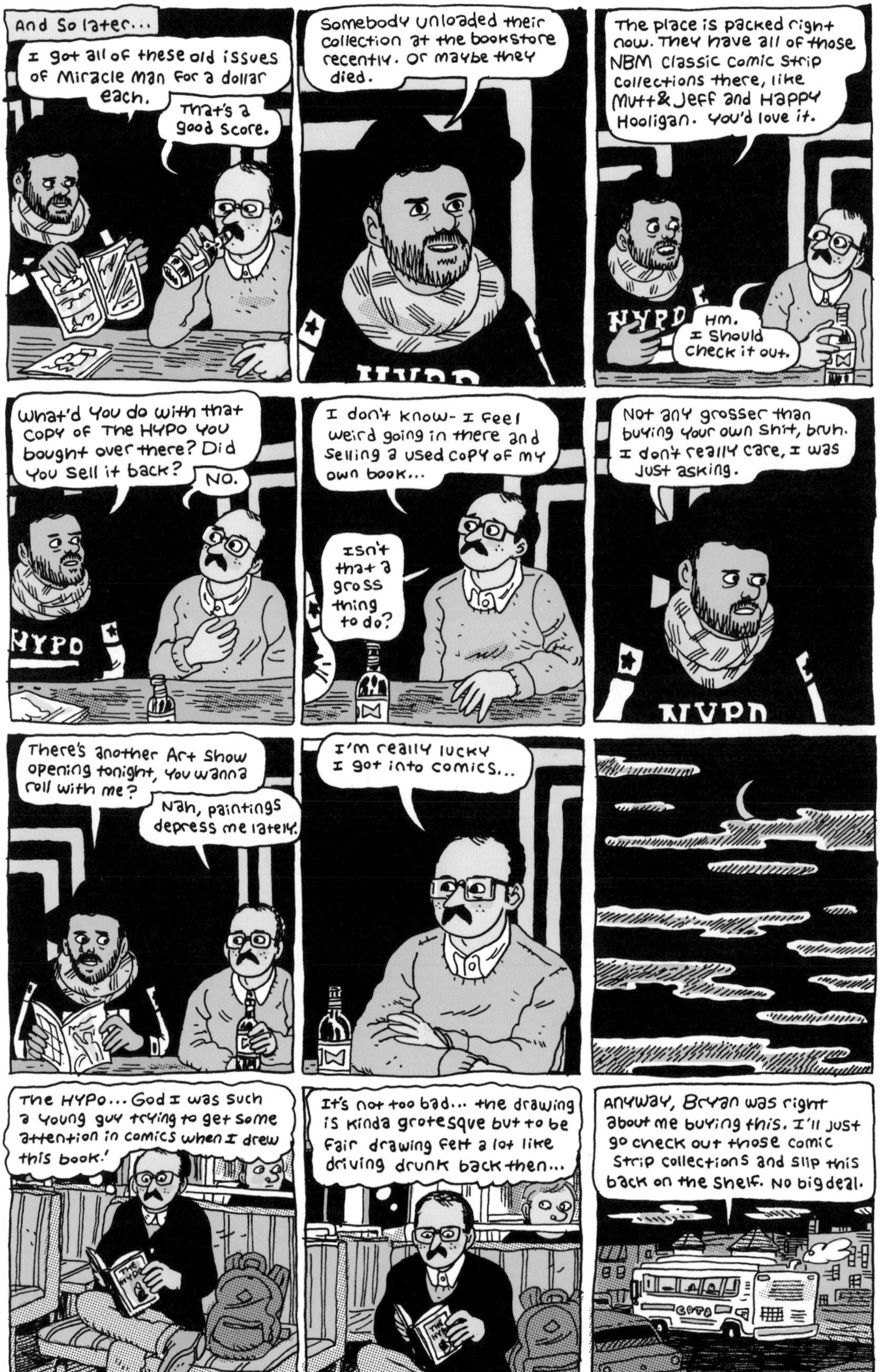
And so later...
I got all of these old issues of Miracle Man for a dollar each.
That's a good score.
Somebody unloaded their collection at the bookstore recently. Or maybe they died.
The place is packed right now. They have all of those NBM classic comic strip collections there, like Mutt & Jeff and Happy Hooligan. You'd love it.
NYPD
Hm. I should check it out.
What'd you do with that copy of The HYPO you bought over there? Did you sell it back?
No.
NYPD
I don't know- I feel weird going in there and selling a used copy of my own book...
Isn't that a gross thing to do?
Not any grosser than buying your own shit, bruh. I don't really care, I was just asking.
NYPD
There's another Art Show opening tonight, you wanna roll with me?
Nah, paintings depress me lately.
I'm really lucky I got into comics...
The HYPO... God I was such a young guy trying to get some attention in comics when I drew this book!
It's not too bad... the drawing is kinda grotesque but to be fair drawing felt a lot like driving drunk back then...
Anyway, Bryan was right about me buying this. I'll just go check out those comic strip collections and slip this back on the shelf. No big deal.

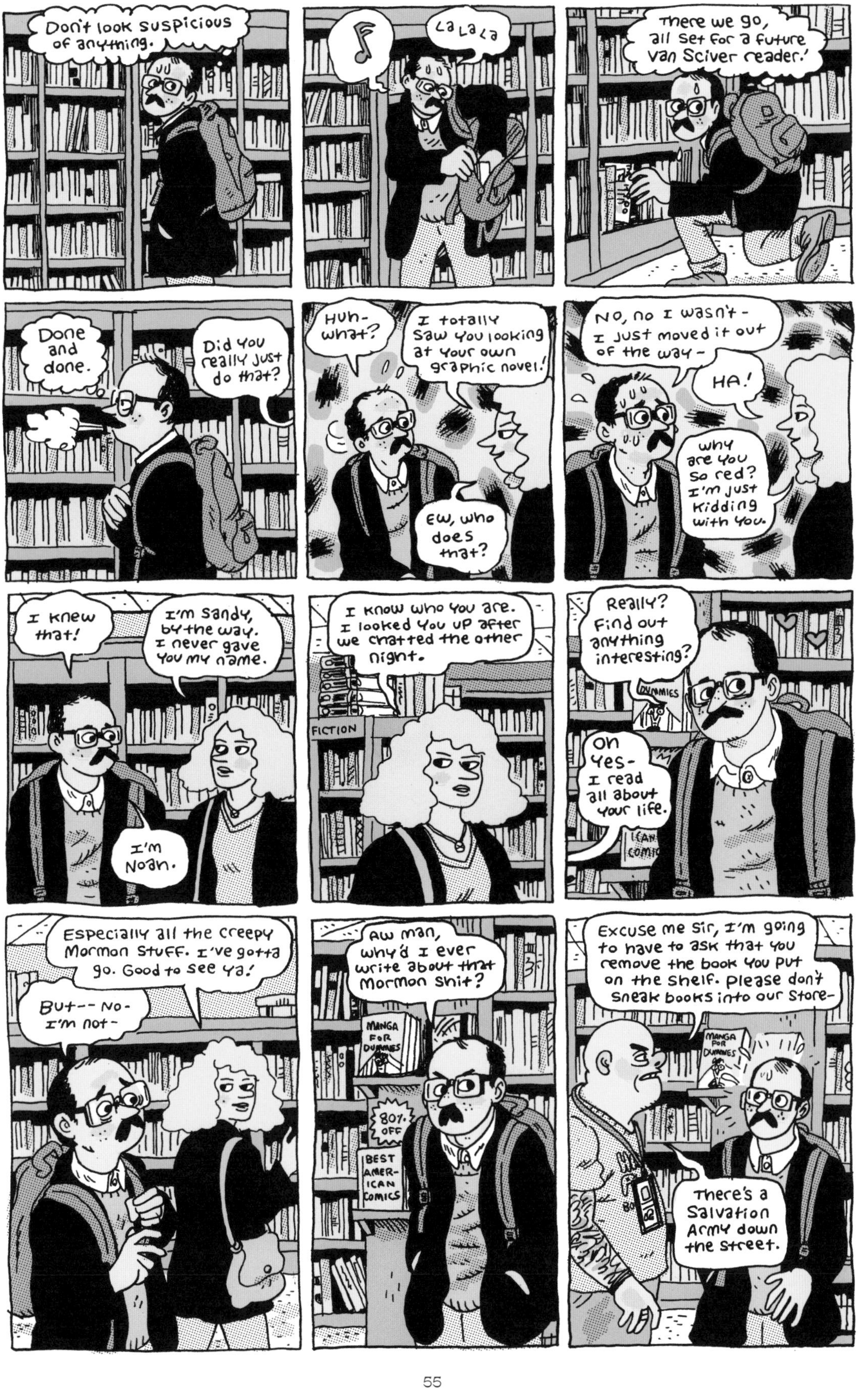
Don't look suspicious of anything.
LA LA LA
There we go, all set for a future Van Sciver reader.
Done and done.
Did you really just do that?
Huh-what?
I totally saw you looking at your own graphic novel!
Ew, who does that?
No, no I wasn't- I just moved it out of the way-
HA!
Why are you so red? I'm just kidding with you.
I knew that!
I'm Sandy, by the way. I never gave you my name.
I'm Noah.
I know who you are. I looked you up after we chatted the other night.
FICTION
Really? Find out anything interesting?
DUMMIES
Oh yes- I read all about your life.
Especially all the creepy Mormon stuff. I've gotta go. Good to see ya!
But-- No- I'm not-
Aw man, why'd I ever write about that Mormon shit?
MANGA FOR DUMMIES
80% OFF
BEST AMERICAN COMICS
Excuse me sir, I'm going to have to ask that you remove the book you put on the shelf. Please don't sneak books into our store-
MANGA FOR DUMMIES
There's a Salvation Army down the street.

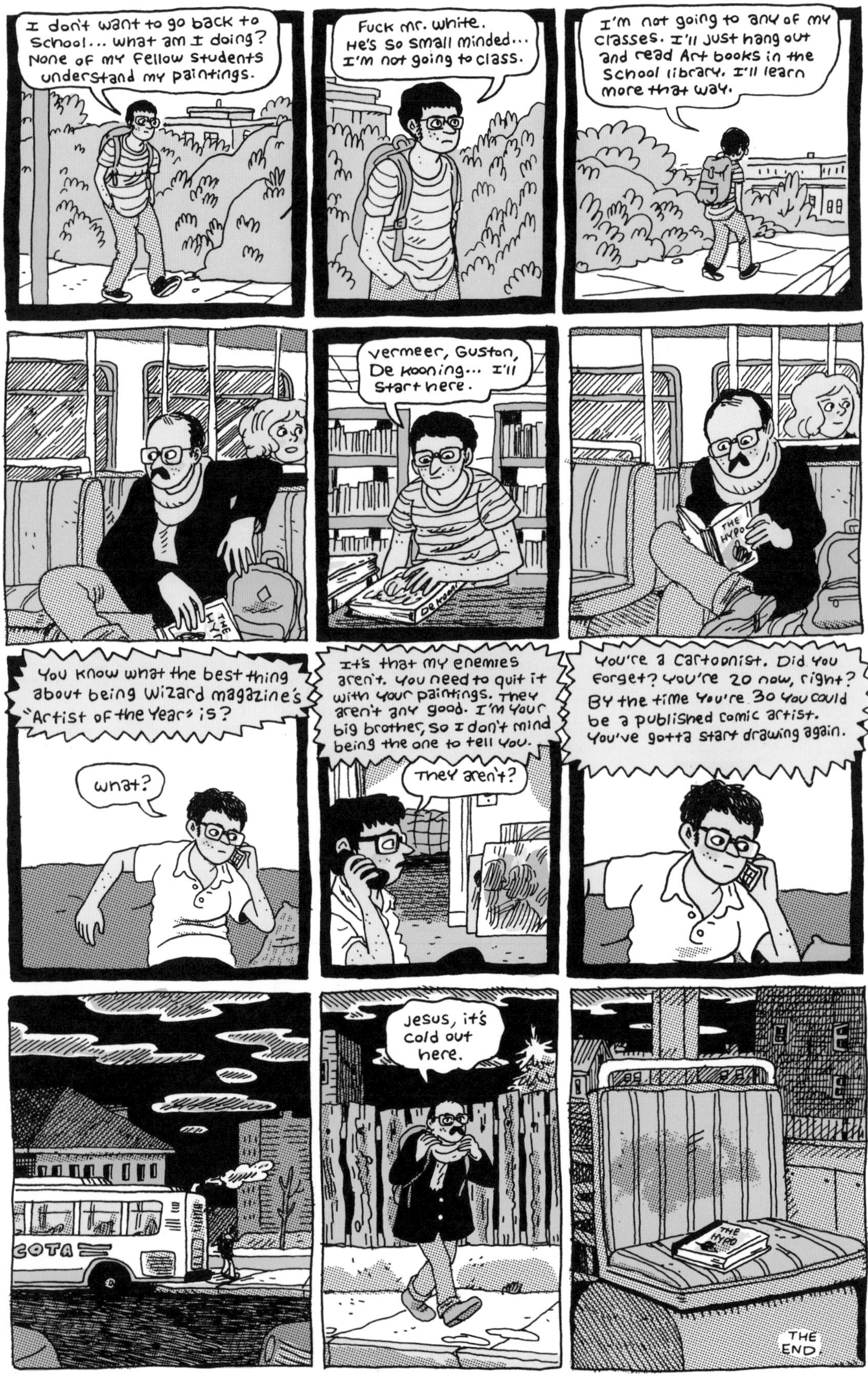
I don't want to go back to school... what am I doing? None of my fellow students understand my paintings.
Fuck Mr. White. He's so small minded... I'm not going to class.
I'm not going to any of my classes. I'll just hang out and read Art books in the school library. I'll learn more that way.
Vermeer, Guston, De Kooning... I'll start here.
De Kooning
THE HYPO
You know what the best thing about being Wizard magazine's "Artist of the Year" is?
What?
It's that my enemies aren't. You need to quit it with your paintings. They aren't any good. I'm your big brother, so I don't mind being the one to tell you.
They aren't?
You're a cartoonist. Did you forget? You're 20 now, right? By the time you're 30 you could be a published comic artist. You've gotta start drawing again.
COTA
Jesus, it's cold out here.
THE HYPO
THE END

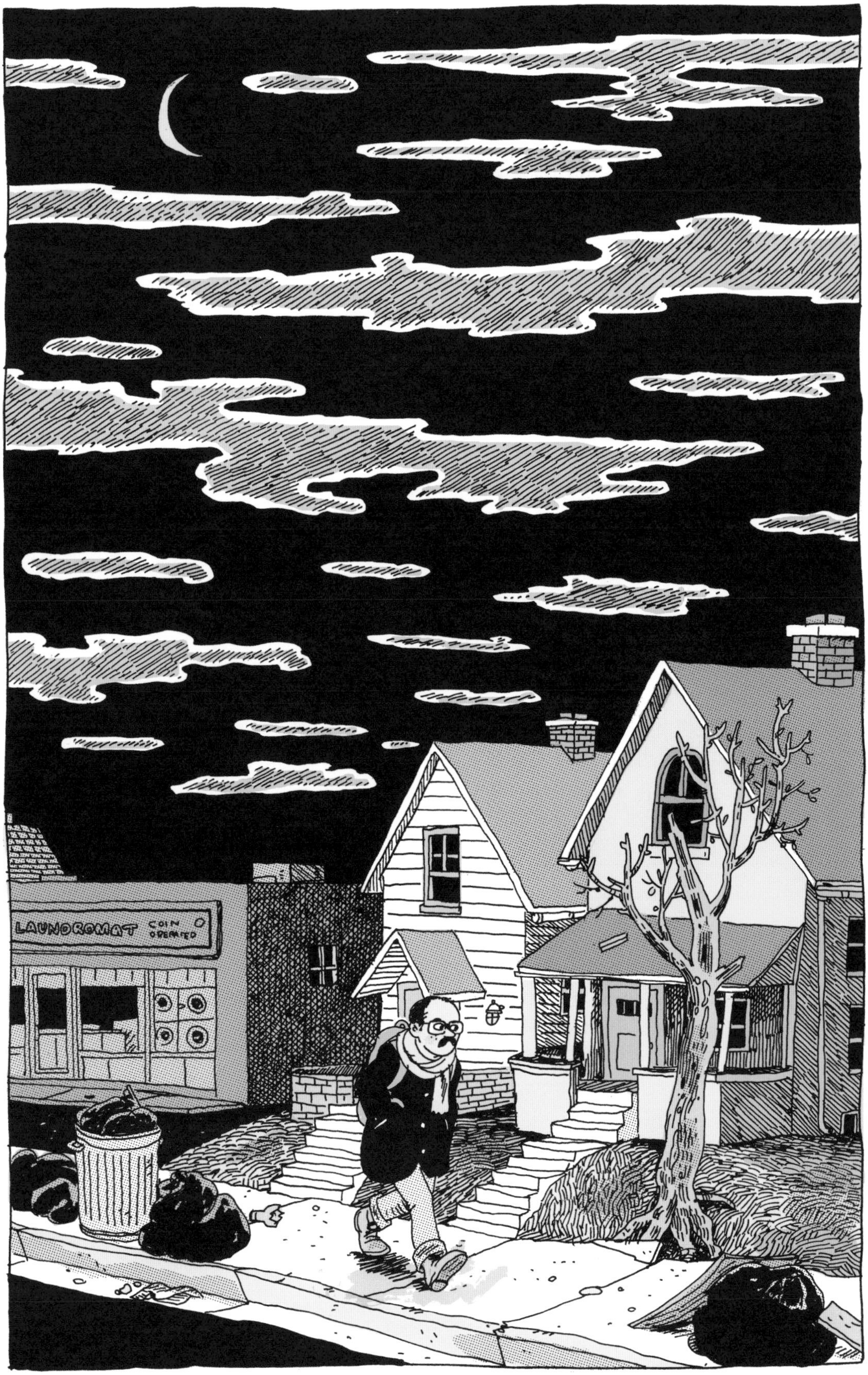
LAUNDROMAT
COIN OPERATED

November 14th 2016

This week I've been reading a biography of peter Arno (famed New Yorker magazine cartoonist). Now I'm fantasizing about working for the magazine myself.

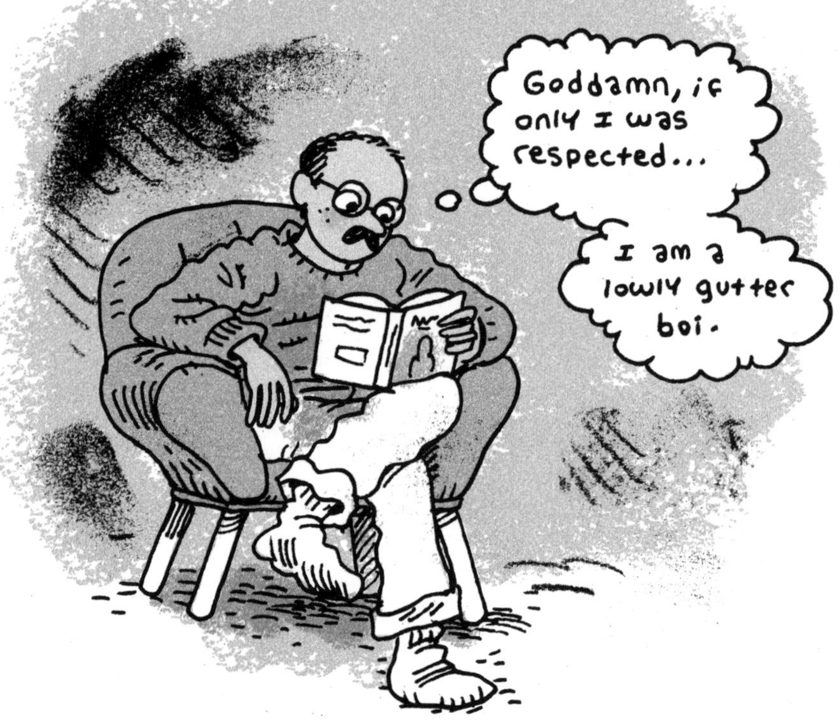
Goddamn, if only I was respected...
I am a lowly gutter boi.

I've dug my own grave, though. I prefer drawing comics like Fante Bukowski or an issue of my beloved Blammo comic book to pursuing anything higher.

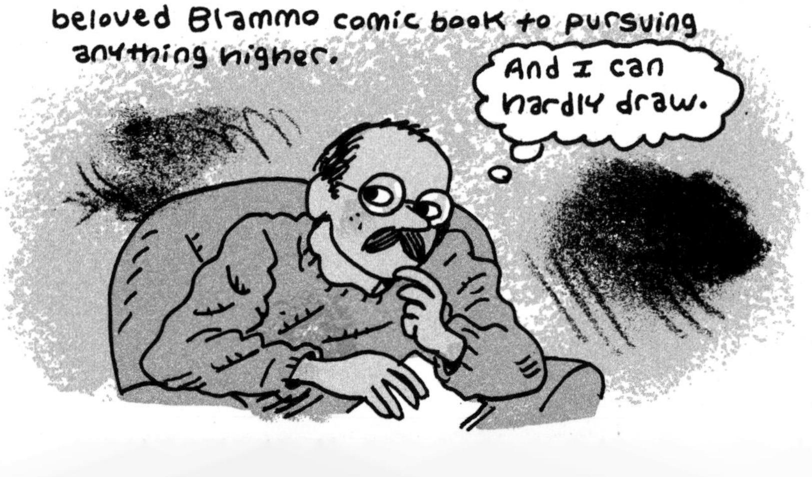
And I can hardly draw.

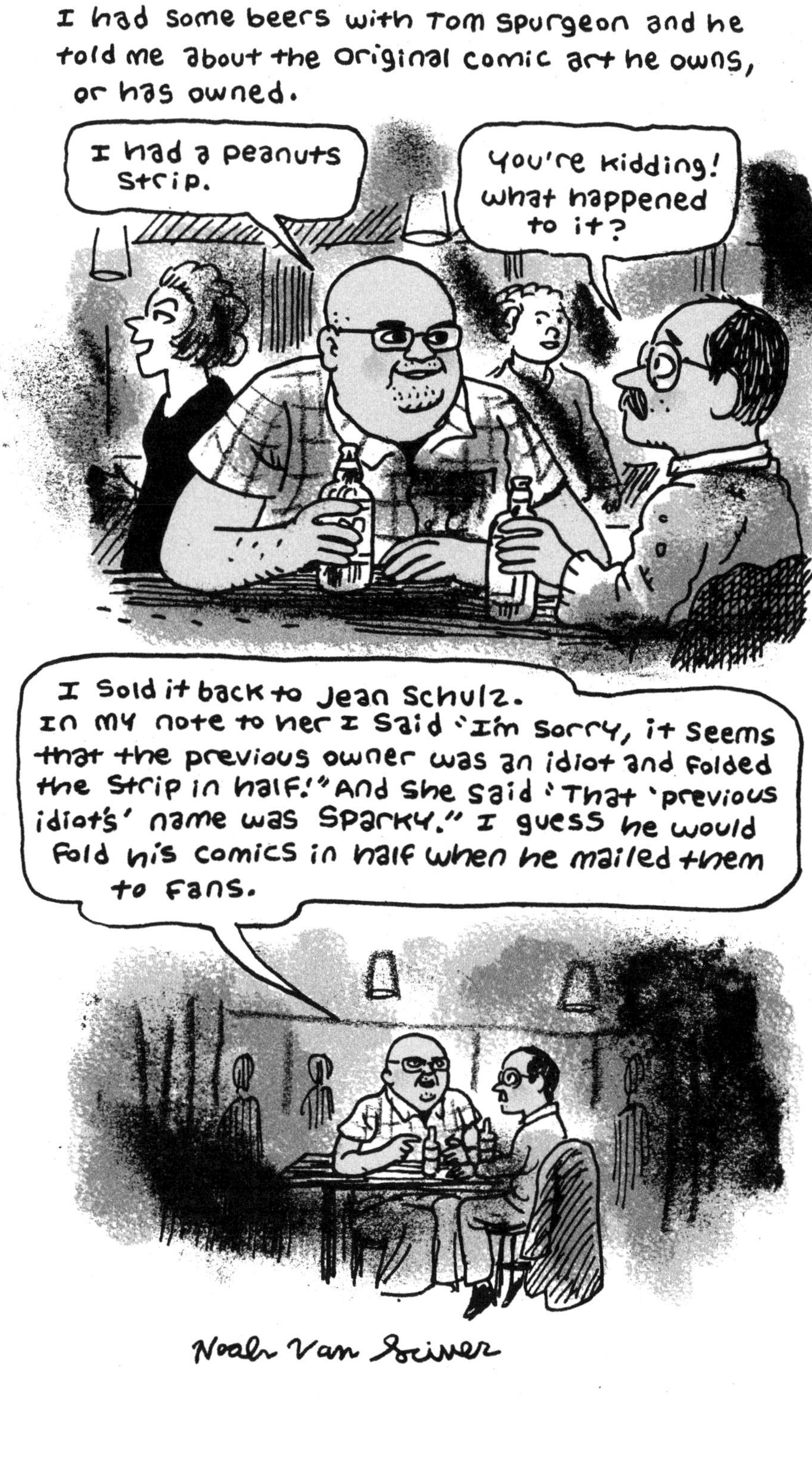
I had some beers with Tom Spurgeon and he told me about the original comic art he owns, or has owned.
I had a peanuts strip.
You're kidding! what happened to it?
I sold it back to Jean Schulz. In my note to her I said "I'm sorry, it seems that the previous owner was an idiot and folded the strip in half!" And she said "That 'previous idiot's' name was Sparky." I guess he would fold his comics in half when he mailed them to fans.
Noah Van Sciver

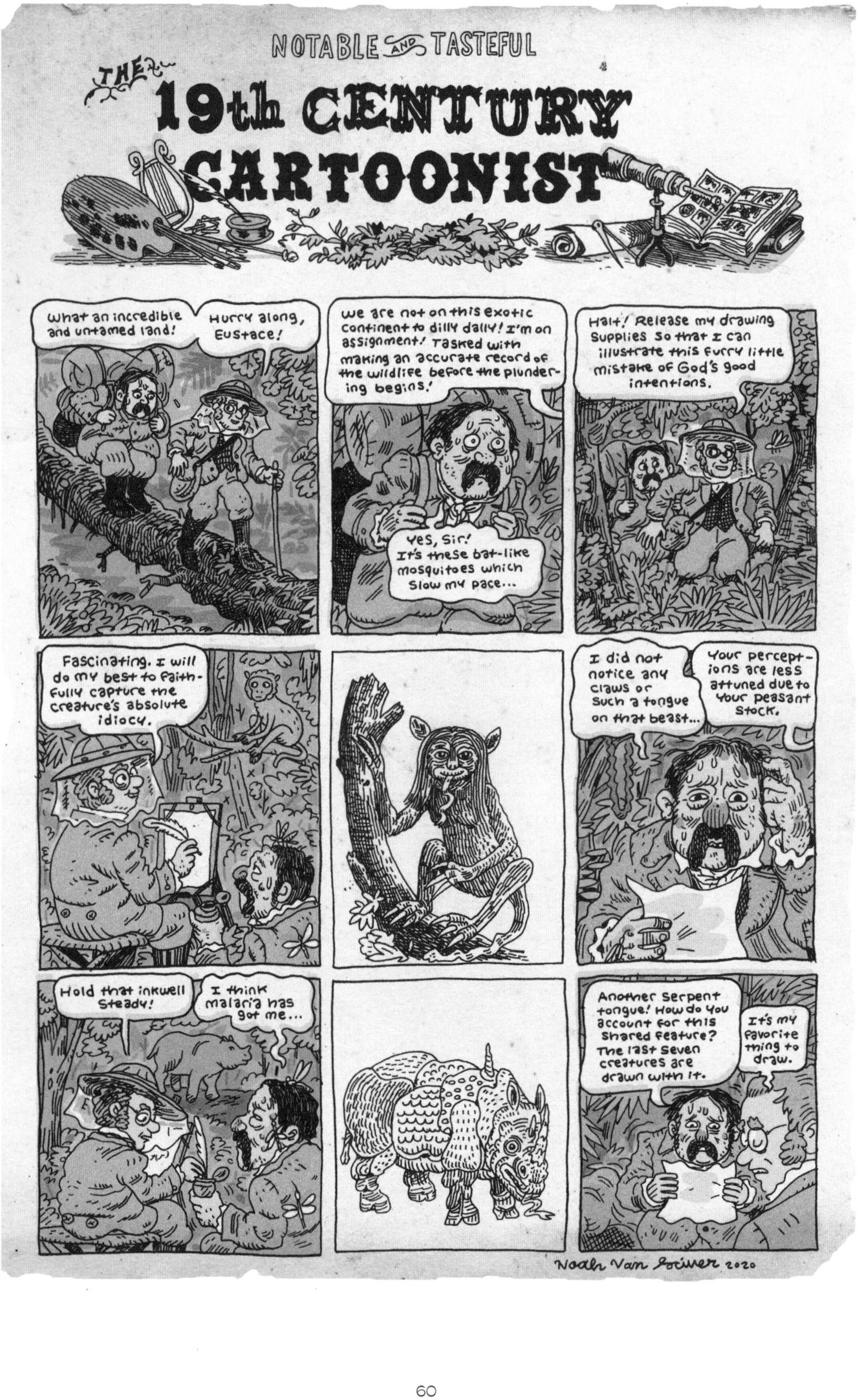
NOTABLE AND TASTEFUL
THE 19th CENTURY CARTOONIST
What an incredible and untamed land!
Hurry along, Eustace!
We are not on this exotic continent to dilly dally! I'm on assignment! Tasked with making an accurate record of the wildlife before the plundering begins!
Yes, Sir! It's these bat-like mosquitoes which slow my pace...
Halt! Release my drawing supplies so that I can illustrate this furry little mistake of God's good intentions.
Fascinating. I will do my best to faithfully capture the creature's absolute idiocy.
I did not notice any claws or such a tongue on that beast...
Your perceptions are less attuned due to your peasant stock.
Hold that inkwell steady!
I think malaria has got me...
Another serpent tongue! How do you account for this shared feature? The last seven creatures are drawn with it.
It's my favorite thing to draw.
Noah Van Sciver 2020

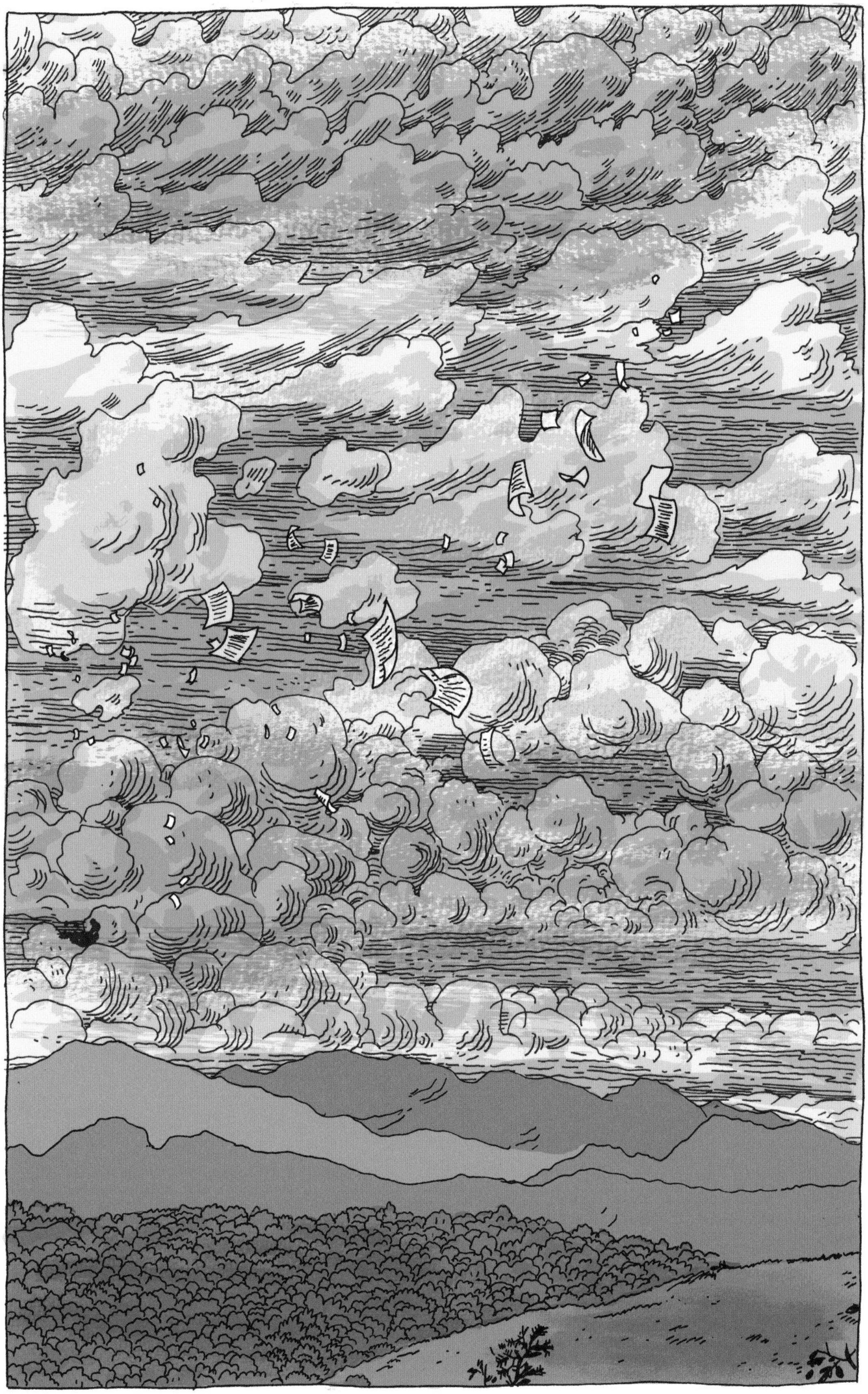

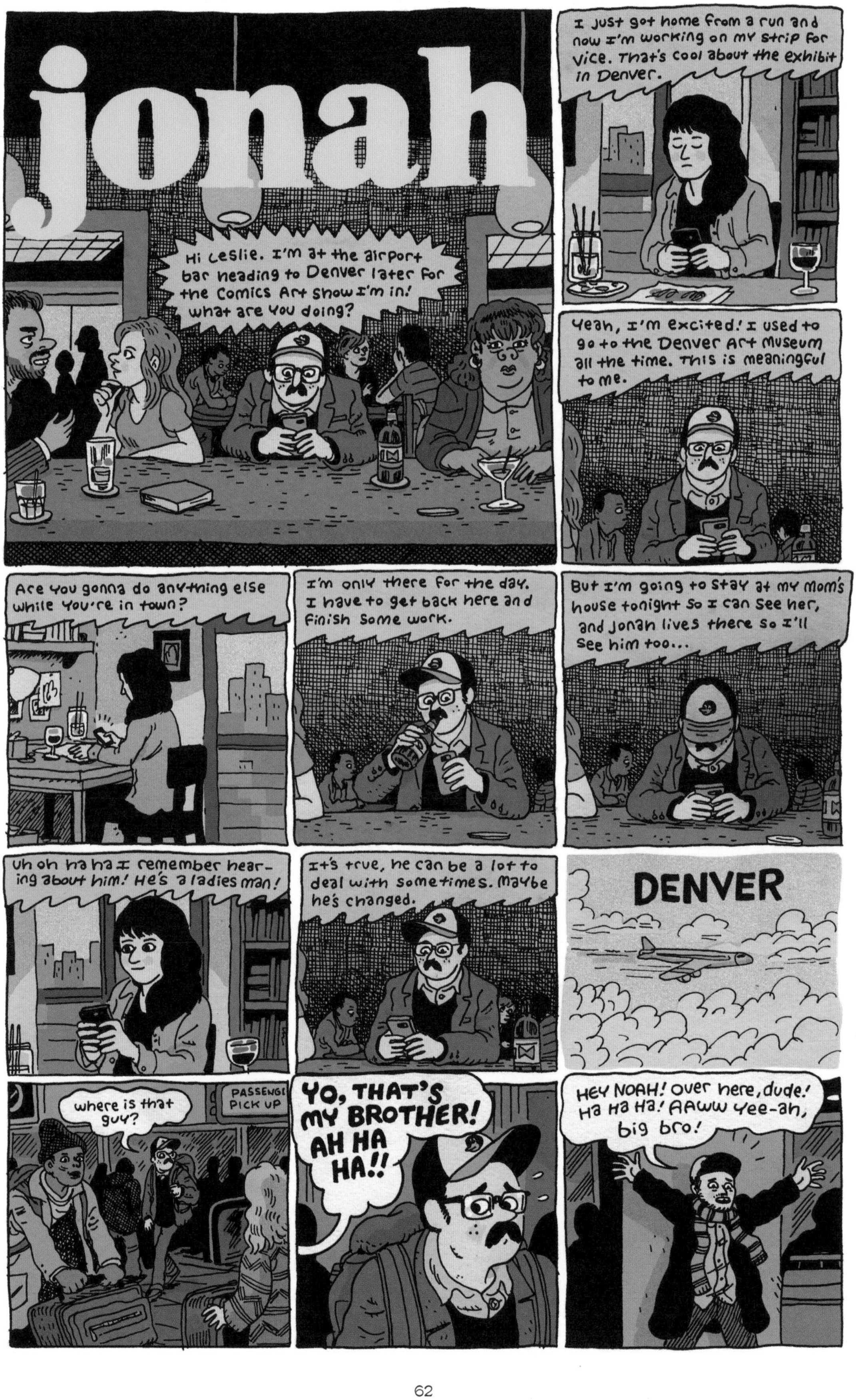
jonah
Hi Leslie. I'm at the airport bar heading to Denver later for the Comics Art show I'm in! what are you doing?
I just got home from a run and now I'm working on my strip for vice. That's cool about the exhibit in Denver.
Yeah, I'm excited! I used to go to the Denver Art Museum all the time. This is meaningful to me.
Are you gonna do anything else while you're in town?
I'm only there for the day. I have to get back here and finish some work.
But I'm going to stay at my mom's house tonight so I can see her, and Jonah lives there so I'll see him too...
Uh oh ha ha I remember hearing about him! He's a ladies man!
It's true, he can be a lot to deal with sometimes. Maybe he's changed.
DENVER
where is that guy?
PASSENG PICK UP
YO, THAT'S MY BROTHER! AH HA HA!!
HEY NOAH! over here, dude! Ha Ha Ha! AAWW yee-ah, big bro!

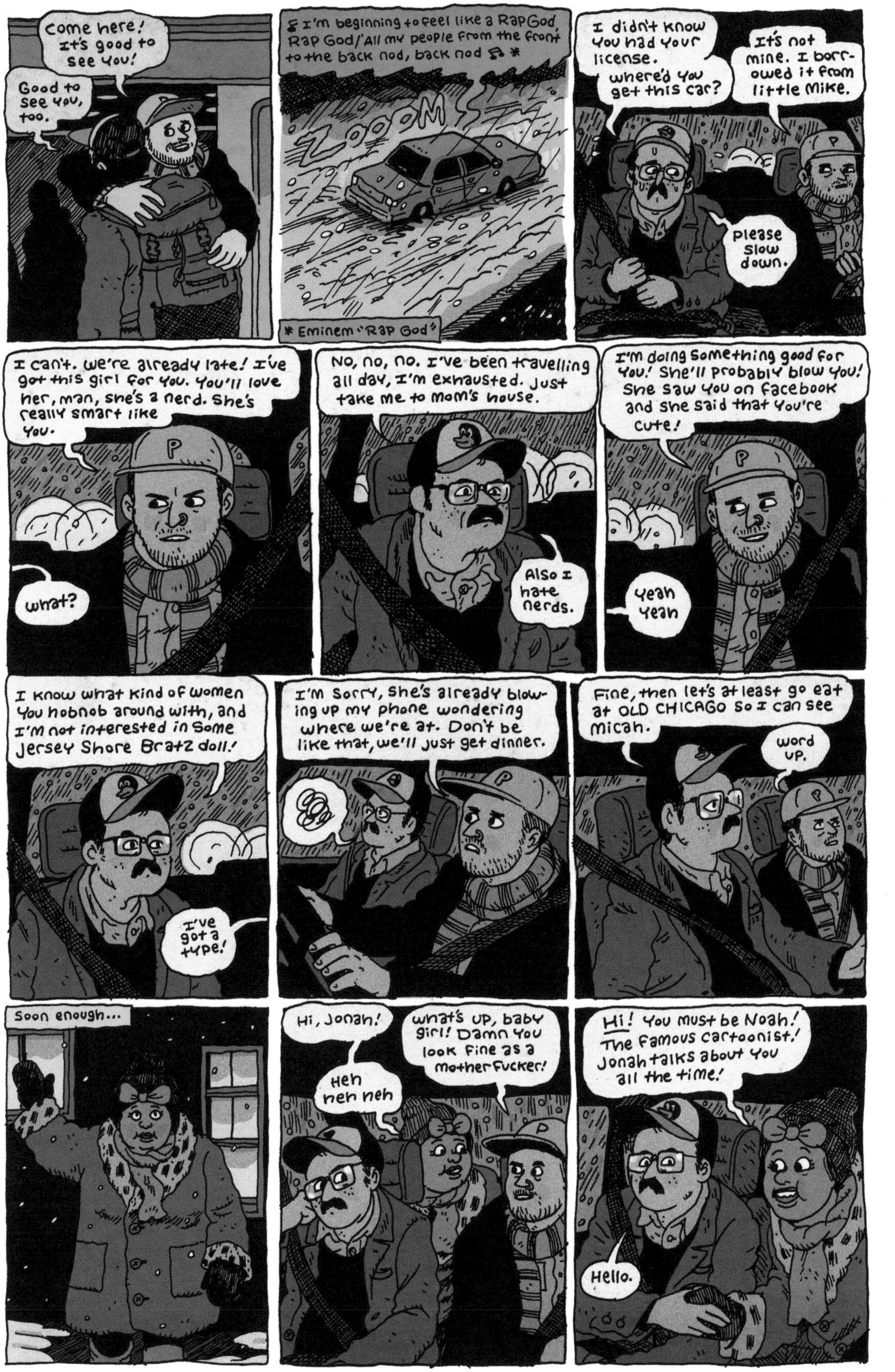
Come here! It's good to see you!
Good to see you, too.
♪ I'm beginning to feel like a Rap God, Rap God/All my people from the front to the back nod, back nod ♫ *
ZOOOM
* Eminem "Rap God"
I didn't know you had your license.
where'd you get this car?
It's not mine. I borrowed it from little Mike.
please slow down.
I can't. we're already late! I've got this girl for you. You'll love her, man, she's a nerd. She's really smart like you.
what?
No, no, no. I've been travelling all day, I'm exhausted. Just take me to mom's house.
Also I hate nerds.
I'm doing something good for you! She'll probably blow you! She saw you on facebook and she said that you're cute!
yeah yeah
I know what kind of women you hobnob around with, and I'm not interested in some Jersey Shore Bratz doll!
I've got a type!
I'm sorry, she's already blowing up my phone wondering where we're at. Don't be like that, we'll just get dinner.
Fine, then let's at least go eat at OLD CHICAGO so I can see Micah.
word up.
Soon enough...
Hi, Jonah!
what's up, baby girl! Damn you look fine as a motherfucker!
Heh heh heh
Hi! You must be Noah! The famous cartoonist! Jonah talks about you all the time!
Hello.

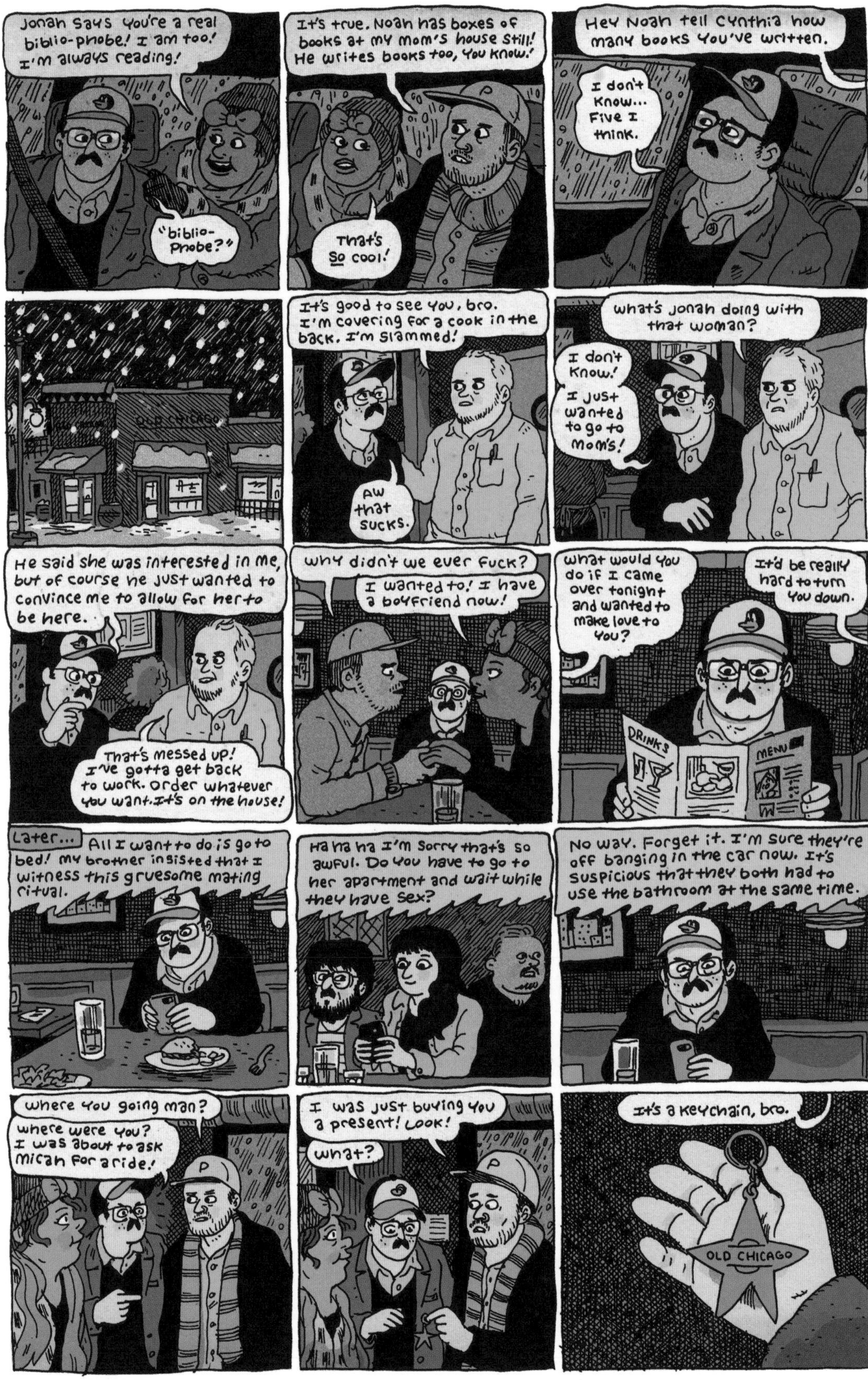
Jonah says you're a real biblio-phobe! I am too! I'm always reading!
"biblio-phobe?"
It's true. Noah has boxes of books at my mom's house still! He writes books too, you know.
That's so cool!
Hey Noah tell Cynthia how many books you've written.
I don't know... Five I think.
OLD CHICAGO
It's good to see you, bro. I'm covering for a cook in the back. I'm slammed!
Aw that sucks.
What's Jonah doing with that woman?
I don't know! I just wanted to go to Mom's!
He said she was interested in me, but of course he just wanted to convince me to allow for her to be here.
That's messed up! I've gotta get back to work. Order whatever you want. It's on the house!
Why didn't we ever fuck?
I wanted to! I have a boyfriend now!
What would you do if I came over tonight and wanted to make love to you?
It'd be really hard to turn you down.
DRINKS
MENU
Later...
All I want to do is go to bed! My brother insisted that I witness this gruesome mating ritual.
Ha ha ha I'm sorry that's so awful. Do you have to go to her apartment and wait while they have sex?
No way. Forget it. I'm sure they're off banging in the car now. It's suspicious that they both had to use the bathroom at the same time.
Where you going man?
Where were you? I was about to ask Micah for a ride!
I was just buying you a present! Look!
What?
It's a keychain, bro.
OLD CHICAGO

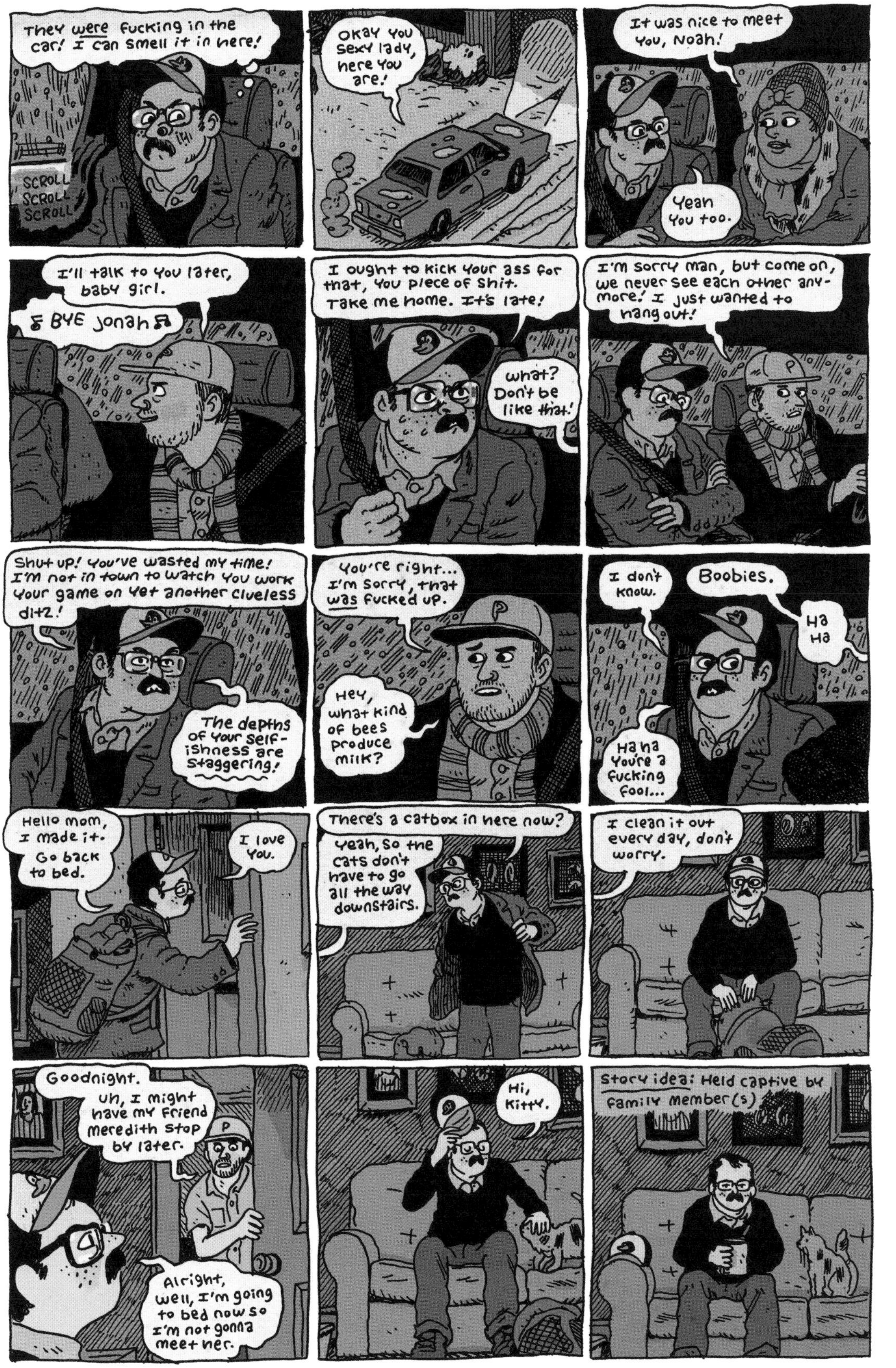
They were fucking in the car! I can smell it in here!
SCROLL SCROLL SCROLL
Okay you sexy lady, here you are!
It was nice to meet you, Noah!
Yeah you too.
I'll talk to you later, baby girl.
BYE Jonah
I ought to kick your ass for that, you piece of shit. Take me home. It's late!
what? Don't be like that!
I'm sorry man, but come on, we never see each other any-more! I just wanted to hang out!
Shut up! You've wasted my time! I'm not in town to watch you work your game on yet another clueless ditz!
The depths of your self-ishness are staggering!
You're right... I'm sorry, that was fucked up.
Hey, what kind of bees produce milk?
I don't know.
Boobies.
Ha ha
Ha ha You're a fucking fool...
Hello mom, I made it. Go back to bed.
I love you.
There's a catbox in here now?
Yeah, so the cats don't have to go all the way downstairs.
I clean it out every day, don't worry.
Goodnight.
Uh, I might have my friend Meredith stop by later.
Alright, well, I'm going to bed now so I'm not gonna meet her.
Hi, Kitty.
Story idea: Held captive by family member(s)

Ssh... be quiet, my brother's sleeping...

Heh heh

Ah yeah, suck it... oon fuck yeah... mmm... fuck...

GOD. DAMN. IT.

mmm yeah girl, suck that dick...

SCRATCH SCRATCH SCRATCH

I'M GONNA PUKE, YOU ASSHOLE! KEEP IT DOWN!

The next morning...

So you got to see Mican at work last night?

For about a minute. He was pretty busy. How are things here, mom?

Things are fine, David still gets his migraines, and we've been considering moving into a one story home.

Really? Aw man, that's sad, I love this house... the stairs are too difficult?

Yeah, they're getting tougher.

What are your plans for the day?

I'll probably just get dressed for the exhibit and head out early. I wanna walk around and visit some old haunts.

It's too bad this visit is so quick.

You know, Jonah is really hoping that you invite him along to the opening this evening.

Couldn't you consider it? He is your brother.

Mom, come on! Why would he want to go? He doesn't even read comics! Plus, he's loud and says crass shit constantly!

He'd embarrass me, I know it!

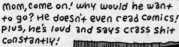
He loves you! He was so happy when he heard you were coming home.

No, absolutely not. I've wanted to see my work hung in the Denver Art Museum for years! This means a lot to me. I don't want Jonah to ruin this.

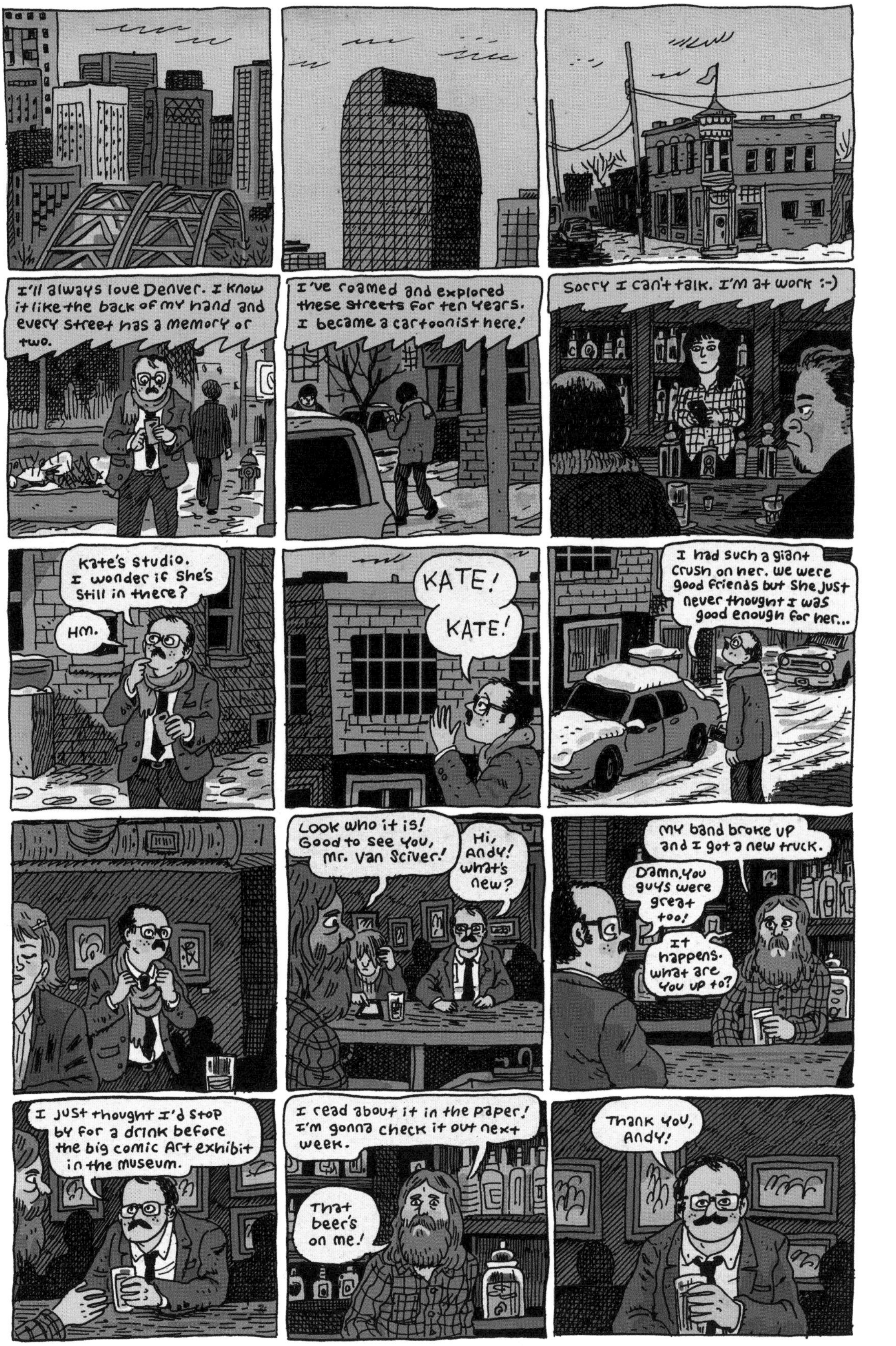
I'll always love Denver. I know it like the back of my hand and every street has a memory or two.
I've roamed and explored these streets for ten years. I became a cartoonist here!
Sorry I can't talk. I'm at work :-)
Kate's studio. I wonder if she's still in there?
Hm.
KATE!
KATE!
I had such a giant crush on her. We were good friends but she just never thought I was good enough for her...
Look who it is! Good to see you, Mr. Van Sciver!
Hi, Andy! What's new?
My band broke up and I got a new truck.
Damn, you guys were great too!
It happens. What are you up to?
I just thought I'd stop by for a drink before the big comic art exhibit in the museum.
I read about it in the paper! I'm gonna check it out next week.
That beer's on me!
Thank you, Andy!

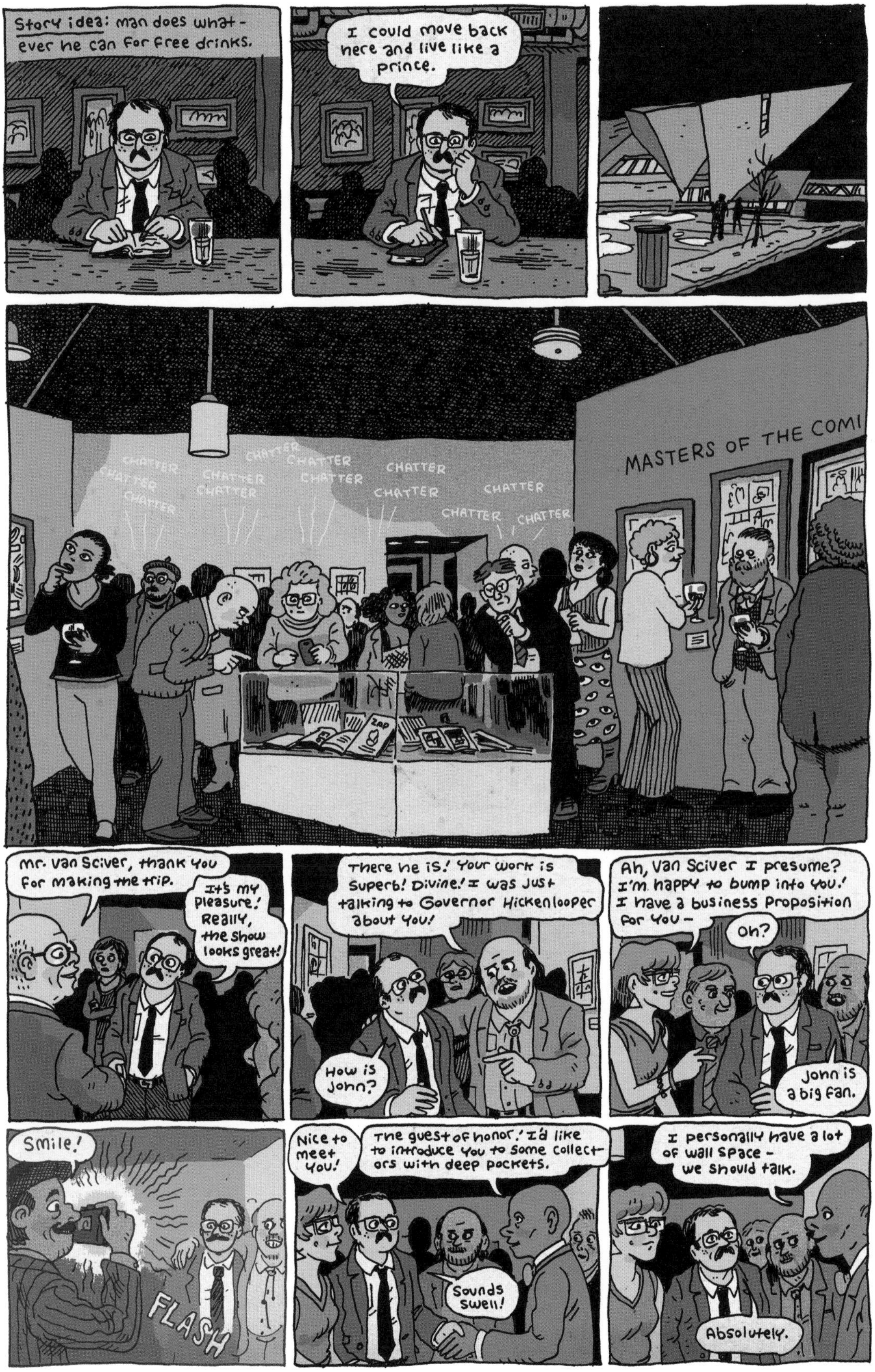
Story idea: man does whatever he can for free drinks.
I could move back here and live like a prince.
CHATTER
CHATTER
CHATTER
CHATTER
CHATTER
CHATTER
CHATTER
CHATTER
CHATTER
CHATTER
CHATTER
CHATTER
MASTERS OF THE COMI
ZAP
Mr. Van Sciver, thank you for making the trip.
It's my pleasure! Really, the show looks great!
There he is! Your work is superb! Divine! I was just talking to Governor Hickenlooper about you!
How is John?
Ah, Van Sciver I presume? I'm happy to bump into you! I have a business proposition for you –
Oh?
John is a big fan.
Smile!
FLASH
Nice to meet you!
The guest of honor! I'd like to introduce you to some collectors with deep pockets.
Sounds swell!
I personally have a lot of wall space – we should talk.
Absolutely.

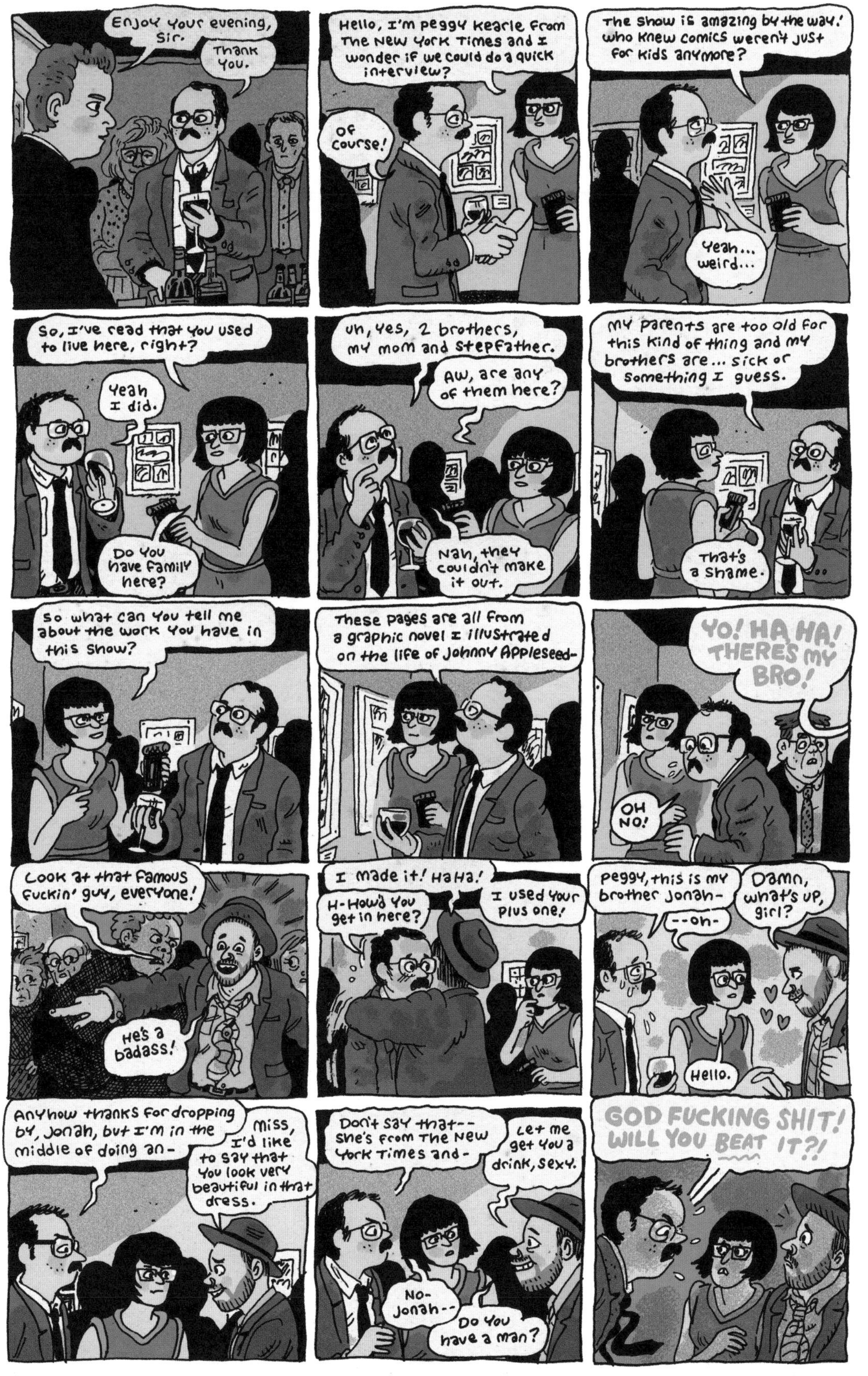
Enjoy your evening, sir.
Thank you.
Hello, I'm Peggy Kearle from the New York Times and I wonder if we could do a quick interview?
Of course!
The show is amazing by the way! Who knew comics weren't just for kids anymore?
Yeah... weird...
So, I've read that you used to live here, right?
Yeah I did.
Do you have family here?
Uh, yes, 2 brothers, my mom and stepfather.
Aw, are any of them here?
Nah, they couldn't make it out.
My parents are too old for this kind of thing and my brothers are... sick or something I guess.
That's a shame.
So what can you tell me about the work you have in this show?
These pages are all from a graphic novel I illustrated on the life of Johnny Appleseed-
YO! HA HA! THERE'S MY BRO!
OH NO!
Look at that famous fuckin' guy, everyone!
He's a badass!
I made it! Ha ha!
H-How'd you get in here?
I used your plus one!
Peggy, this is my brother Jonah-
--oh-
Damn, what's up, girl?
Hello.
Anyhow thanks for dropping by, Jonah, but I'm in the middle of doing an-
Miss, I'd like to say that you look very beautiful in that dress.
Don't say that-- she's from the New York Times and-
Let me get you a drink, sexy.
No- Jonah--
Do you have a man?
GOD FUCKING SHIT! WILL YOU BEAT IT?!

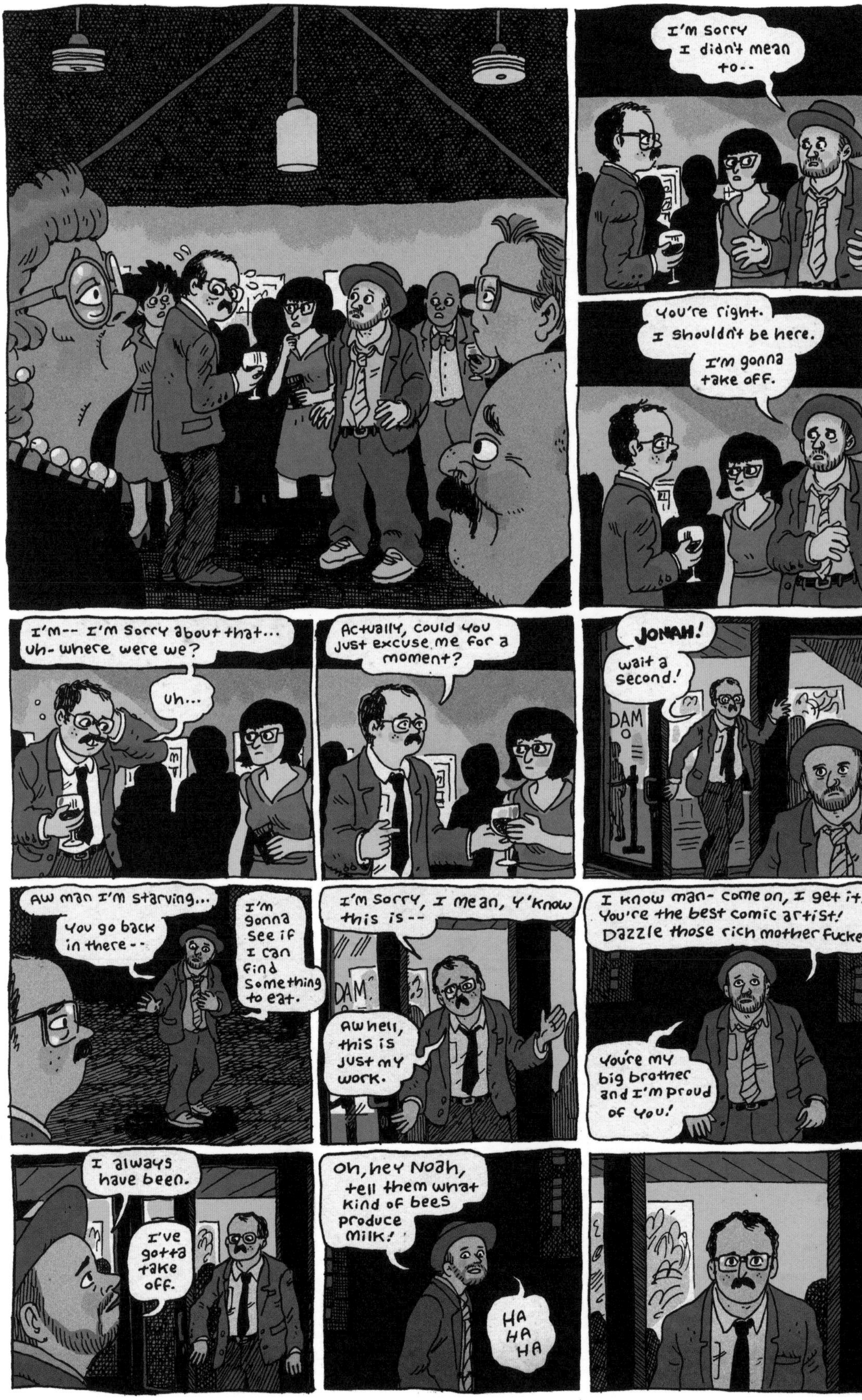
I'm sorry
I didn't mean to--
You're right.
I shouldn't be here.
I'm gonna take off.
I'm-- I'm sorry about that... uh- where were we?
uh...
Actually, could you just excuse me for a moment?
JONAH!
wait a second!
Aw man I'm starving...
You go back in there--
I'm gonna see if I can find something to eat.
I'm sorry, I mean, y'know this is--
Aw hell, this is just my work.
I know man- come on, I get it! You're the best comic artist! Dazzle those rich mother fuckers!
You're my big brother and I'm proud of you!
I always have been.
I've gotta take off.
Oh, hey Noah, tell them what kind of bees produce milk!
HA HA HA

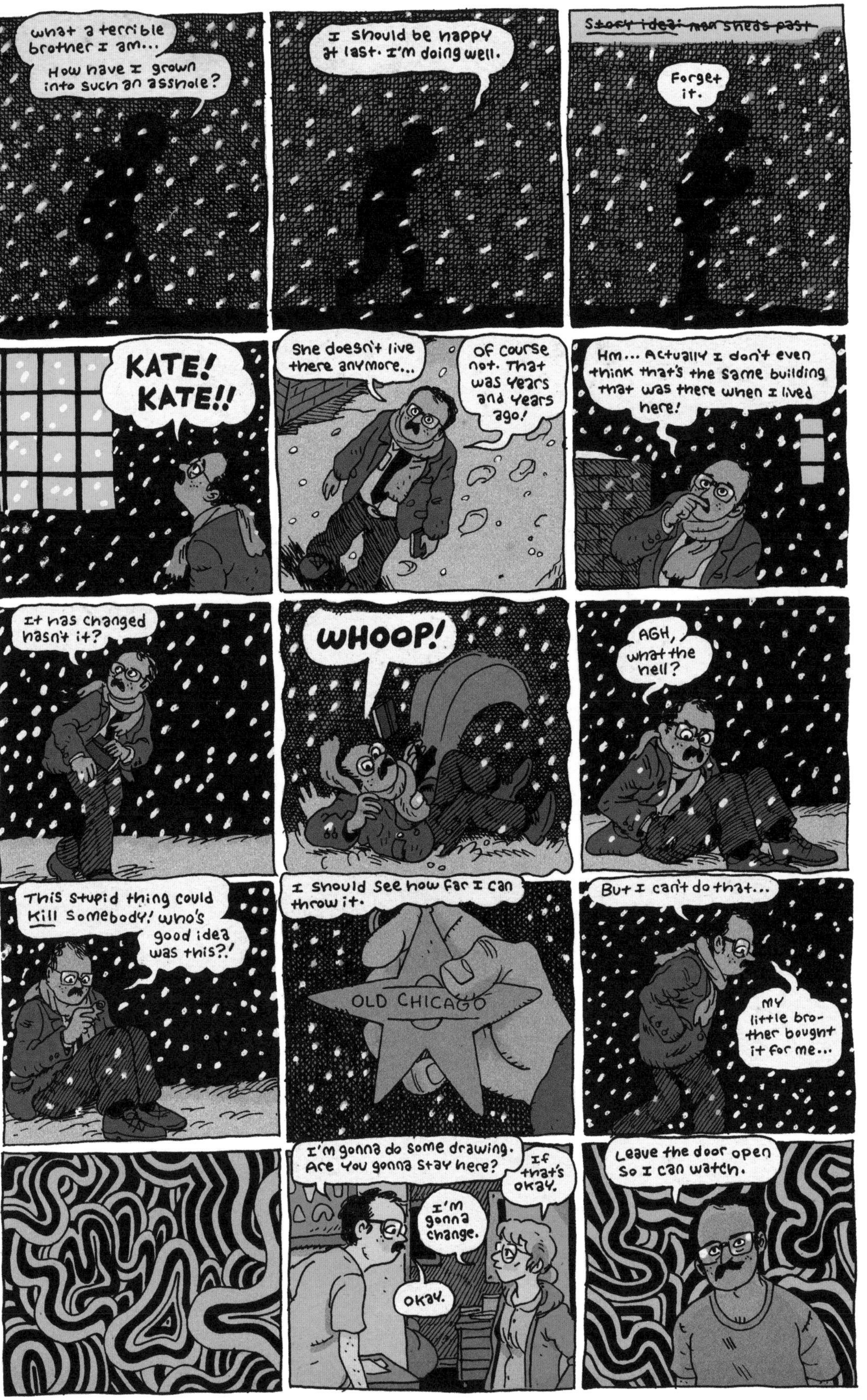
what a terrible brother I am...
How have I grown into such an asshole?
I should be happy at last. I'm doing well.
Story idea: man sneas past
Forget it.
KATE! KATE!!
She doesn't live there anymore...
Of course not. That was years and years ago!
Hm... Actually I don't even think that's the same building that was there when I lived here!
It has changed hasn't it?
WHOOP!
AGH, what the hell?
This stupid thing could Kill somebody! who's good idea was this?!
I should see how far I can throw it.
OLD CHICAGO
But I can't do that...
My little brother bought it for me...
I'm gonna do some drawing. Are you gonna stay here?
If that's okay.
I'm gonna change.
Okay.
Leave the door open so I can watch.

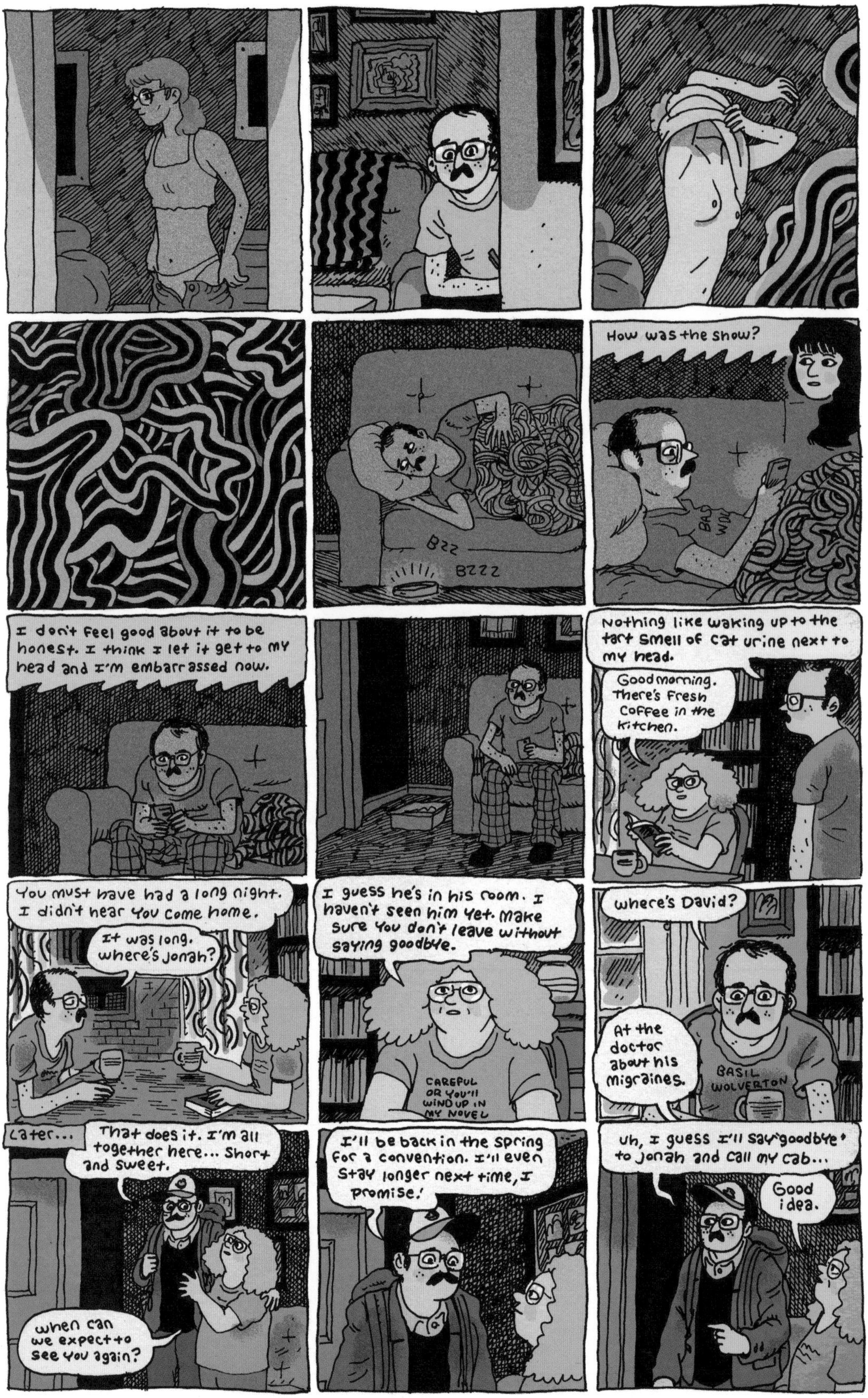
How was the show?
I don't feel good about it to be honest. I think I let it get to my head and I'm embarrassed now.
Nothing like waking up to the tart smell of cat urine next to my head.
Good morning. There's fresh coffee in the kitchen.
You must have had a long night. I didn't hear you come home.
It was long. Where's Jonah?
I guess he's in his room. I haven't seen him yet. Make sure you don't leave without saying goodbye.
CAREFUL OR YOU'LL WIND UP IN MY NOVEL
Where's David?
At the doctor about his migraines.
BASIL WOLVERTON
Later...
That does it. I'm all together here... Short and sweet.
When can we expect to see you again?
I'll be back in the spring for a convention. I'll even stay longer next time, I promise!
Uh, I guess I'll say "goodbye" to Jonah and call my cab...
Good idea.

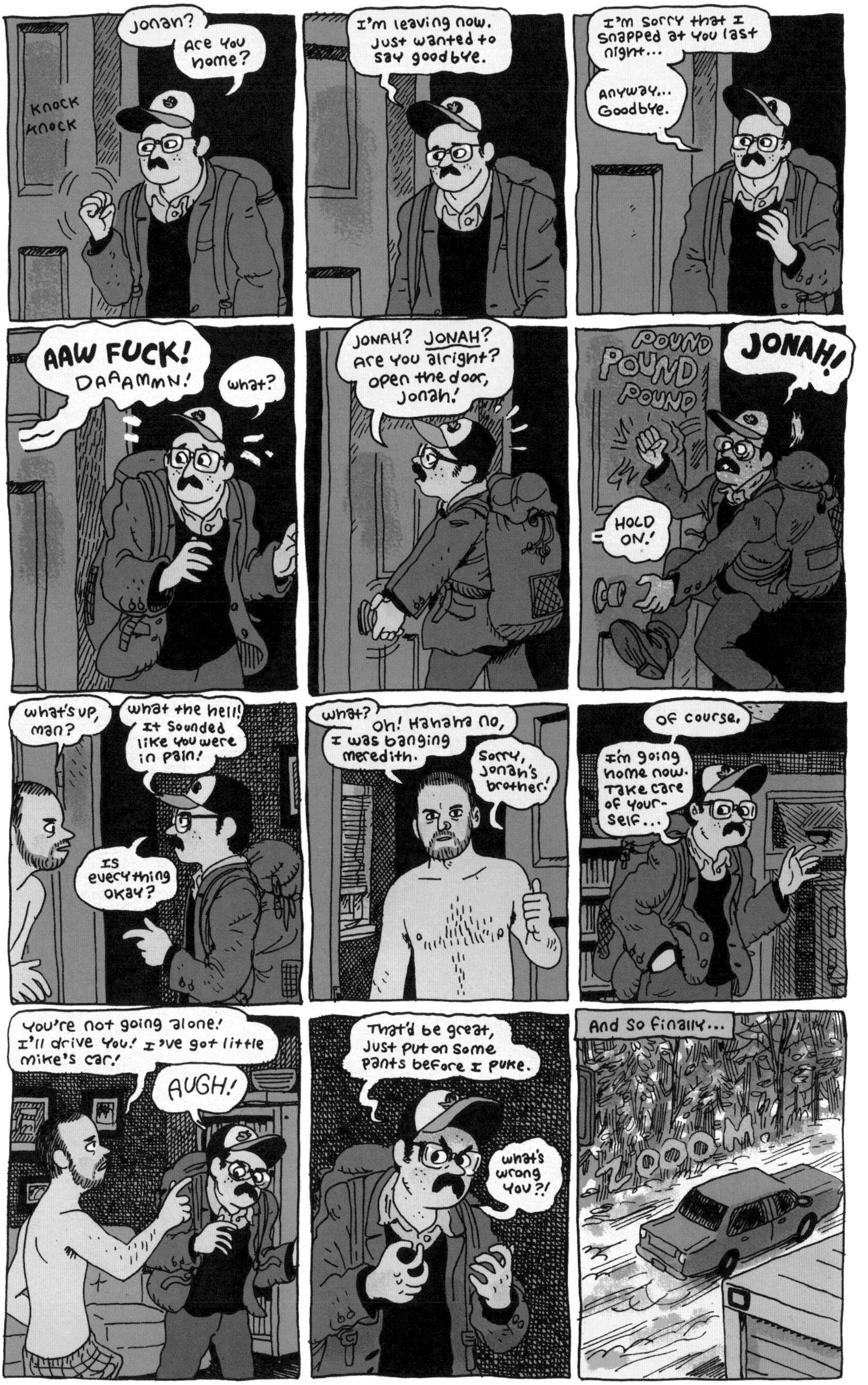
Jonah?
Are you home?
KNOCK KNOCK
I'm leaving now. Just wanted to say goodbye.
I'm sorry that I snapped at you last night...
Anyway... Goodbye.
AAW FUCK! DAAAMMN!
what?
JONAH? JONAH? Are you alright? open the door, Jonah!
POUND POUND POUND
JONAH!
HOLD ON!
what's up, man?
what the hell! It sounded like you were in pain!
Is everything okay?
what? Oh! Hahaha no, I was banging meredith.
Sorry, Jonah's brother!
Of course.
I'm going home now. Take care of your-self...
You're not going alone! I'll drive you! I've got little mike's car!
AUGH!
That'd be great, Just put on some pants before I puke.
what's wrong you?!
And so finally...
ZOOOOM

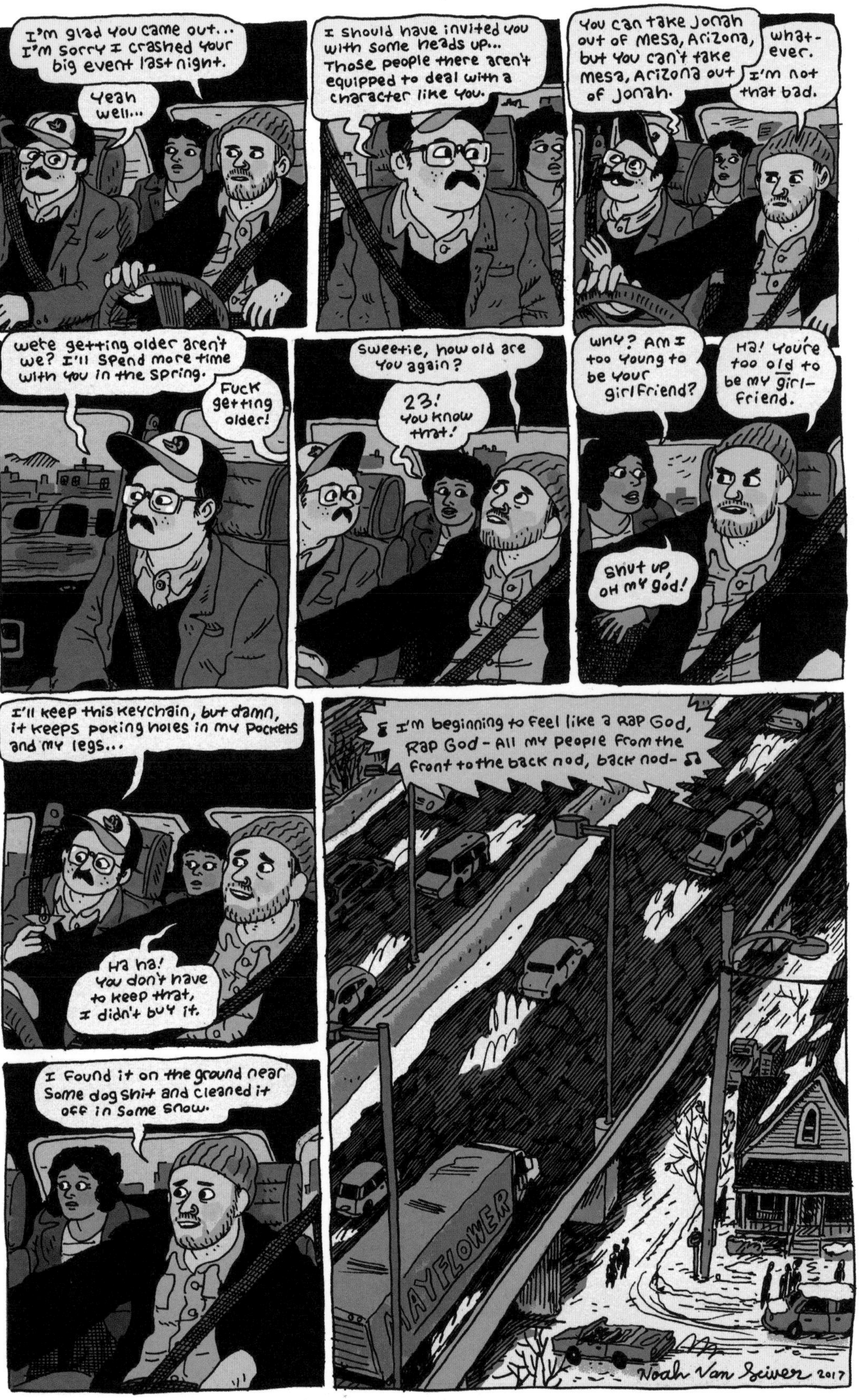
I'm glad you came out... I'm sorry I crashed your big event last night.
Yeah well...
I should have invited you with some heads up... Those people there aren't equipped to deal with a character like you.
You can take Jonah out of Mesa, Arizona, but you can't take Mesa, Arizona out of Jonah.
what-ever. I'm not that bad.
We're getting older aren't we? I'll spend more time with you in the spring.
Fuck getting older!
Sweetie, how old are you again?
23! You know that!
Why? Am I too young to be your girlfriend?
Ha! You're too old to be my girl-friend.
Shut up, oh my god!
I'll keep this keychain, but damn, it keeps poking holes in my pockets and my legs...
Ha ha! You don't have to keep that, I didn't buy it.
I found it on the ground near some dog shit and cleaned it off in some snow.
I'm beginning to feel like a Rap God, Rap God - All my people from the front to the back nod, back nod-
MAYFLOWER
Noah Van Sciver 2017

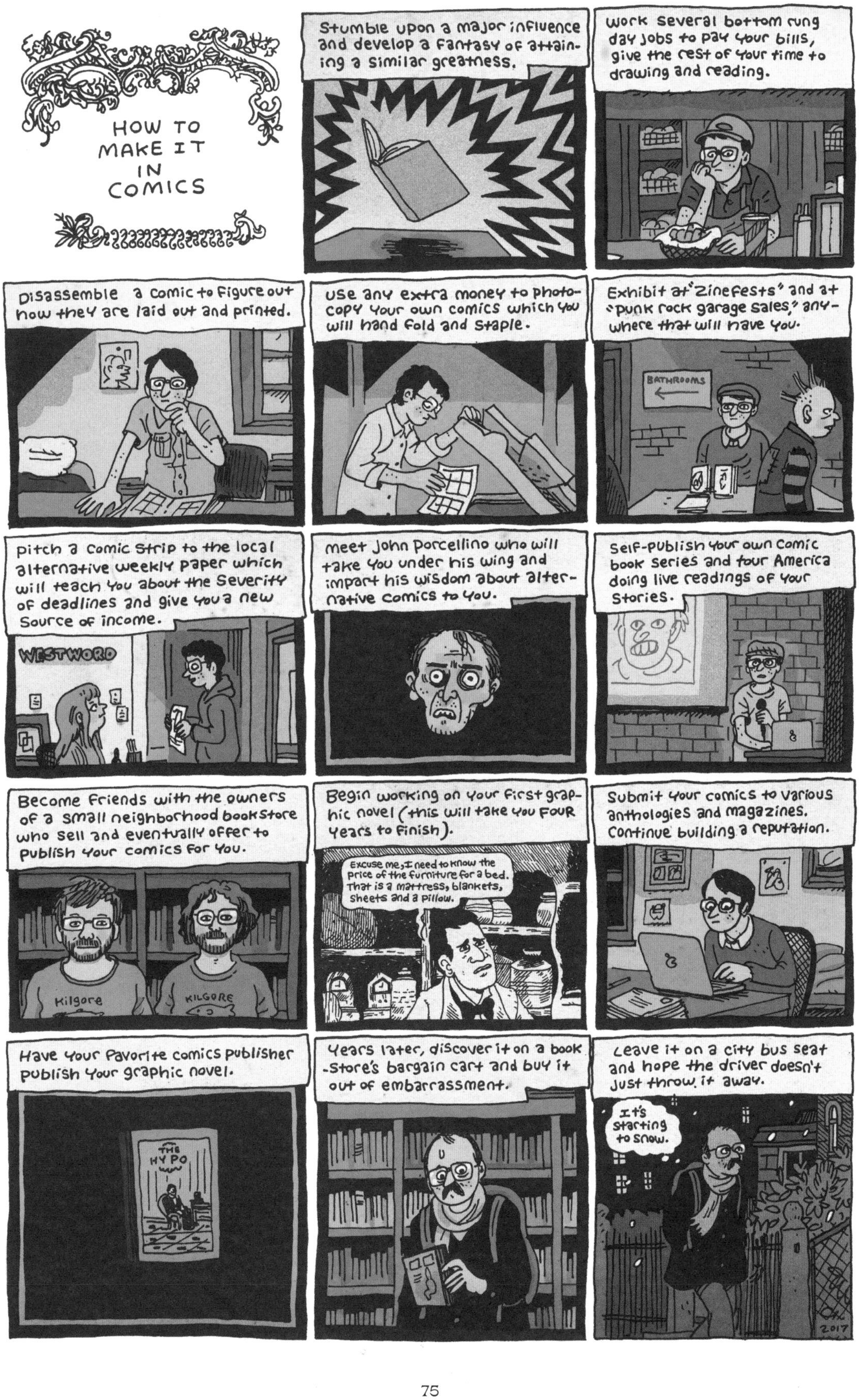
HOW TO MAKE IT IN COMICS
Stumble upon a major influence and develop a fantasy of attaining a similar greatness.
Work several bottom rung day jobs to pay your bills, give the rest of your time to drawing and reading.
Disassemble a comic to figure out how they are laid out and printed.
Use any extra money to photocopy your own comics which you will hand fold and staple.
Exhibit at "Zinefests" and at "punk rock garage sales," anywhere that will have you.
BATHROOMS
Pitch a comic strip to the local alternative weekly paper which will teach you about the severity of deadlines and give you a new source of income.
WESTWORD
Meet John Porcellino who will take you under his wing and impart his wisdom about alternative comics to you.
Self-publish your own comic book series and tour America doing live readings of your stories.
Become friends with the owners of a small neighborhood bookstore who sell and eventually offer to publish your comics for you.
Kilgore
KILGORE
Begin working on your first graphic novel (this will take you FOUR years to finish).
Excuse me, I need to know the price of the furniture for a bed. That is a mattress, blankets, sheets and a pillow.
Submit your comics to various anthologies and magazines. Continue building a reputation.
Have your favorite comics publisher publish your graphic novel.
THE HYPO
Years later, discover it on a book-store's bargain cart and buy it out of embarrassment.
Leave it on a city bus seat and hope the driver doesn't just throw it away.
It's starting to snow.
2017

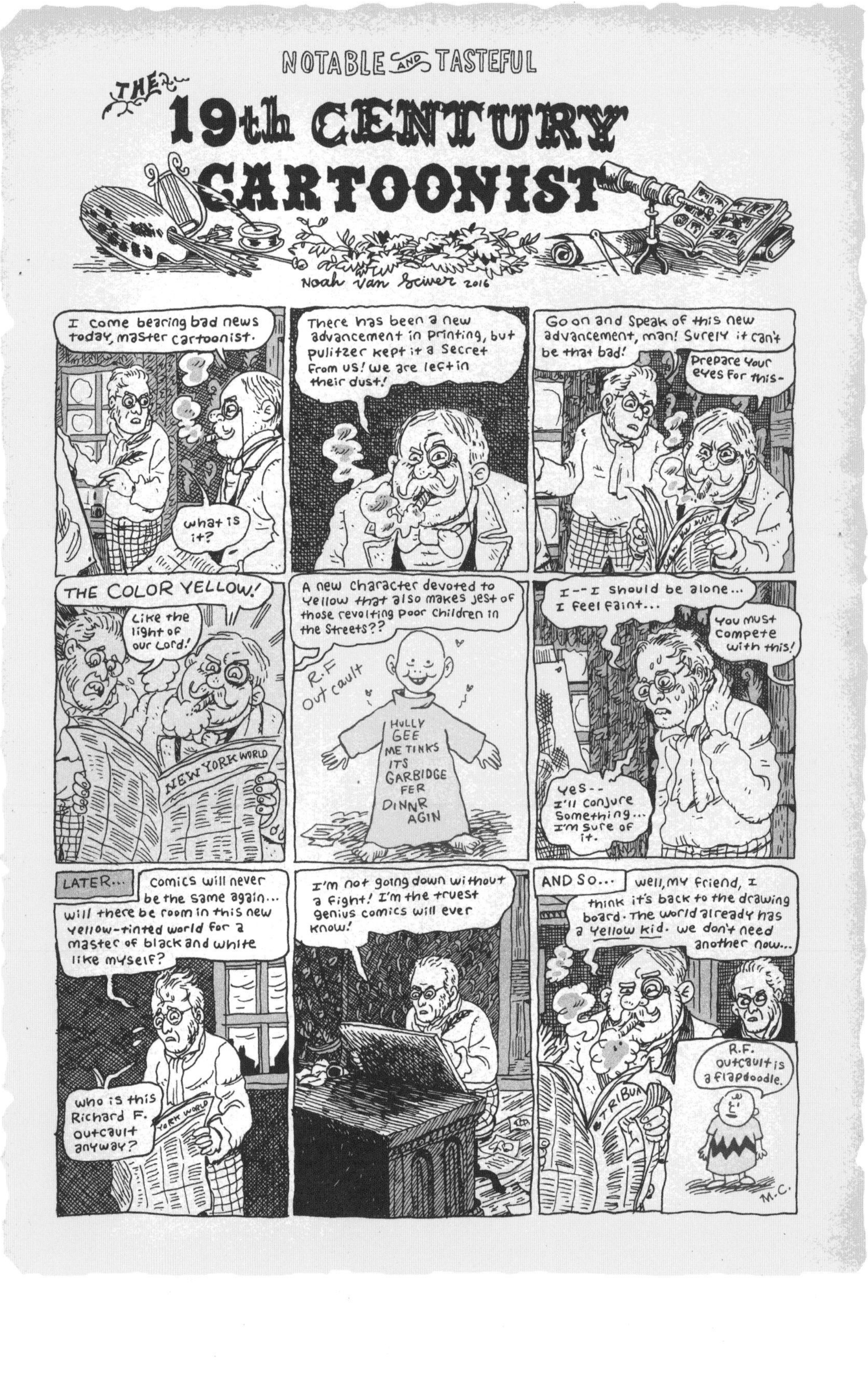
NOTABLE AND TASTEFUL
THE 19th CENTURY CARTOONIST
Noah Van Sciver 2016
I come bearing bad news today, master cartoonist.
what is it?
There has been a new advancement in printing, but pulitzer kept it a secret from us! we are left in their dust!
Go on and speak of this new advancement, man! Surely it can't be that bad!
Prepare your eyes for this-
THE COLOR YELLOW!
Like the light of our Lord!
NEW YORK WORLD
A new character devoted to yellow that also makes jest of those revolting poor children in the streets??
R.F Out cault
HULLY GEE ME TINKS ITS GARBIDGE FER DINNR AGIN
I-- I should be alone... I feel faint...
You must compete with this!
Yes-- I'll conjure something... I'm sure of it.
LATER...
comics will never be the same again... will there be room in this new yellow-tinted world for a master of black and white like myself?
who is this Richard F. outcault anyway?
YORK WORLD
I'm not going down without a fight! I'm the truest genius comics will ever know!
AND SO...
well, my friend, I think it's back to the drawing board. The world already has a Yellow kid. we don't need another now...
TRIBU
R.F. outcault is a flapdoodle.
M.C.

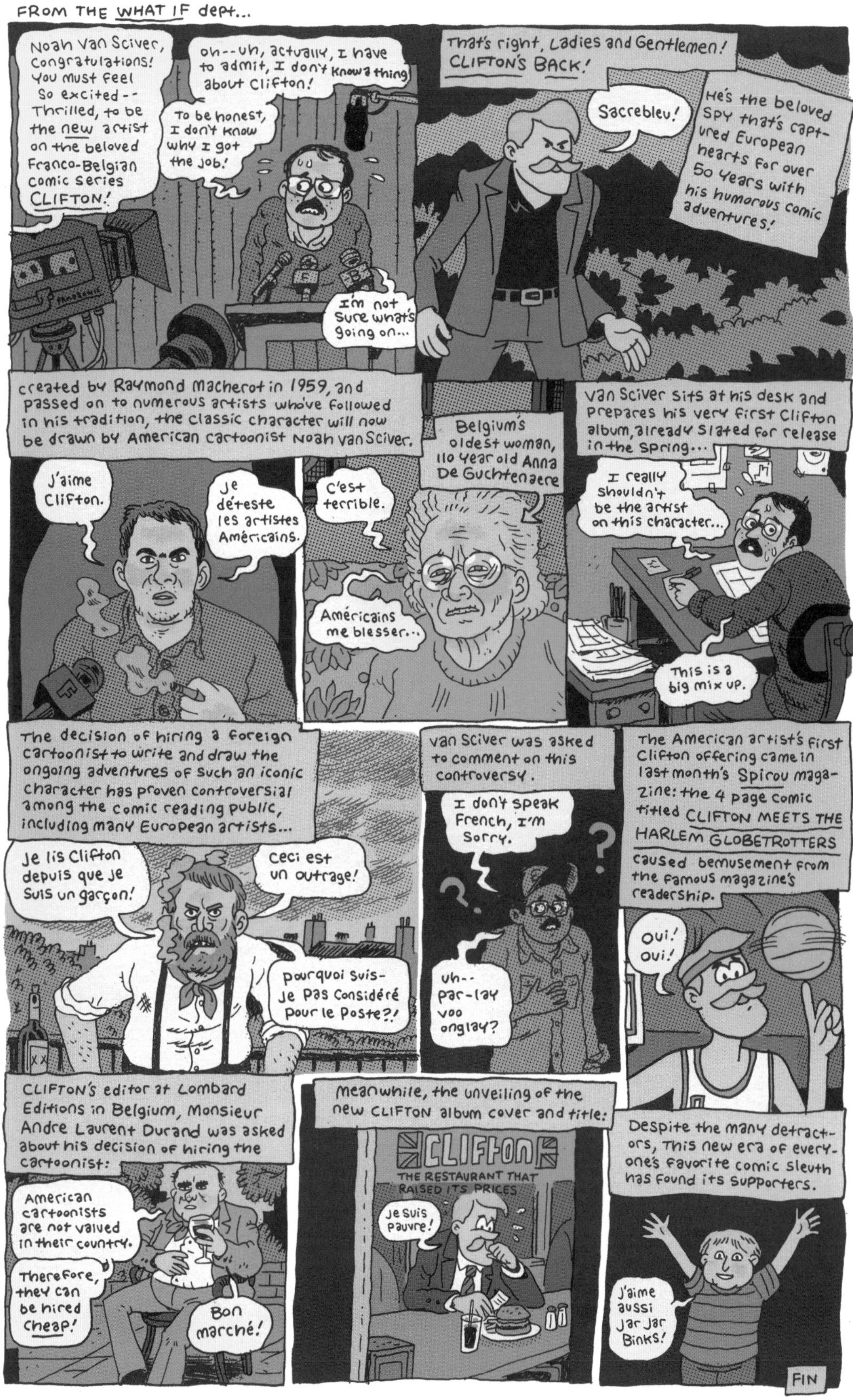
FROM THE WHAT IF dept...
Noah Van Sciver, Congratulations! You must feel so excited -- Thrilled, to be the new artist on the beloved Franco-Belgian comic series CLIFTON!
oh--uh, actually, I have to admit, I don't know a thing about Clifton!
To be honest, I don't know why I got the job!
I'm not sure what's going on...
That's right, Ladies and Gentlemen! CLIFTON'S BACK!
Sacrebleu!
He's the beloved spy that's captured European hearts for over 50 years with his humorous comic adventures!
created by Raymond Macherot in 1959, and passed on to numerous artists who've followed in his tradition, the classic character will now be drawn by American cartoonist Noah van Sciver.
J'aime Clifton.
Je déteste les artistes Américains.
Belgium's oldest woman, 110 year old Anna De Guchtenaere
C'est terrible.
Américains me blesser...
Van Sciver sits at his desk and prepares his very first Clifton album, already slated for release in the spring...
I really shouldn't be the artist on this character...
This is a big mix up.
The decision of hiring a foreign cartoonist to write and draw the ongoing adventures of such an iconic character has proven controversial among the comic reading public, including many European artists...
Je lis Clifton depuis que je suis un garçon!
Ceci est un outrage!
pourquoi suis-je pas considéré pour le poste?!
Van Sciver was asked to comment on this controversy.
I don't speak French, I'm sorry.
uh-- par-lay voo onglay?
The American artist's first Clifton offering came in last month's Spirou magazine: the 4 page comic titled CLIFTON MEETS THE HARLEM GLOBETROTTERS caused bemusement from the famous magazine's readership.
Oui! Oui!
CLIFTON's editor at Lombard Editions in Belgium, Monsieur Andre Laurent Durand was asked about his decision of hiring the cartoonist:
American cartoonists are not valued in their country.
Therefore, they can be hired cheap!
Bon marché!
Meanwhile, the unveiling of the new CLIFTON album cover and title:
CLIFTON
THE RESTAURANT THAT RAISED ITS PRICES
Je suis pauvre!
Despite the many detractors, this new era of everyone's favorite comic sleuth has found its supporters.
J'aime aussi Jar Jar Binks!
FIN

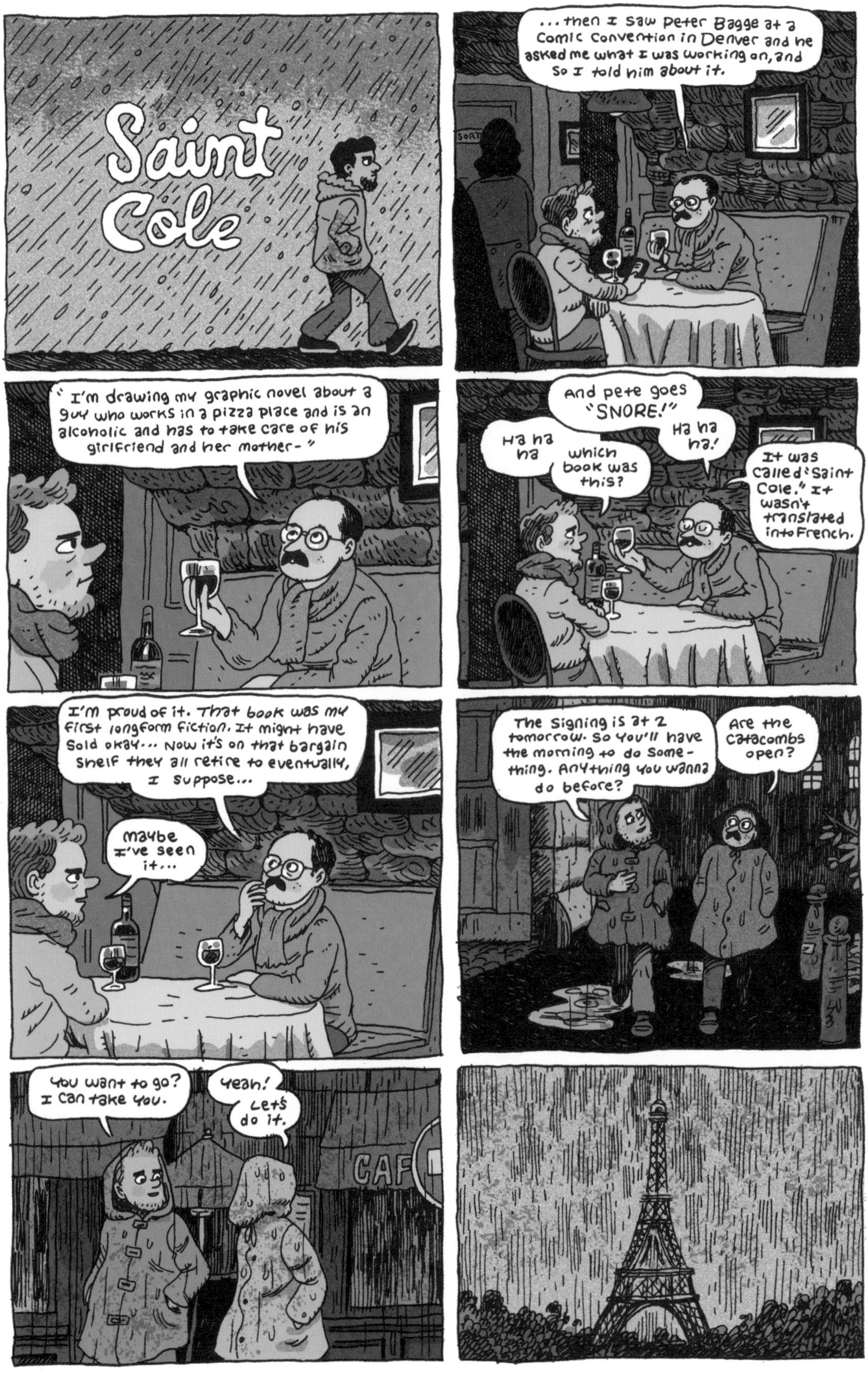
Saint Cole
...then I saw Peter Bagge at a Comic Convention in Denver and he asked me what I was working on, and so I told him about it.
SORT
"I'm drawing my graphic novel about a guy who works in a pizza place and is an alcoholic and has to take care of his girlfriend and her mother-"
And pete goes "SNORE!"
Ha ha ha
Ha ha ha!
which book was this?
It was called "Saint Cole." It wasn't translated into French.
I'm proud of it. That book was my first longform fiction. It might have sold okay... Now it's on that bargain shelf they all retire to eventually, I suppose...
maybe I've seen it...
The signing is at 2 tomorrow. So you'll have the morning to do something. Anything you wanna do before?
Are the catacombs open?
You want to go? I can take you.
Yeah! Let's do it.
CAF

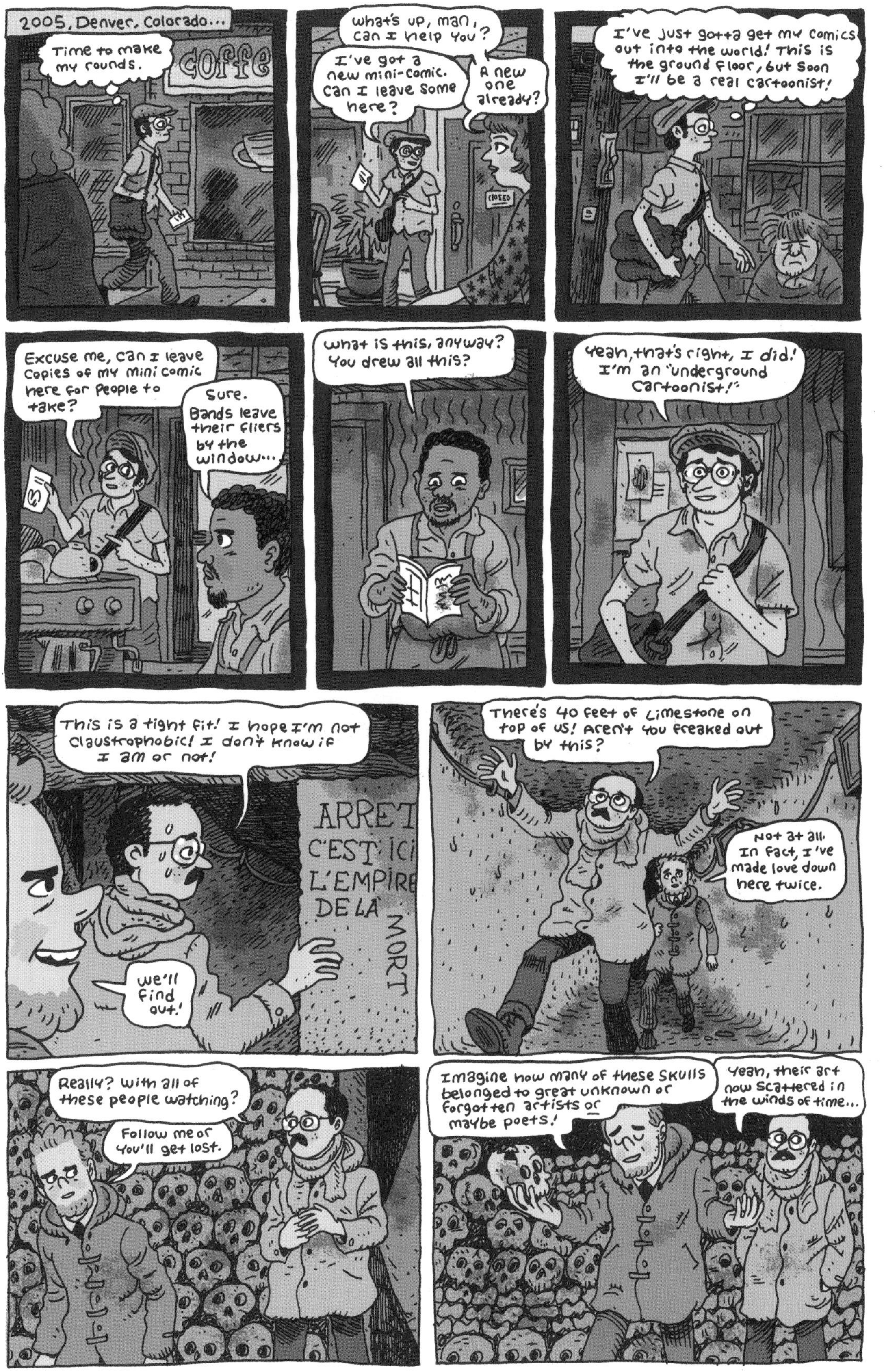
2005, Denver, Colorado...
Time to make my rounds.
coffe
What's up, man, can I help you?
I've got a new mini-comic. Can I leave some here?
A new one already?
CLOSED
I've just gotta get my comics out into the world! This is the ground floor, but soon I'll be a real cartoonist!
Excuse me, can I leave copies of my mini comic here for people to take?
Sure. Bands leave their fliers by the window...
What is this, anyway? You drew all this?
Yeah, that's right, I did! I'm an "underground cartoonist!"
This is a tight fit! I hope I'm not claustrophobic! I don't know if I am or not!
ARRET C'EST ICI L'EMPIRE DE LA MORT
We'll find out!
There's 40 feet of limestone on top of us! Aren't you freaked out by this?
Not at all. In fact, I've made love down here twice.
Really? With all of these people watching?
Follow me or you'll get lost.
Imagine how many of these skulls belonged to great unknown or forgotten artists or maybe poets!
Yeah, their art now scattered in the winds of time...

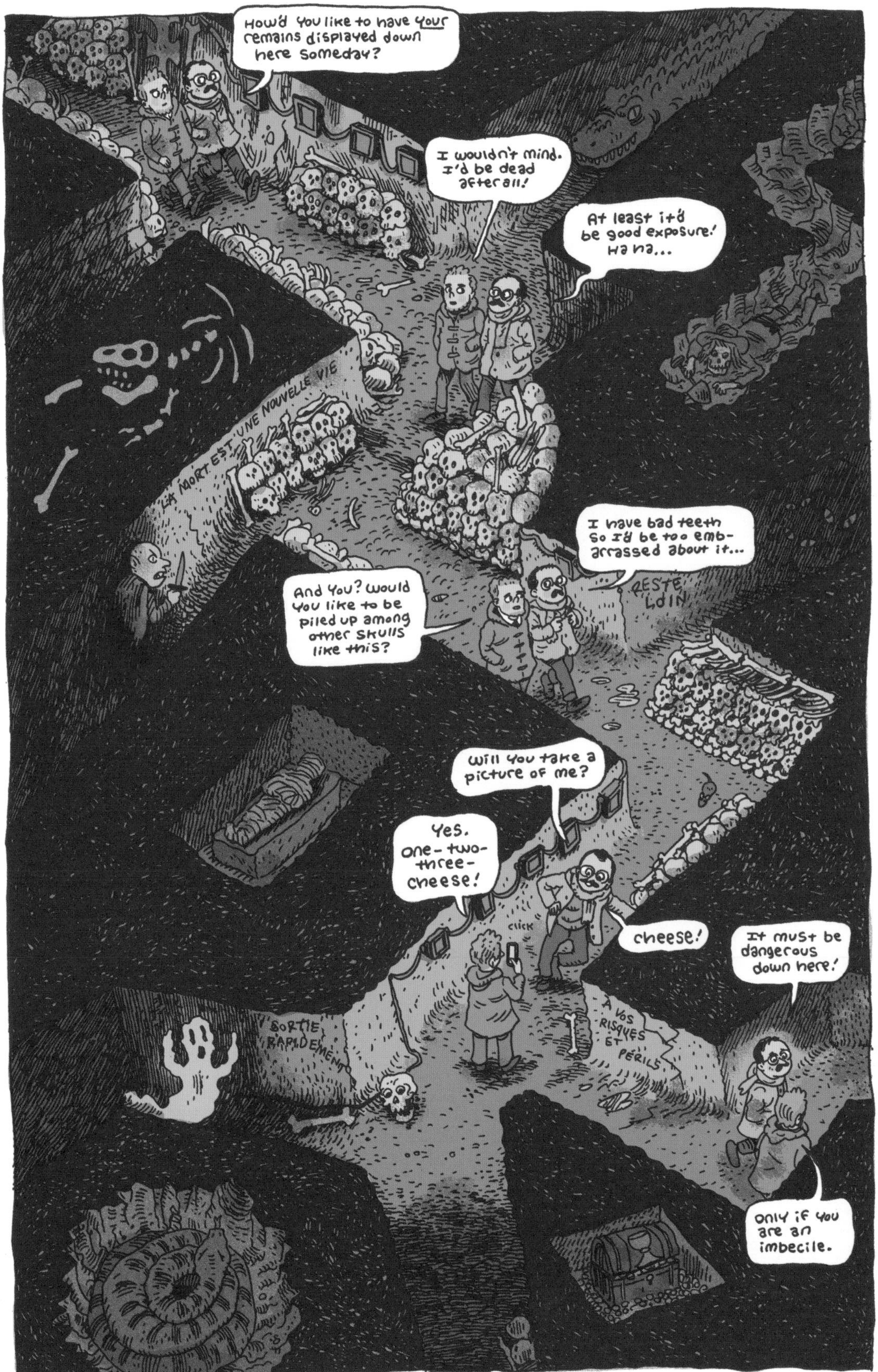
How'd you like to have YOUR remains displayed down here someday?
I wouldn't mind. I'd be dead after all!
At least it'd be good exposure! Ha ha...
LA MORT EST UNE NOUVELLE VIE
I have bad teeth so I'd be too embarrassed about it...
RESTE LOIN
And you? Would you like to be piled up among other skulls like this?
Will you take a picture of me?
Yes. One-two-three-cheese!
CLICK
Cheese!
It must be dangerous down here!
SORTIE RAPIDEMENT
À VOS RISQUES ET PÉRILS
Only if you are an imbecile.

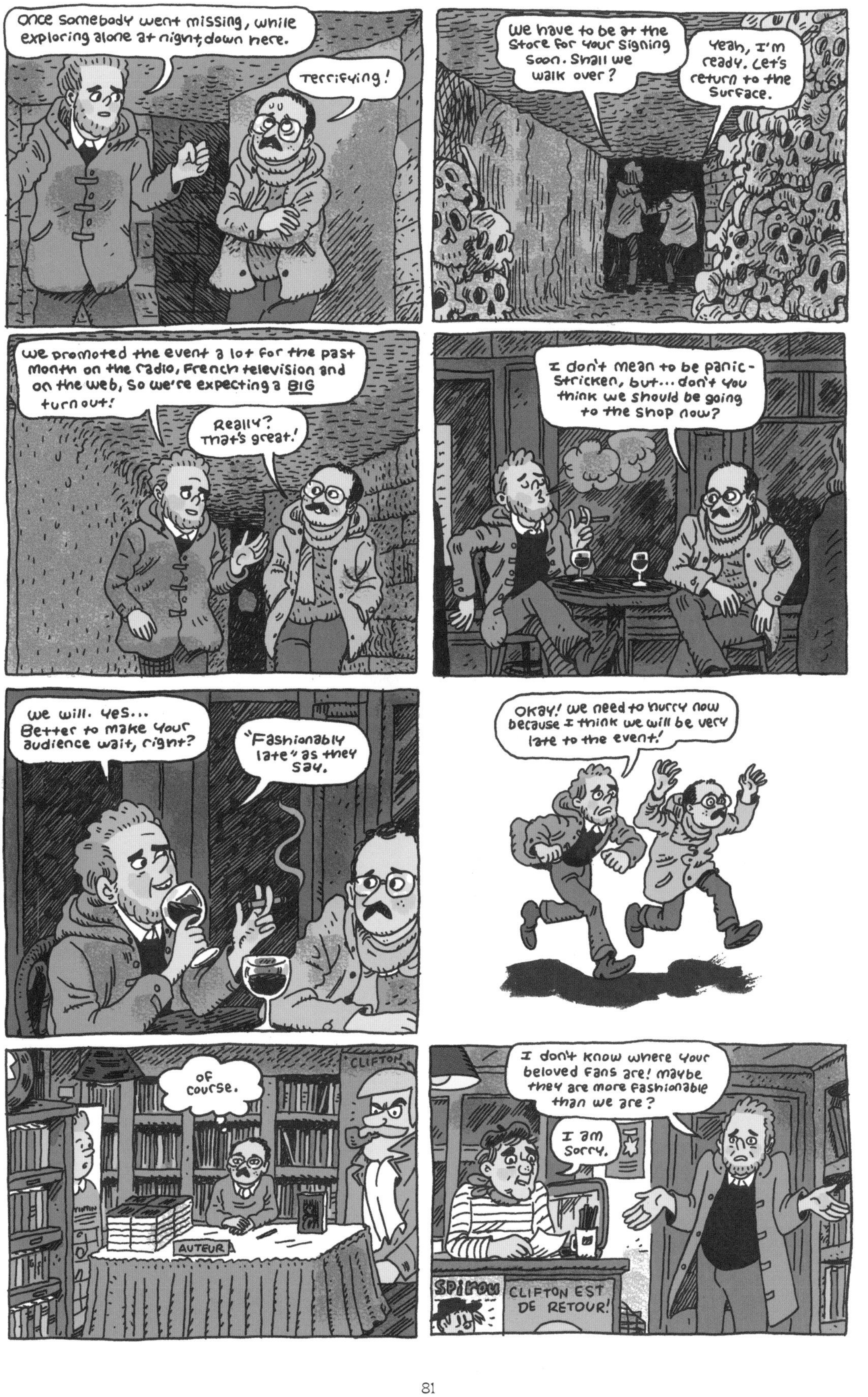
Once somebody went missing, while exploring alone at night, down here.
Terrifying!
We have to be at the store for your signing soon. Shall we walk over?
Yeah, I'm ready. Let's return to the surface.
We promoted the event a lot for the past month on the radio, French television and on the web, so we're expecting a BIG turnout!
Really? That's great!
I don't mean to be panic-stricken, but... don't you think we should be going to the shop now?
We will. Yes... Better to make your audience wait, right?
"Fashionably late" as they say.
Okay! We need to hurry now because I think we will be very late to the event!
Of course.
CLIFTON
AUTEUR
I don't know where your beloved fans are! Maybe they are more fashionable than we are?
I am sorry.
SPIROU
CLIFTON EST DE RETOUR!

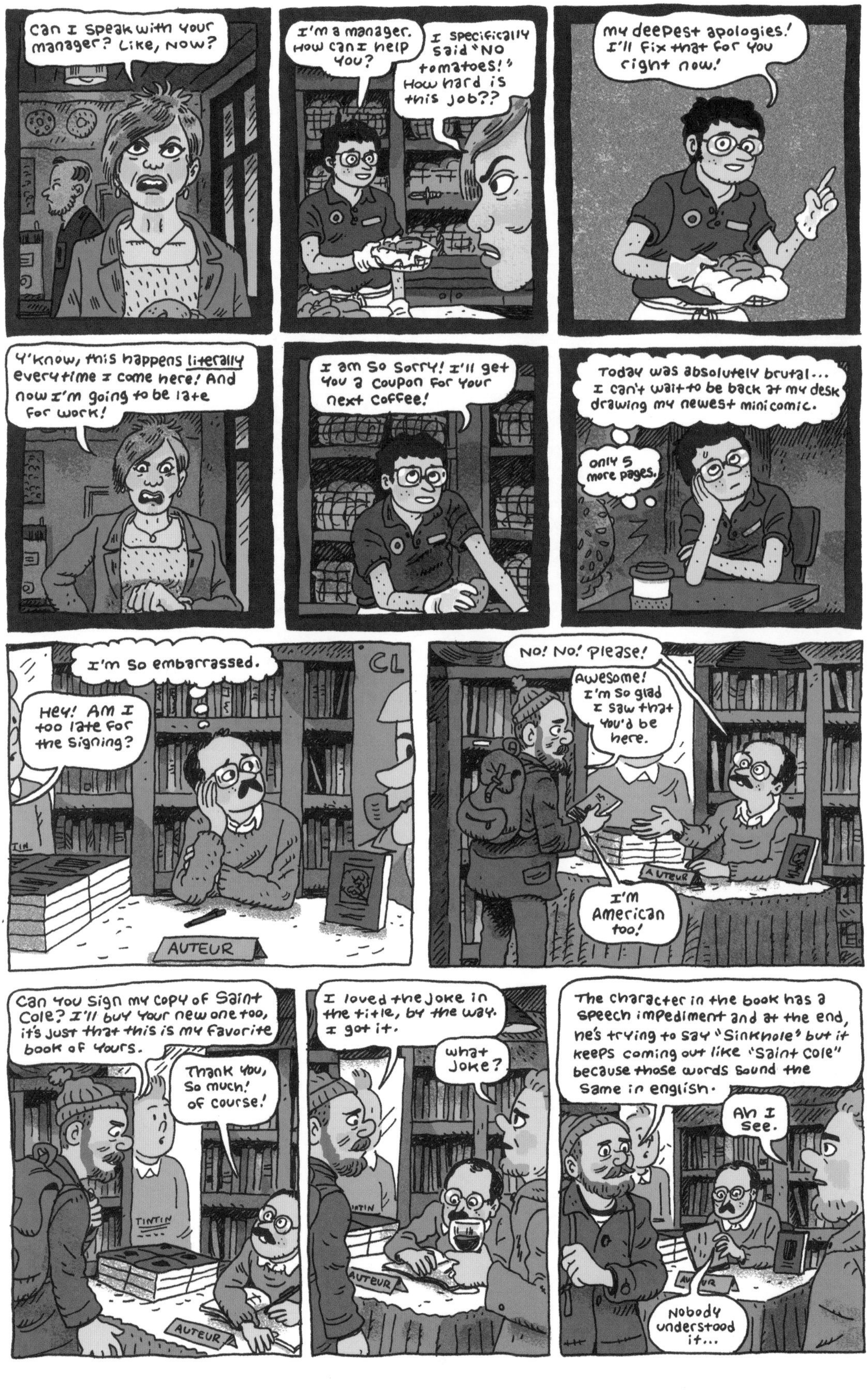
Can I speak with your manager? Like, now?
I'm a manager. How can I help you?
I specifically said "No tomatoes!" How hard is this job??
My deepest apologies! I'll fix that for you right now!
Y'know, this happens literally everytime I come here! And now I'm going to be late for work!
I am so sorry! I'll get you a coupon for your next coffee!
Today was absolutely brutal... I can't wait to be back at my desk drawing my newest minicomic.
Only 5 more pages.
I'm so embarrassed.
Hey! Am I too late for the signing?
AUTEUR
No! No! Please!
Awesome! I'm so glad I saw that you'd be here.
I'm American too!
AUTEUR
Can you sign my copy of Saint Cole? I'll buy your new one too, it's just that this is my favorite book of yours.
Thank you, so much! Of course!
TINTIN
AUTEUR
I loved the joke in the title, by the way. I got it.
What joke?
AUTEUR
The character in the book has a speech impediment and at the end, he's trying to say "Sinkhole" but it keeps coming out like "Saint Cole" because those words sound the same in english.
Ah I see.
Nobody understood it...

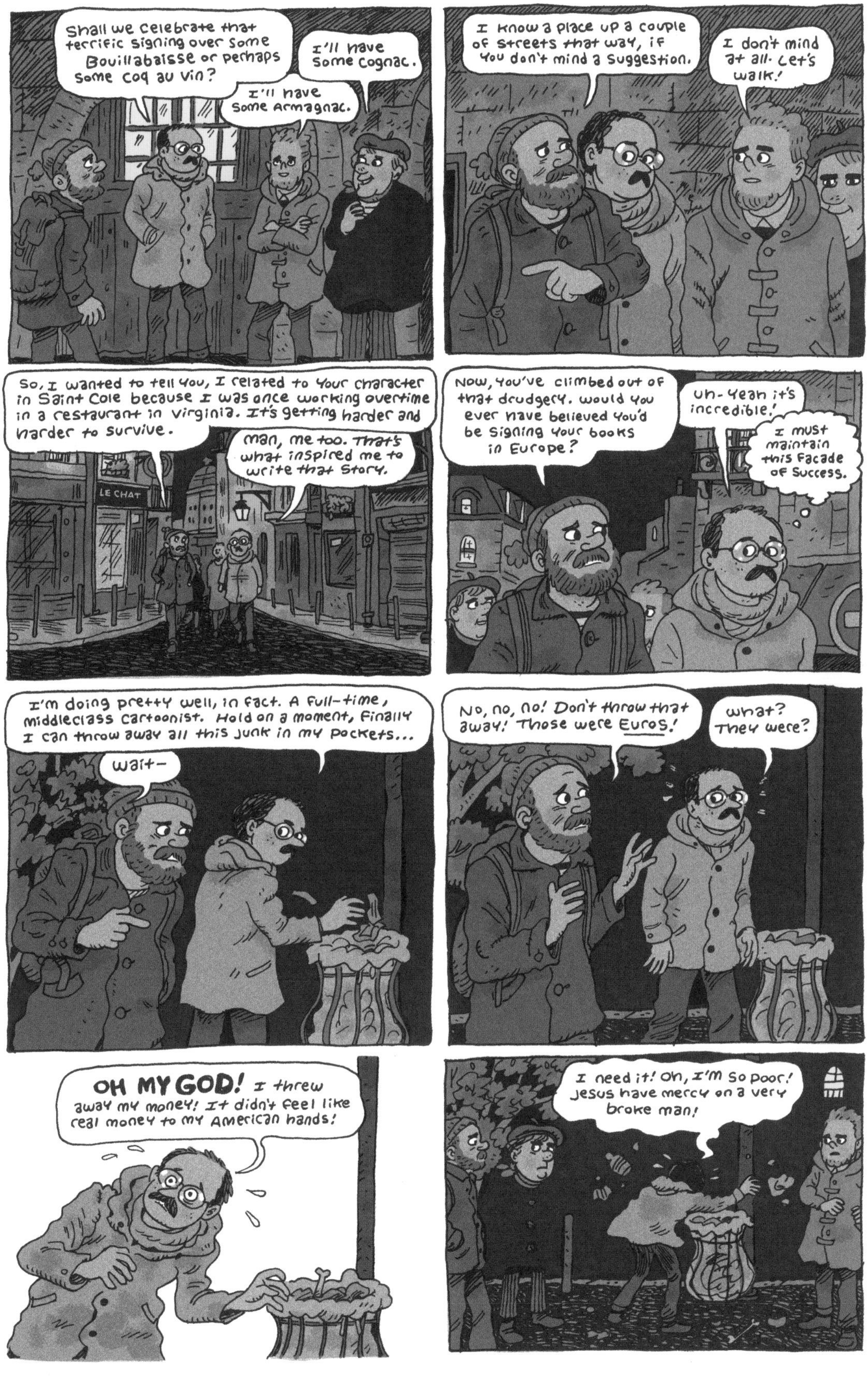
Shall we celebrate that terrific signing over some Bouillabaisse or perhaps some coq au vin?
I'll have some Armagnac.
I'll have some cognac.
I know a place up a couple of streets that way, if you don't mind a suggestion.
I don't mind at all. Let's walk!
So, I wanted to tell you, I related to your character in Saint Cole because I was once working overtime in a restaurant in Virginia. It's getting harder and harder to survive.
Man, me too. That's what inspired me to write that story.
LE CHAT
Now, you've climbed out of that drudgery. Would you ever have believed you'd be signing your books in Europe?
Uh- Yeah it's incredible!
I must maintain this facade of success.
I'm doing pretty well, in fact. A full-time, middleclass cartoonist. Hold on a moment, finally I can throw away all this junk in my pockets...
Wait-
No, no, no! Don't throw that away! Those were Euros!
What? They were?
OH MY GOD! I threw away my money! It didn't feel like real money to my American hands!
I need it! Oh, I'm so poor! Jesus have mercy on a very broke man!

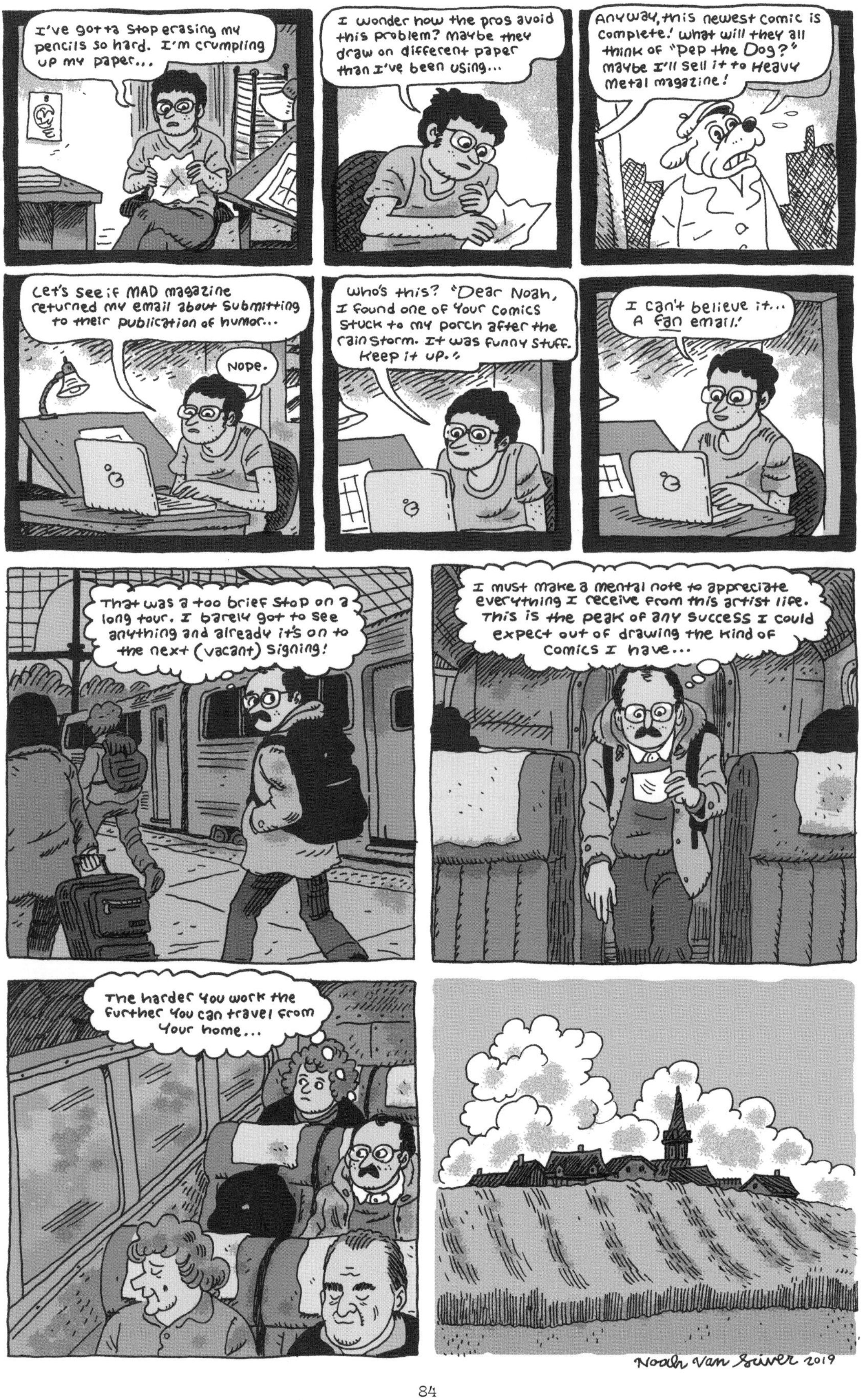
I've gotta stop erasing my pencils so hard. I'm crumpling up my paper...
I wonder how the pros avoid this problem? Maybe they draw on different paper than I've been using...
Anyway, this newest comic is complete! What will they all think of "Pep the Dog?" Maybe I'll sell it to Heavy Metal magazine!
Let's see if MAD magazine returned my email about submitting to their publication of humor...
Nope.
Who's this? "Dear Noah, I found one of your comics stuck to my porch after the rainstorm. It was funny stuff. Keep it up."
I can't believe it... A fan email!
That was a too brief stop on a long tour. I barely got to see anything and already it's on to the next (vacant) signing!
I must make a mental note to appreciate everything I receive from this artist life. This is the peak of any success I could expect out of drawing the kind of comics I have...
The harder you work the further you can travel from your home...
Noah Van Sciver 2019

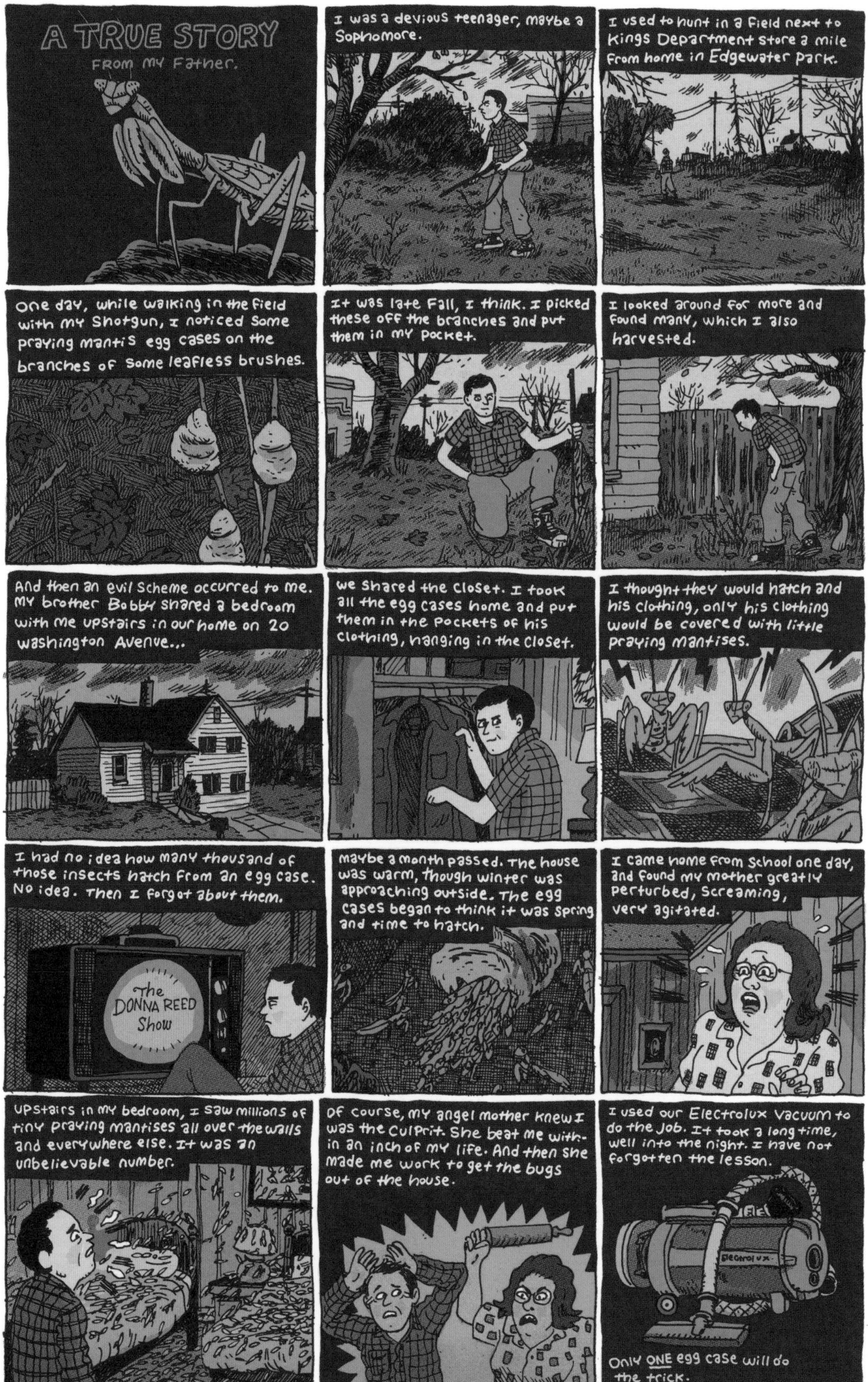
A TRUE STORY
FROM MY FATHER.
I was a devious teenager, maybe a Sophomore.
I used to hunt in a field next to Kings Department store a mile from home in Edgewater park.
One day, while walking in the field with my shotgun, I noticed some praying mantis egg cases on the branches of some leafless brushes.
It was late Fall, I think. I picked these off the branches and put them in my pocket.
I looked around for more and found many, which I also harvested.
And then an evil scheme occurred to me. My brother Bobby shared a bedroom with me upstairs in our home on 20 Washington Avenue...
We shared the closet. I took all the egg cases home and put them in the pockets of his clothing, hanging in the closet.
I thought they would hatch and his clothing, only his clothing would be covered with little praying mantises.
I had no idea how many thousand of those insects hatch from an egg case. No idea. Then I forgot about them.
The DONNA REED Show
Maybe a month passed. The house was warm, though winter was approaching outside. The egg cases began to think it was Spring and time to hatch.
I came home from school one day, and found my mother greatly perturbed, screaming, very agitated.
Upstairs in my bedroom, I saw millions of tiny praying mantises all over the walls and everywhere else. It was an unbelievable number.
Of course, my angel mother knew I was the culprit. She beat me within an inch of my life. And then she made me work to get the bugs out of the house.
I used our Electrolux vacuum to do the job. It took a long time, well into the night. I have not forgotten the lesson.
Electrolux
Only ONE egg case will do the trick.
2016

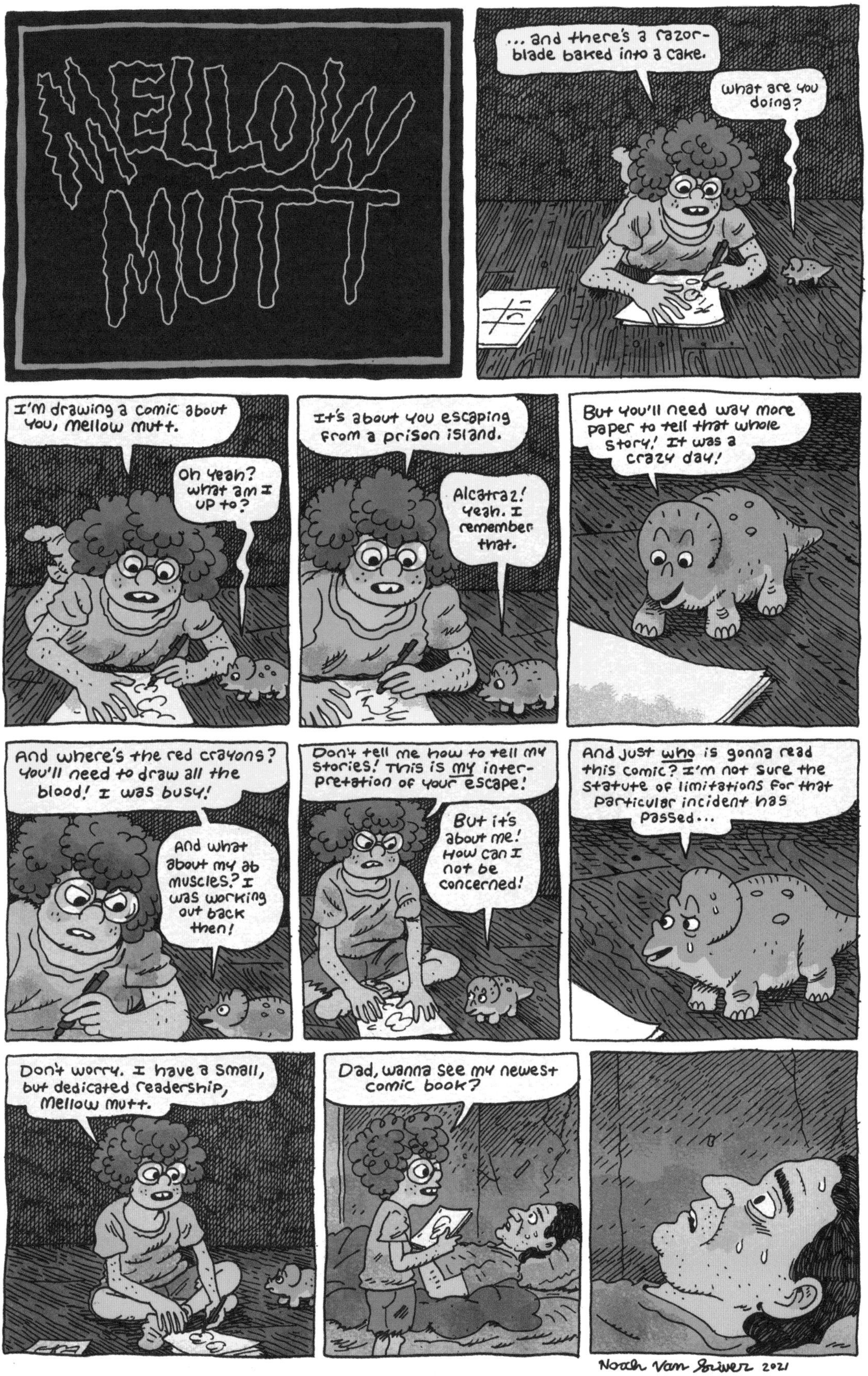
MELLOW MUTT
... and there's a razor-blade baked into a cake.
What are you doing?
I'm drawing a comic about you, Mellow Mutt.
Oh yeah? what am I up to?
It's about you escaping from a prison island.
Alcatraz! Yeah. I remember that.
But you'll need way more paper to tell that whole story! It was a crazy day!
And where's the red crayons? You'll need to draw all the blood! I was busy!
And what about my ab muscles? I was working out back then!
Don't tell me how to tell my stories! This is my interpretation of your escape!
But it's about me! How can I not be concerned!
And just who is gonna read this comic? I'm not sure the statute of limitations for that particular incident has passed...
Don't worry. I have a small, but dedicated readership, Mellow Mutt.
Dad, wanna see my newest comic book?
Noah Van Sciver 2021

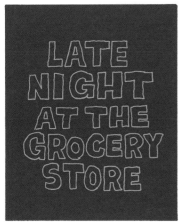

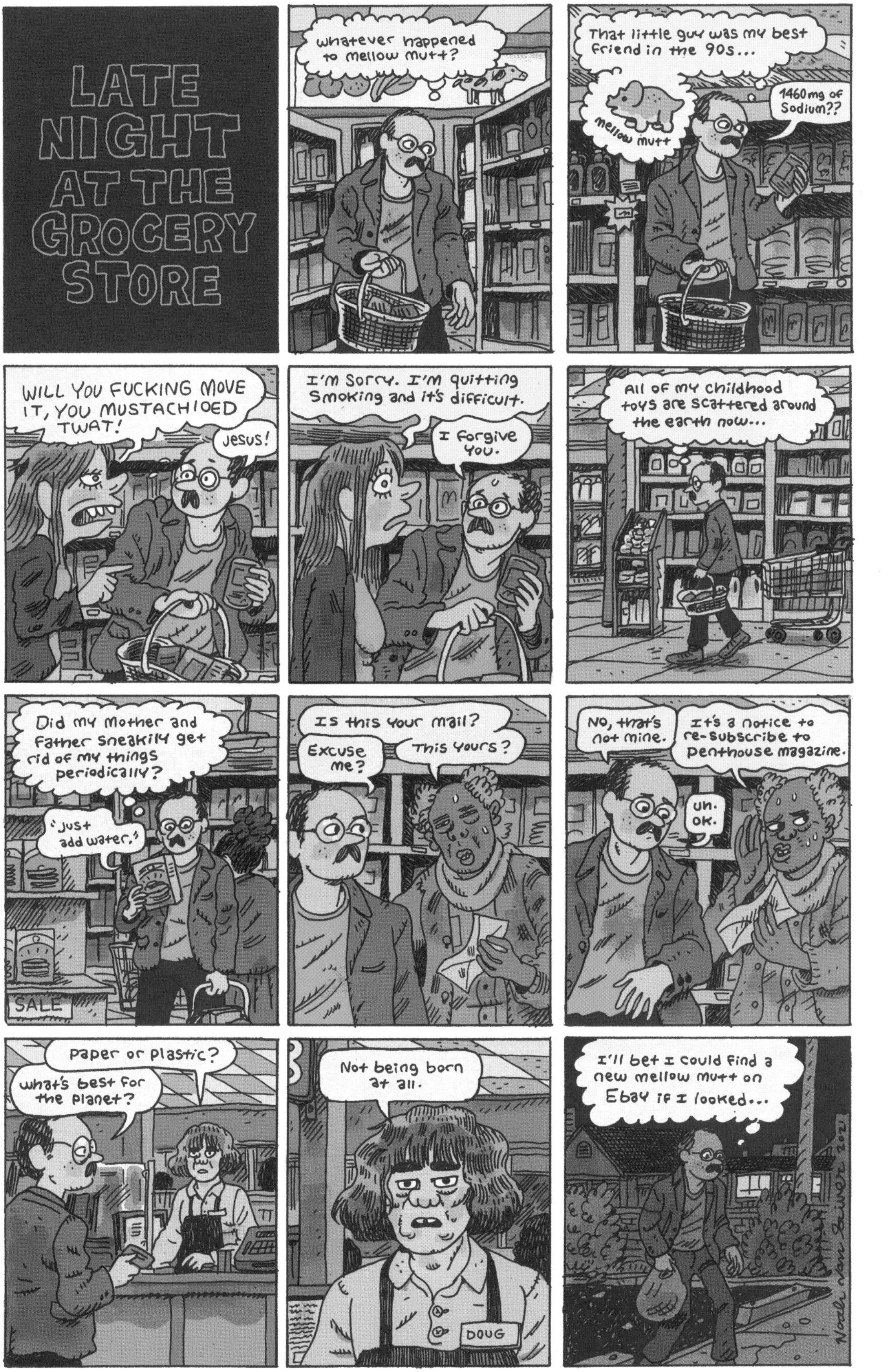
LATE NIGHT AT THE GROCERY STORE
whatever happened to mellow mutt?
That little guy was my best friend in the 90s...
mellow mutt
1460mg of Sodium??
WILL YOU FUCKING MOVE IT, YOU MUSTACHIOED TWAT!
JESUS!
I'm sorry. I'm quitting smoking and it's difficult.
I forgive you.
All of my childhood toys are scattered around the earth now...
Did my mother and father sneakily get rid of my things periodically?
"just add water."
SALE
Is this your mail?
Excuse me?
This yours?
No, that's not mine.
It's a notice to re-subscribe to penthouse magazine.
uh. ok.
paper or plastic?
what's best for the planet?
Not being born at all.
DOUG
I'll bet I could find a new mellow mutt on Ebay if I looked...

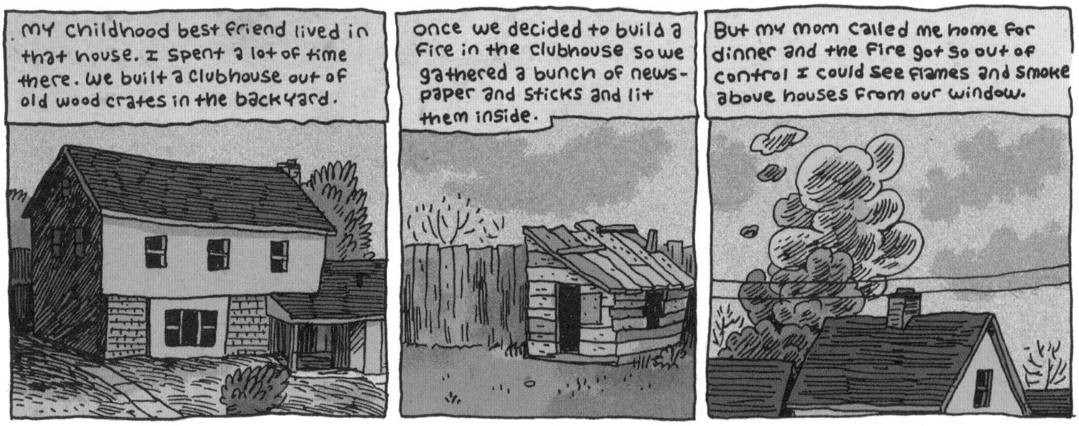
MY childhood best friend lived in that house. I spent a lot of time there. We built a clubhouse out of old wood crates in the backyard.
Once we decided to build a fire in the clubhouse so we gathered a bunch of newspaper and sticks and lit them inside.
But my mom called me home for dinner and the fire got so out of control I could see flames and smoke above houses from our window.

BEVERLY NEW JERSEY

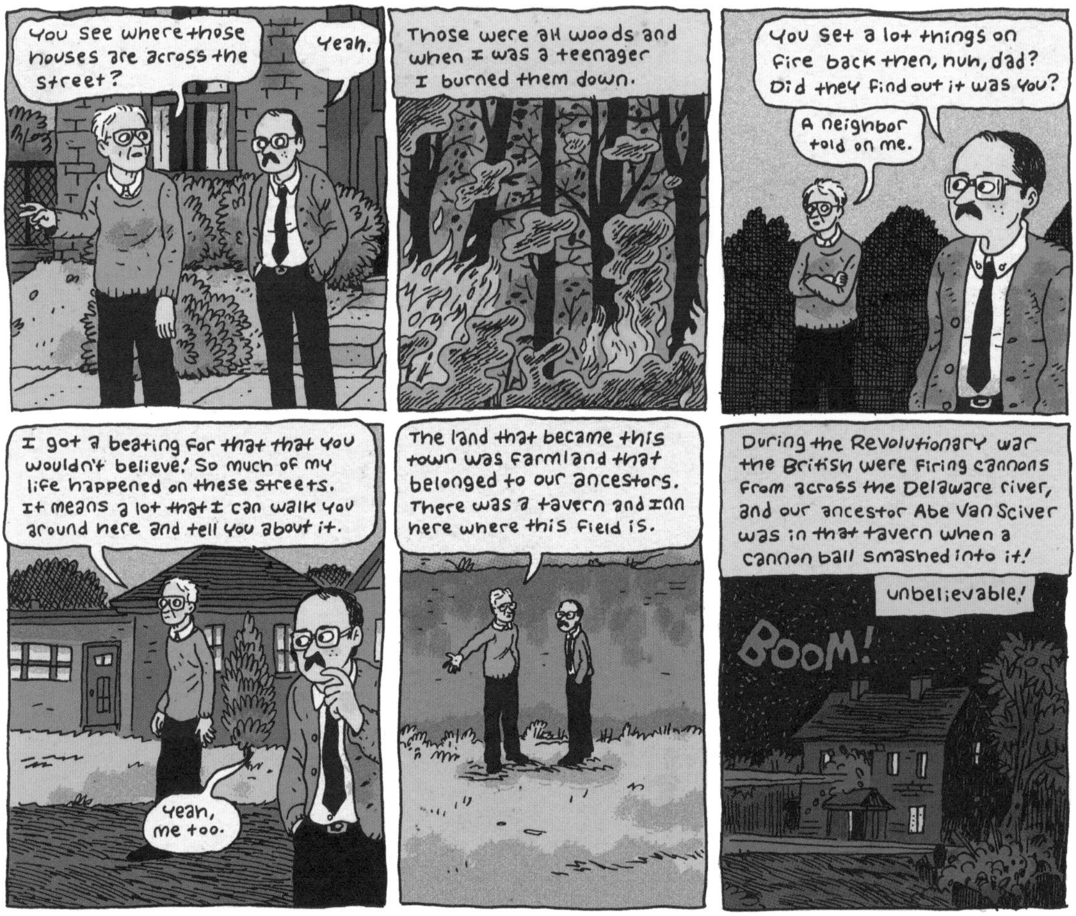
You see where those houses are across the street?
Yeah.
Those were all woods and when I was a teenager I burned them down.
You set a lot things on fire back then, huh, dad? Did they find out it was you?
A neighbor told on me.
I got a beating for that that you wouldn't believe! So much of my life happened on these streets. It means a lot that I can walk you around here and tell you about it.
Yeah, me too.
The land that became this town was farmland that belonged to our ancestors. There was a tavern and Inn here where this field is.
During the Revolutionary war the British were firing cannons from across the Delaware river, and our ancestor Abe Van Sciver was in that tavern when a cannon ball smashed into it!
unbelievable!
BOOM!

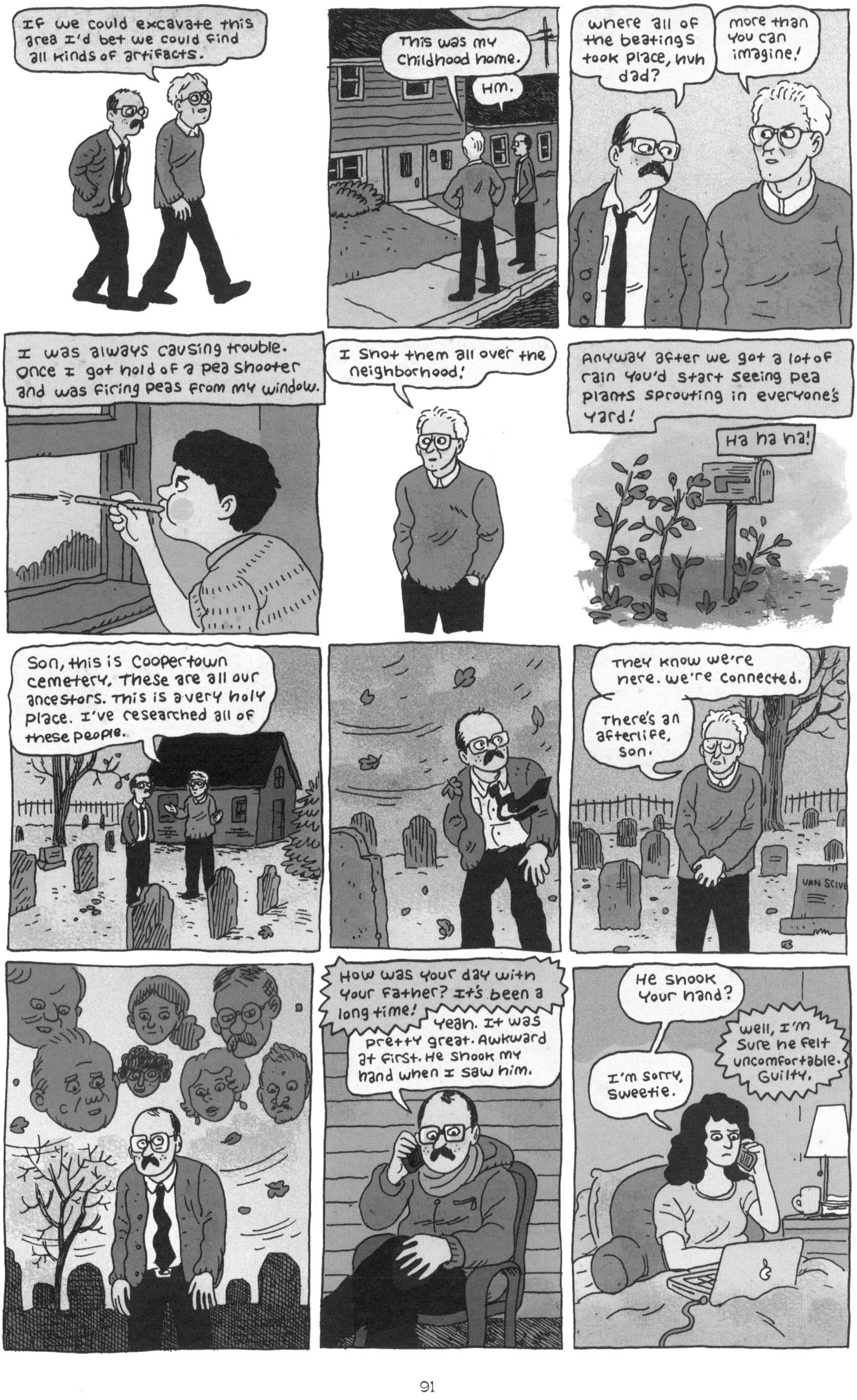
If we could excavate this area I'd bet we could find all kinds of artifacts.
This was my Childhood home.
Hm.
where all of the beatings took place, huh dad?
more than you can imagine!
I was always causing trouble. Once I got hold of a pea shooter and was firing peas from my window.
I shot them all over the neighborhood!
Anyway after we got a lot of rain you'd start seeing pea plants sprouting in everyone's yard!
Ha ha ha!
Son, this is Coopertown cemetery. These are all our ancestors. This is a very holy place. I've researched all of these people.
They know we're here. we're connected.
There's an afterlife, son.
VAN SCIVE
How was your day with your father? It's been a long time!
Yeah. It was pretty great. Awkward at first. He shook my hand when I saw him.
He shook your hand?
I'm sorry, sweetie.
well, I'm sure he felt uncomfortable. Guilty.

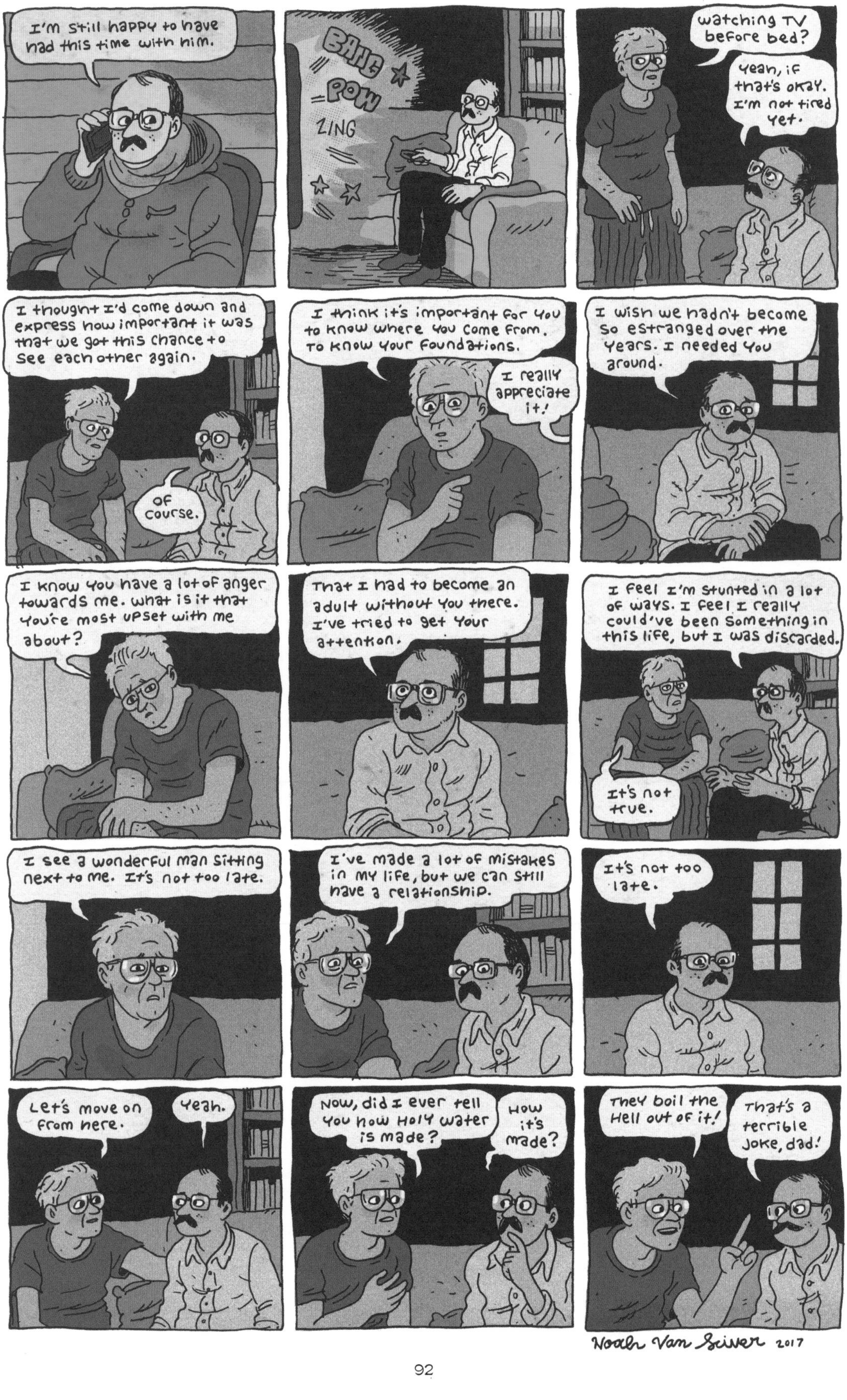
I'm still happy to have had this time with him.
BANG
POW
ZING
watching TV before bed?
Yeah, if that's okay. I'm not tired yet.
I thought I'd come down and express how important it was that we got this chance to see each other again.
Of course.
I think it's important for you to know where you come from. To know your foundations.
I really appreciate it!
I wish we hadn't become so estranged over the years. I needed you around.
I know you have a lot of anger towards me. what is it that you're most upset with me about?
That I had to become an adult without you there. I've tried to get your attention.
I feel I'm stunted in a lot of ways. I feel I really could've been something in this life, but I was discarded.
It's not true.
I see a wonderful man sitting next to me. It's not too late.
I've made a lot of mistakes in my life, but we can still have a relationship.
It's not too late.
Let's move on from here.
Yeah.
Now, did I ever tell you how Holy water is made?
How it's made?
They boil the Hell out of it!
That's a terrible joke, dad!
Noah Van Sciver 2017

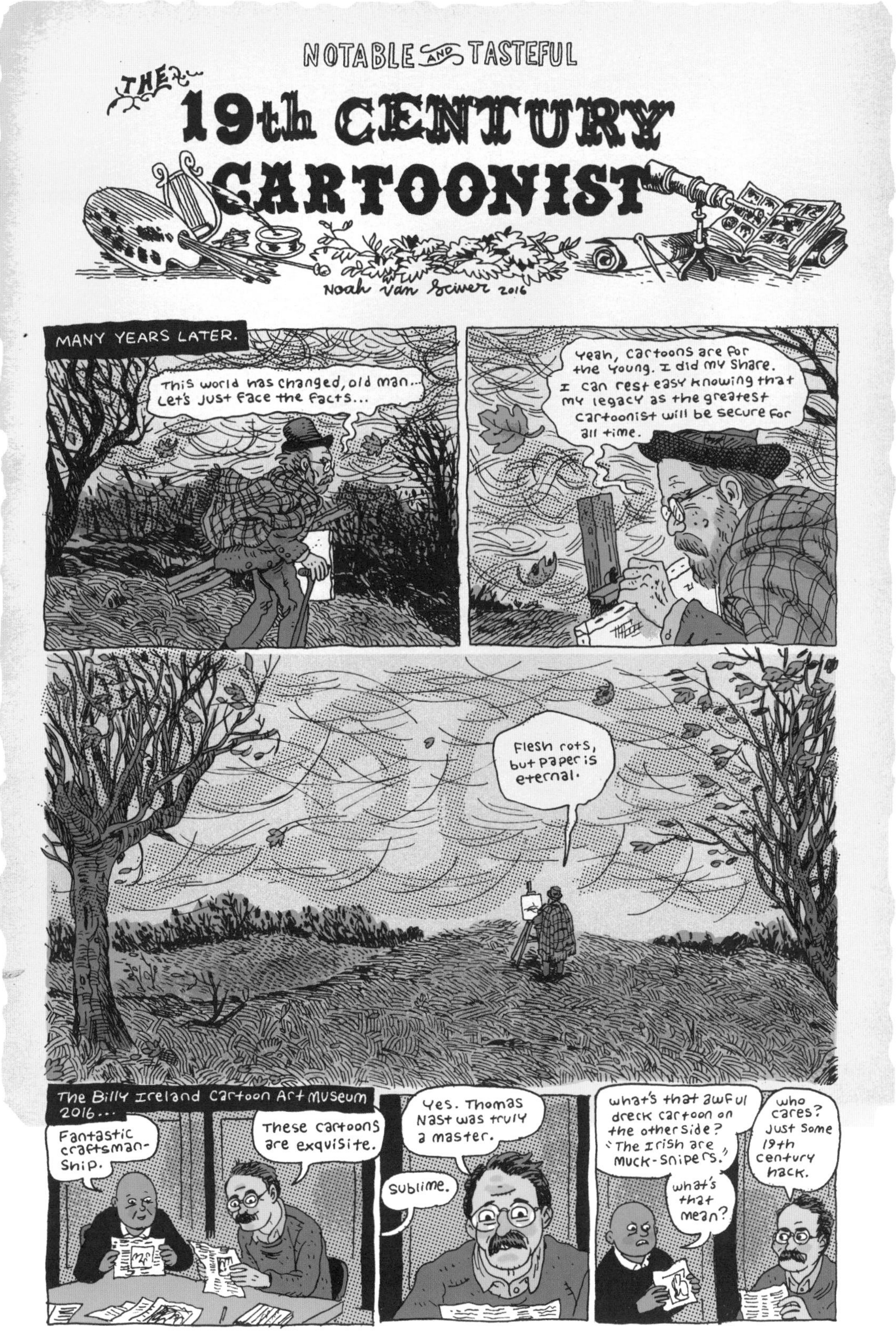
NOTABLE AND TASTEFUL
THE 19th CENTURY CARTOONIST
Noah Van Sciver 2016
MANY YEARS LATER.
This world has changed, old man... Let's just face the facts...
Yeah, cartoons are for the young. I did my share. I can rest easy knowing that my legacy as the greatest cartoonist will be secure for all time.
Flesh rots, but paper is eternal.
The Billy Ireland Cartoon Art Museum 2016...
Fantastic craftsmanship.
These cartoons are exquisite.
Yes. Thomas Nast was truly a master.
Sublime.
What's that awful dreck cartoon on the other side? "The Irish are muck-snipers."
What's that mean?
Who cares? Just some 19th century hack.

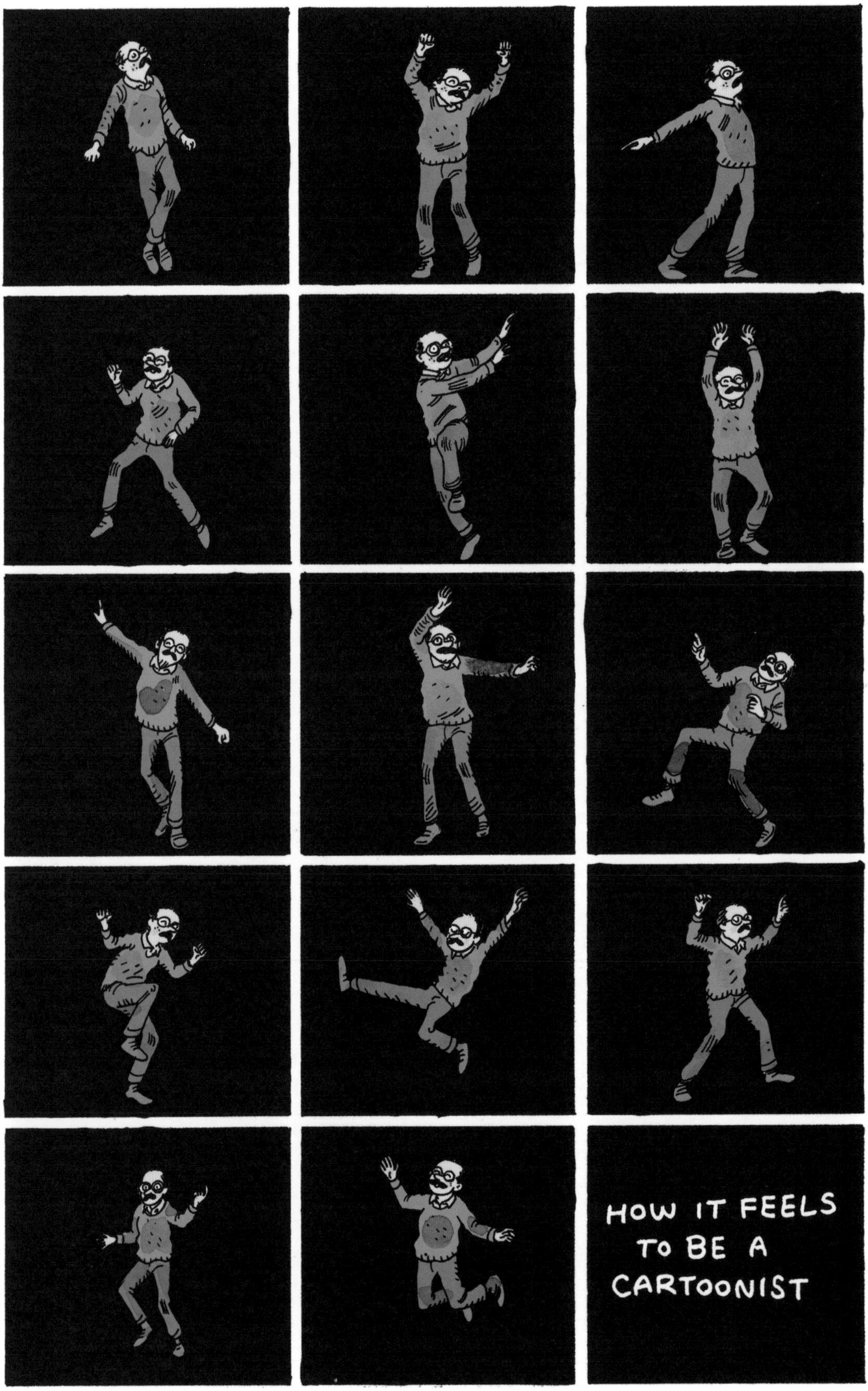
HOW IT FEELS TO BE A CARTOONIST

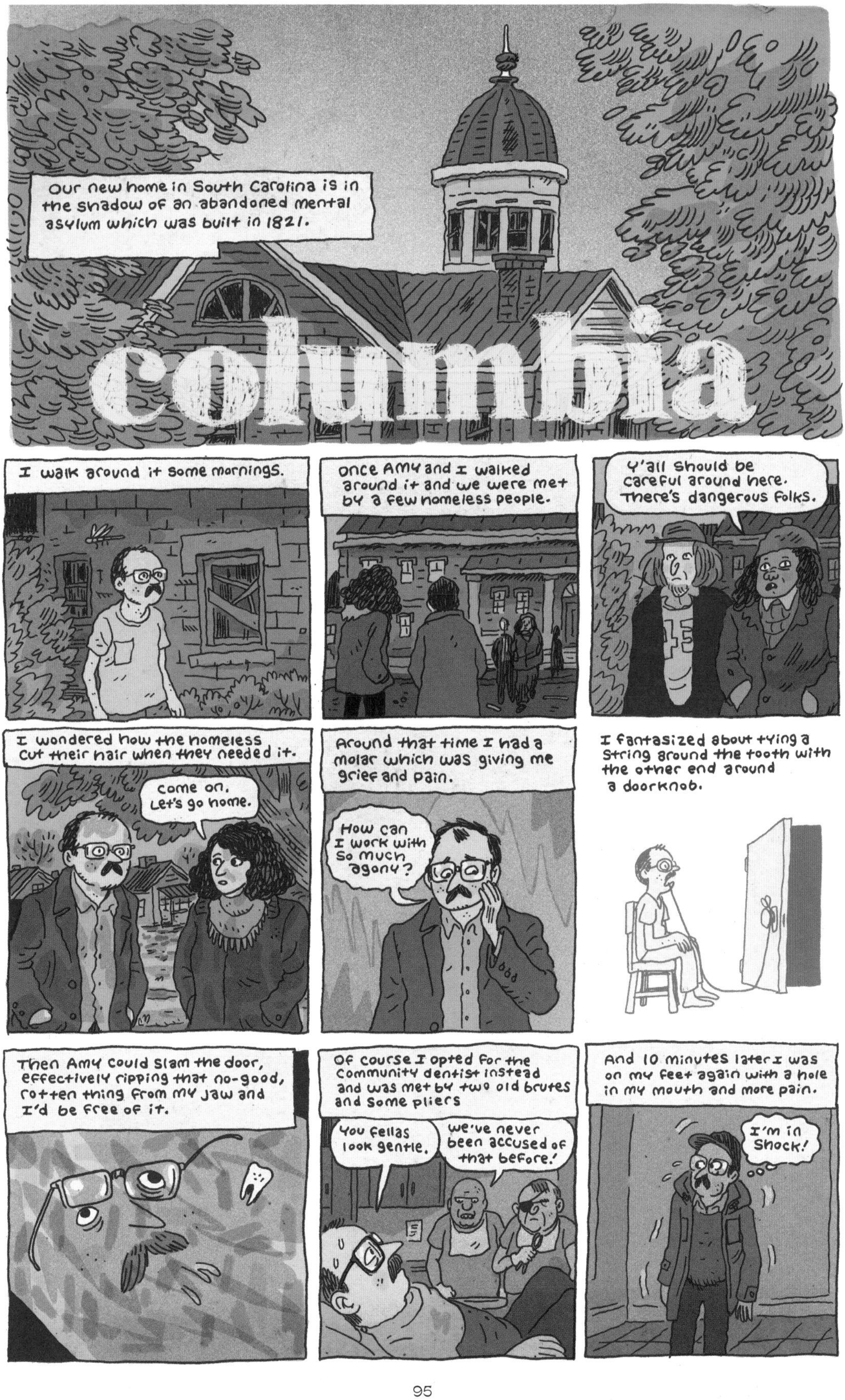
Our new home in South Carolina is in the shadow of an abandoned mental asylum which was built in 1821.
columbia
I walk around it some mornings.
Once Amy and I walked around it and we were met by a few homeless people.
Y'all should be careful around here. There's dangerous folks.
I wondered how the homeless cut their hair when they needed it.
Come on. Let's go home.
Around that time I had a molar which was giving me grief and pain.
How can I work with so much agony?
I fantasized about tying a string around the tooth with the other end around a doorknob.
Then Amy could slam the door, effectively ripping that no-good, rotten thing from my jaw and I'd be free of it.
Of course I opted for the community dentist instead and was met by two old brutes and some pliers
You fellas look gentle.
We've never been accused of that before!
And 10 minutes later I was on my feet again with a hole in my mouth and more pain.
I'm in shock!

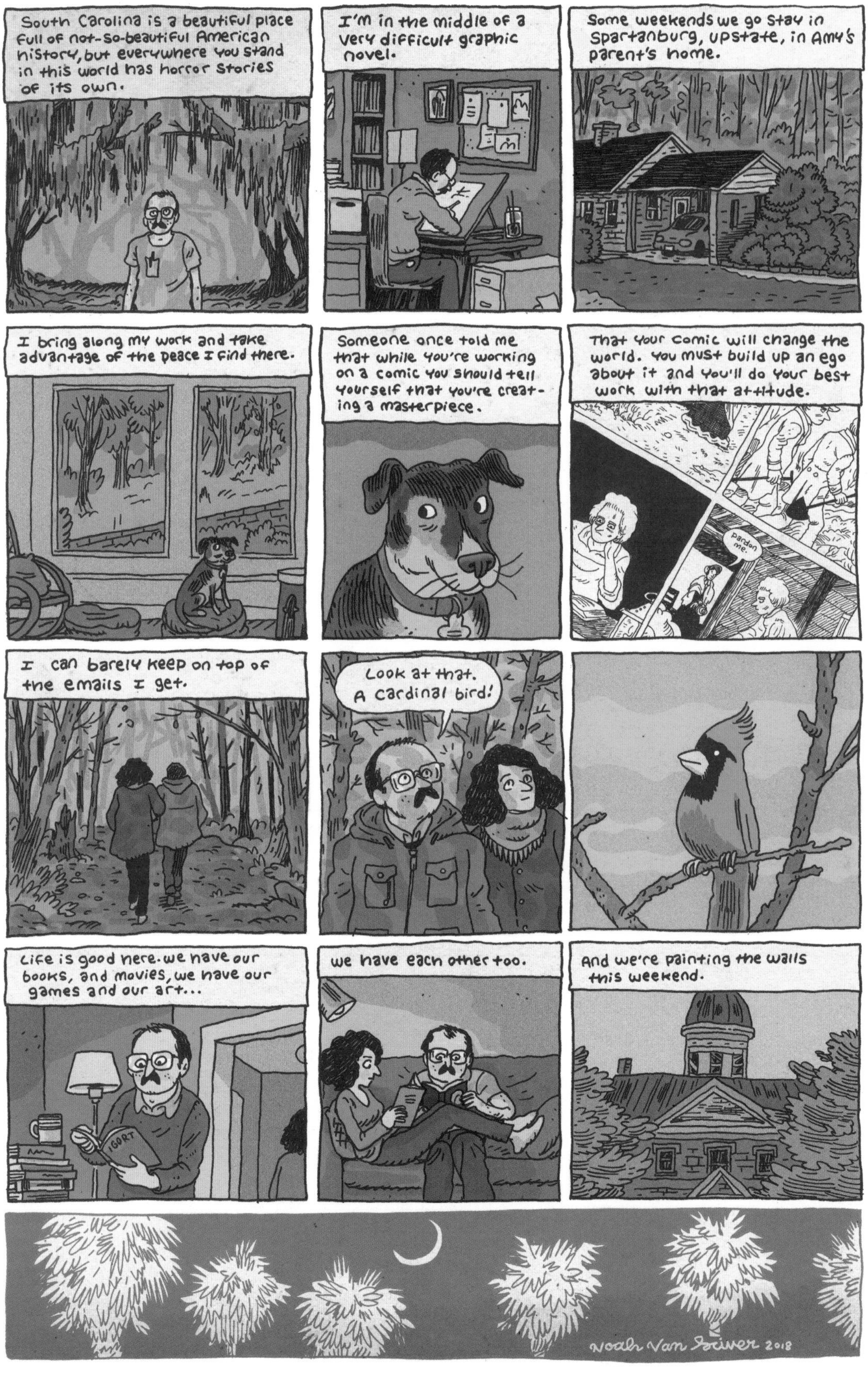
South Carolina is a beautiful place full of not-so-beautiful American history, but everywhere you stand in this world has horror stories of its own.
I'm in the middle of a very difficult graphic novel.
Some weekends we go stay in Spartanburg, upstate, in Amy's parent's home.
I bring along my work and take advantage of the peace I find there.
Someone once told me that while you're working on a comic you should tell yourself that you're creating a masterpiece.
That your comic will change the world. You must build up an ego about it and you'll do your best work with that attitude.
Pardon me.
I can barely keep on top of the emails I get.
Look at that. A cardinal bird!
Life is good here. we have our books, and movies, we have our games and our art...
IGORT
we have each other too.
And we're painting the walls this weekend.
Noah Van Sciver 2018

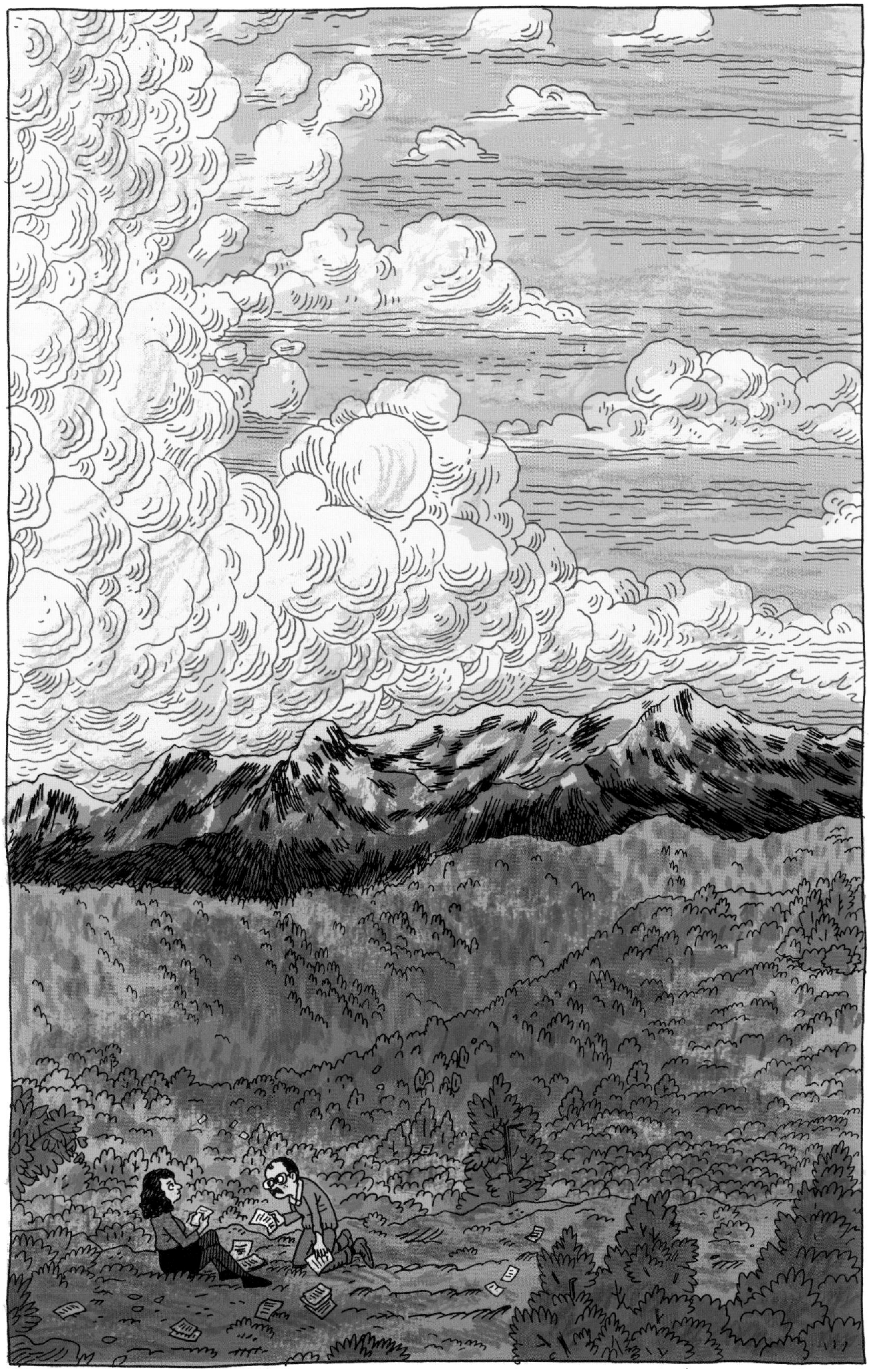

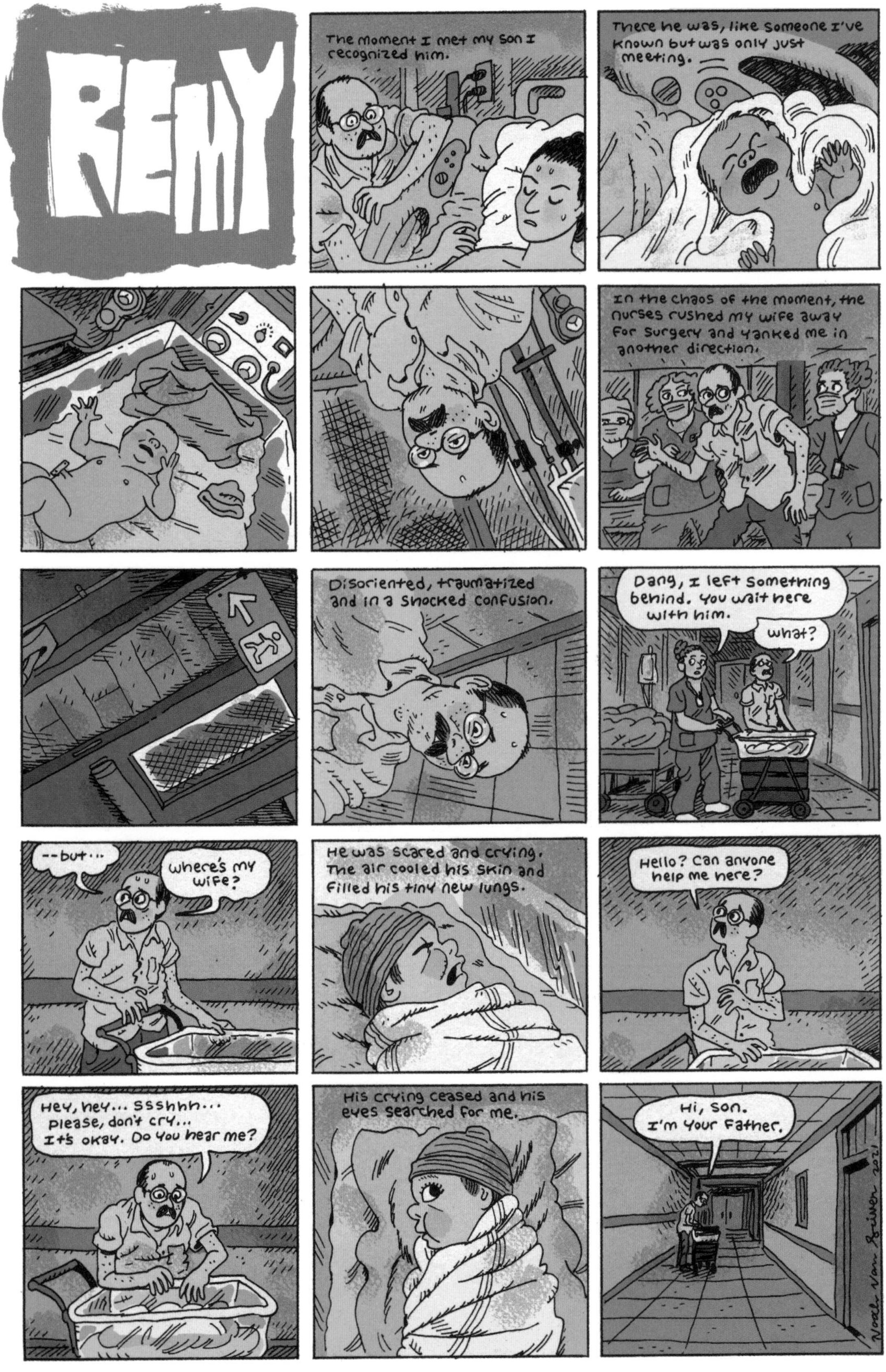
REMY
The moment I met my son I recognized him.
There he was, like someone I've known but was only just meeting.
In the chaos of the moment, the nurses rushed my wife away for surgery and yanked me in another direction.
Disoriented, traumatized and in a shocked confusion.
Dang, I left something behind. You wait here with him.
What?
--but...
Where's my wife?
He was scared and crying. The air cooled his skin and filled his tiny new lungs.
Hello? Can anyone help me here?
Hey, hey... ssshhh... please, don't cry... It's okay. Do you hear me?
His crying ceased and his eyes searched for me.
Hi, son. I'm your father.
Noah Van Sciver 2021

Noah Van Sciver is a multiple award-winning cartoonist who first came to comic reader's attention for his comic book series BLAMMO.

He was a regular contributor to MAD magazine, and has written and drawn numerous best-selling graphic novels, including ONE DIRTY TREE, FANTE BUKOWSKI, and the epic origin of the Latter-day Saints; JOSEPH SMITH AND THE MORMONS.

Van Sciver served as the 2015-16 Fellow at Vermont's Center FOR CARTOON STUDIES where his presence increased the school's enrollment to an all-time high.

He lives in Columbia, South Carolina with his wife AMY and son Remy.

- DRAWING OF NOAH REACHING FOR BOOKS (TADDLE CREEK COVER)
- Cartoonists of history drawings (never published)
- 19th century cartoonist (BIAMMO 9)
- Mellow MUTT (never published)
- Drawing of MY COLUMBUS, Ohio workspace (CONSTANT Companion) sketchbook
- White River Junction (BIAMMO 9)
- Nature drawings (never published)
- Mellow MUTT (NOW 9)
- Self Portrait 19th Century Style (never published)
- FISHING (never published)
- Fante Bukowski (never published)
- Comics Festival 2016 (BIAMMO 9)
- My Dad's ghost story (BIAMMO 9)
- Nature drawing (never published)
- Van Sciver moves to Columbus feels depressed (never published)
- 3 page diary (never published)
- THE HYPO (BIAMMO 10)
- 19th century Cartoonist (never published)
- Nature with paper Floating (BIAMMO 10)
- Jonah (previously titled "Wall of Shame") (NOW 1)
- HOW TO MAKE IT IN COMICS (never published
- 19th century cartoonist (BIAMMO 9)
- Clifton (never published)
- Saint Cole (NOW 8)
- Mellow Mutt (never published)
- Beverly New Jersey (BIAMMO 10)
- 19th century cartoonist (BIAMMO 9)
- How it feels to be a cartoonist (sold as a print)
- COLUMBIA (mineshaft)
- Remy (never published)
- Glossary of Favorite Comics (never published)

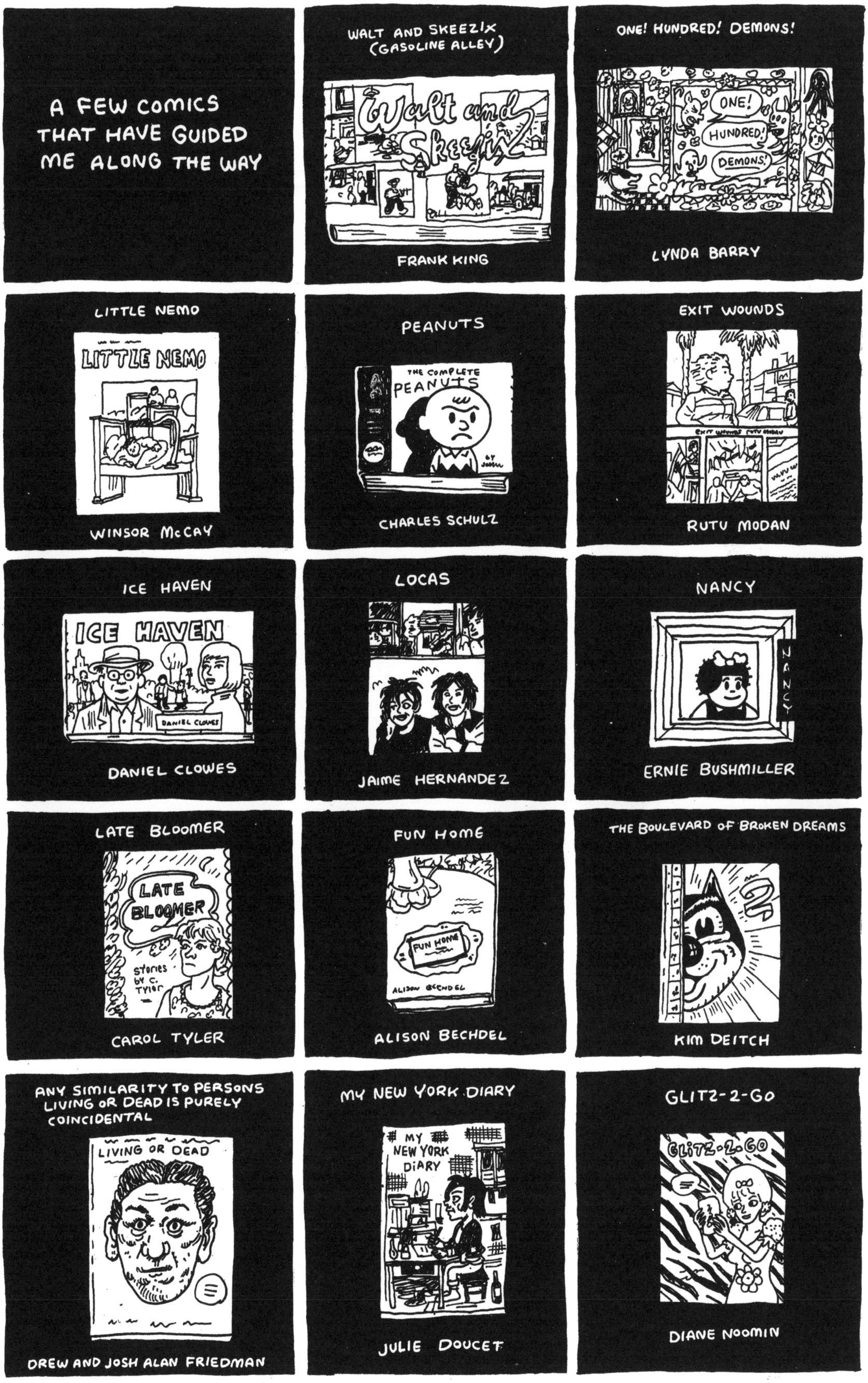
A FEW COMICS THAT HAVE GUIDED ME ALONG THE WAY
WALT AND SKEEZIX (GASOLINE ALLEY)
Walt and Skeezix
FRANK KING
ONE! HUNDRED! DEMONS!
ONE!
HUNDRED!
DEMONS!
LYNDA BARRY
LITTLE NEMO
LITTLE NEMO
WINSOR McCAY
PEANUTS
THE COMPLETE PEANUTS
CHARLES SCHULZ
EXIT WOUNDS
RUTU MODAN
ICE HAVEN
ICE HAVEN
DANIEL CLOWES
DANIEL CLOWES
LOCAS
JAIME HERNANDEZ
NANCY
NANCY
ERNIE BUSHMILLER
LATE BLOOMER
LATE BLOOMER
stories by C. Tyler
CAROL TYLER
FUN HOME
FUN HOME
ALISON BECHDEL
ALISON BECHDEL
THE BOULEVARD OF BROKEN DREAMS
KIM DEITCH
ANY SIMILARITY TO PERSONS LIVING OR DEAD IS PURELY COINCIDENTAL
LIVING OR DEAD
DREW AND JOSH ALAN FRIEDMAN
MY NEW YORK DIARY
MY NEW YORK DIARY
JULIE DOUCET
GLITZ-2-GO
GLITZ-2-GO
DIANE NOOMIN

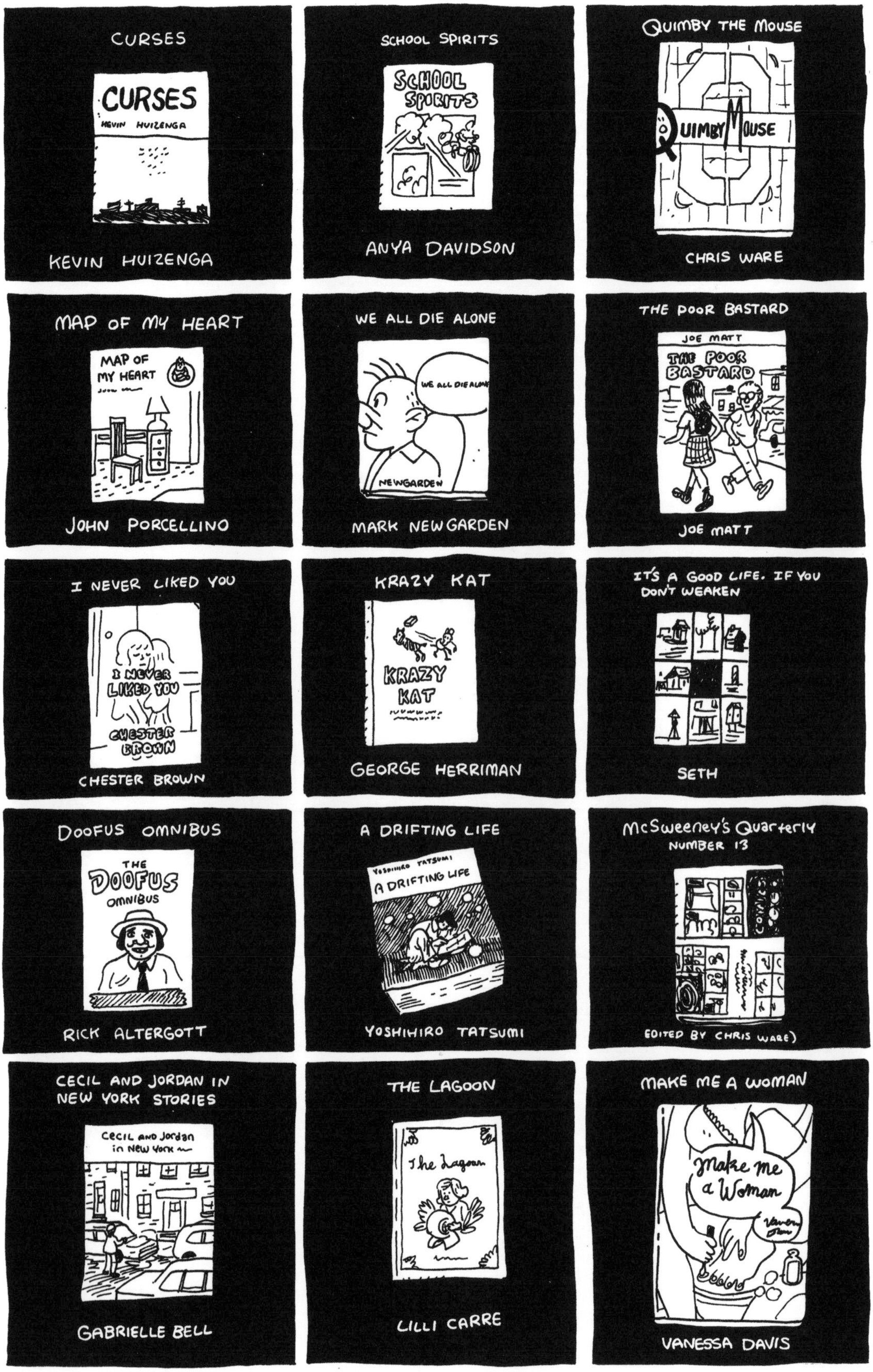
CURSES
CURSES
KEVIN HUIZENGA
KEVIN HUIZENGA
SCHOOL SPIRITS
SCHOOL SPIRITS
ANYA DAVIDSON
QUIMBY THE MOUSE
QUIMBY MOUSE
CHRIS WARE
MAP OF MY HEART
MAP OF MY HEART
JOHN PORCELLINO
WE ALL DIE ALONE
WE ALL DIE ALONE
NEWGARDEN
MARK NEWGARDEN
THE POOR BASTARD
JOE MATT
THE POOR BASTARD
JOE MATT
I NEVER LIKED YOU
I NEVER LIKED YOU
CHESTER BROWN
CHESTER BROWN
KRAZY KAT
KRAZY KAT
GEORGE HERRIMAN
IT'S A GOOD LIFE, IF YOU DON'T WEAKEN
SETH
DOOFUS OMNIBUS
THE DOOFUS OMNIBUS
RICK ALTERGOTT
A DRIFTING LIFE
YOSHIHIRO TATSUMI
A DRIFTING LIFE
YOSHIHIRO TATSUMI
McSweeney's Quarterly NUMBER 13
COMICS
EDITED BY CHRIS WARE)
CECIL AND JORDAN IN NEW YORK STORIES
Cecil and Jordan in New York
GABRIELLE BELL
THE LAGOON
The Lagoon
LILLI CARRE
MAKE ME A WOMAN
Make me a Woman
VANESSA DAVIS

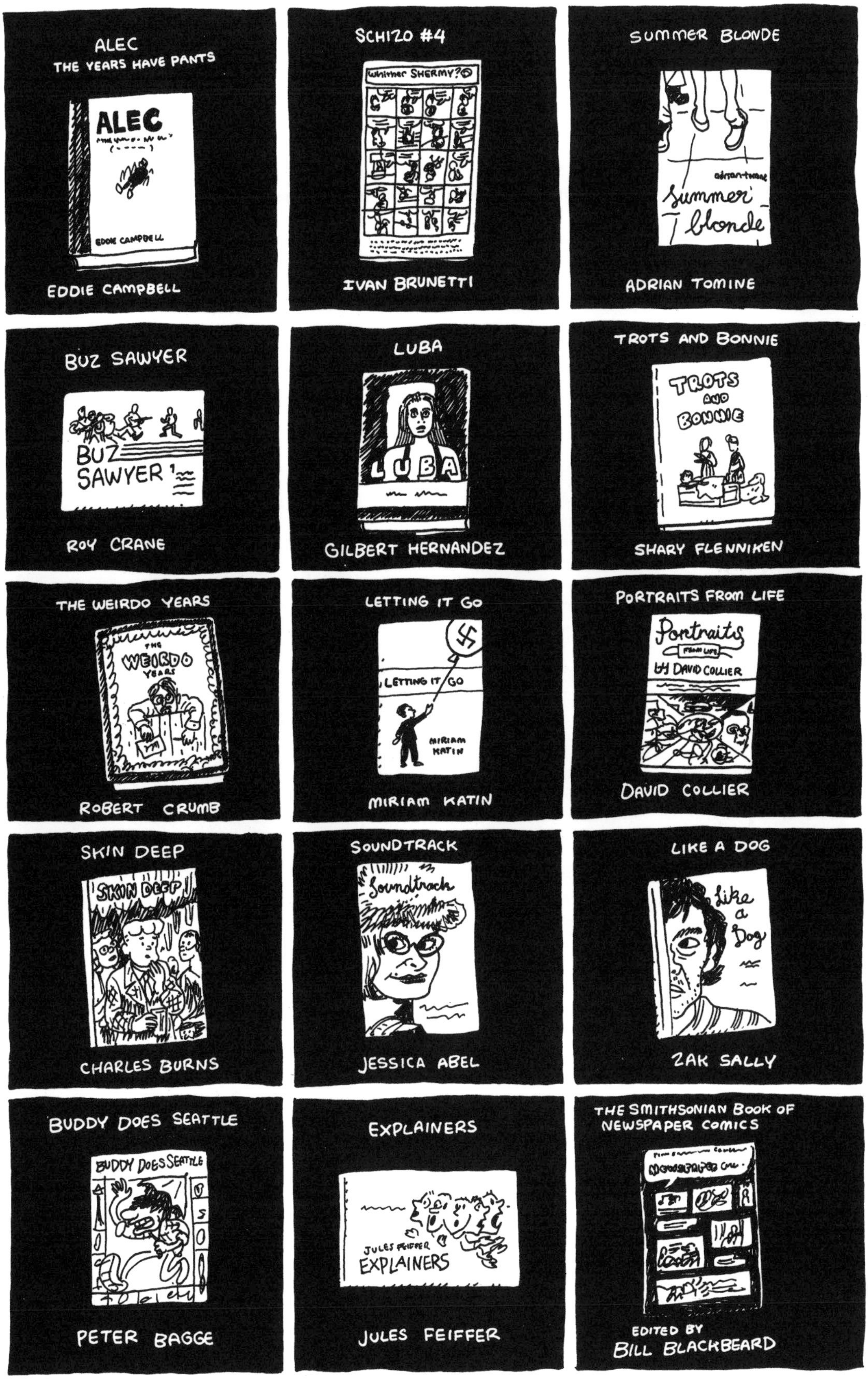

ALEC
THE YEARS HAVE PANTS
ALEC
EDDIE CAMPBELL
EDDIE CAMPBELL
SCHIZO #4
Whither SHERMY?
IVAN BRUNETTI
SUMMER BLONDE
adrian tomine
summer blonde
ADRIAN TOMINE
BUZ SAWYER
BUZ SAWYER
ROY CRANE
LUBA
LUBA
GILBERT HERNANDEZ
TROTS AND BONNIE
TROTS AND BONNIE
SHARY FLENNIKEN
THE WEIRDO YEARS
THE WEIRDO YEARS
ROBERT CRUMB
LETTING IT GO
LETTING IT GO
MIRIAM KATIN
MIRIAM KATIN
PORTRAITS FROM LIFE
Portraits
FROM LIFE
by DAVID COLLIER
DAVID COLLIER
SKIN DEEP
SKIN DEEP
CHARLES BURNS
SOUNDTRACK
Soundtrack
JESSICA ABEL
LIKE A DOG
Like a Dog
ZAK SALLY
BUDDY DOES SEATTLE
BUDDY DOES SEATTLE
PETER BAGGE
EXPLAINERS
JULES FEIFFER
EXPLAINERS
JULES FEIFFER
THE SMITHSONIAN BOOK OF NEWSPAPER COMICS
EDITED BY
BILL BLACKBEARD

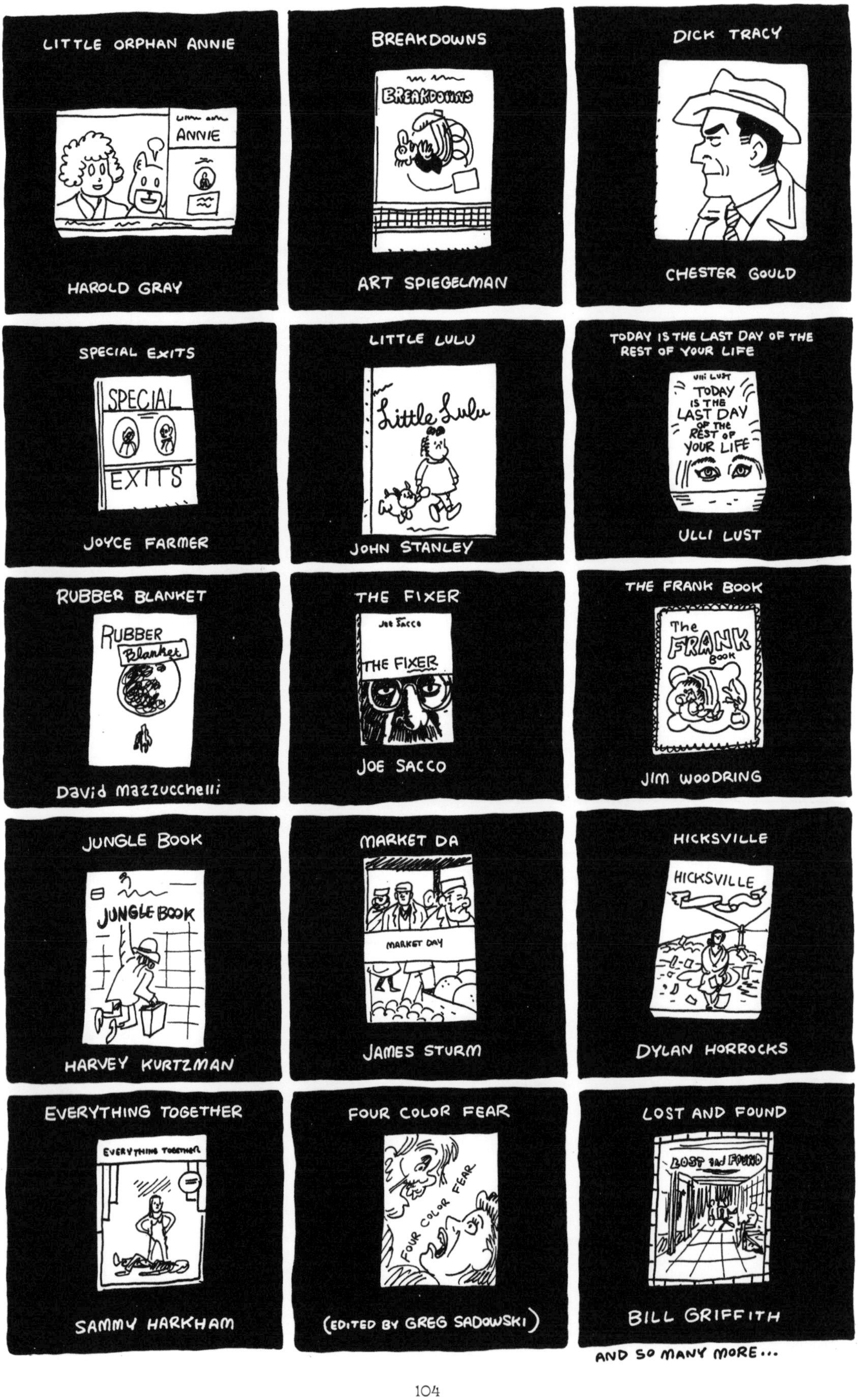

LITTLE ORPHAN ANNIE
ANNIE
HAROLD GRAY
BREAKDOWNS
BREAKDOWNS
ART SPIEGELMAN
DICK TRACY
CHESTER GOULD
SPECIAL EXITS
SPECIAL
EXITS
JOYCE FARMER
LITTLE LULU
Little Lulu
JOHN STANLEY
TODAY IS THE LAST DAY OF THE REST OF YOUR LIFE
ULLI LUST
TODAY IS THE LAST DAY OF THE REST OF YOUR LIFE
ULLI LUST
RUBBER BLANKET
RUBBER Blanket
David Mazzucchelli
THE FIXER
JOE SACCO
THE FIXER
JOE SACCO
THE FRANK BOOK
The FRANK Book
JIM WOODRING
JUNGLE BOOK
JUNGLE BOOK
HARVEY KURTZMAN
MARKET DA
MARKET DAY
JAMES STURM
HICKSVILLE
HICKSVILLE
DYLAN HORROCKS
EVERYTHING TOGETHER
EVERYTHING TOGETHER
SAMMY HARKHAM
FOUR COLOR FEAR
FOUR COLOR FEAR
(EDITED BY GREG SADOWSKI)
LOST AND FOUND
LOST and FOUND
BILL GRIFFITH
AND SO MANY MORE...

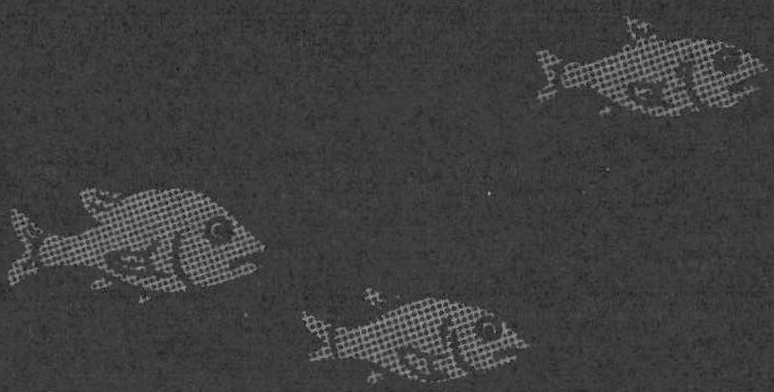
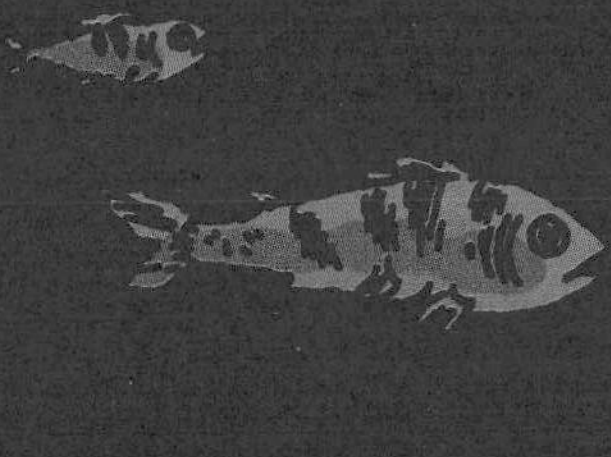